P9-CAN-601

Ready for Reference

TEACHING LIBRARY MEDIA RESEARCH AND INFORMATION SKILLS SERIES

Edited by Paula Kay Montgomery

Library Media Skills: Strategies for Instructing Primary Students. By Alice R. Seaver.

Media Skills for Middle Schools: Strategies for Library Media Specialists and Teachers. By Lucille W. Van Vliet.

Ready for Reference: Media Skills for Intermediate Students. By Barbara Bradley Zlotnick.

READY FOR REFERENCE

Media Skills for Intermediate Students

BARBARA BRADLEY ZLOTNICK

EDITED BY
PAULA KAY MONTGOMERY

1984
Libraries Unlimited, Inc.
Littleton, Colorado

LIBRARIES UNLIMITED, INC.
P.O. Box 263
Littleton, Colorado 80160-0263

Library of Congress Cataloging in Publication Data

Zlotnick, Barbara Bradley, 1946-
   Ready for reference.

   (Teaching library media research and information
skills series)
   Bibliography: p. 255
   Includes index.
   1. School children--Library orientation.
2. Instructional materials centers--User education.
3. School libraries (Elementary school) 4. Media
programs (Education) I. Montgomery, Paula Kay.
II. Title. III. Series.
Z675.S3Z54   1984   025.5'678222   84-11222
ISBN 0-87287-411-7

Libraries Unlimited books are bound with Type II nonwoven material that meets and exceeds National Association of State Textbook Administrators' Type II nonwoven material specifications Class A through E.

31.02

Table of Contents

List of Illustrations

Figure

Foreword

Teaching library media research and study skills within the context of regular classroom instruction when student motivation and interest are at a peak should be a primary goal of educators. The instruction of library media research skills that is integrated with all facets of the curriculum represents a sound method for introducing and reinforcing students' learning.

In 1977 *Teaching Media Skills* by H. Thomas Walker and Paula Kay Montgomery (Littleton, CO: Libraries Unlimited) presented a model for an integrated approach to library skills instruction in grades K through 8. Other books have also espoused this integrated approach during the past ten years. School systems throughout the United States have developed curriculum documents that acknowledge the crucial nature of library media skills for learning in all subject areas. Many of these documents provide scope and sequence charts, suggested activities, and tests for school library media specialists to use in their instructional programs.

Continued interest in this subject and a basic need voiced by school library media specialists and teachers encouraged the development of the series, *Teaching Library Media Research and Information Skills*. The major purpose of the series is to provide specific advice to library media specialists and teachers at each instructional level. This book offers strategies for broad implementation of an integrated approach to library media skills instruction and creative strategies for assessing and instructing students.

Ready for Reference: Media Skills for Intermediate Students is by Barbara Bradley Zlotnick, a successful elementary classroom teacher who has taught for sixteen years in Montgomery County Public Schools in Rockville, Maryland. The focus of the book is on the cooperative effort required in planning and implementing a library media skills program for upper elementary grades. Teaching roles for both library media specialists and teachers are suggested. Practical suggestions and sample activities are provided for use with students in all subject areas.

As the title suggests, students in grades three through six should be ready for instruction in the basic library media skills that will sustain independent learning with materials from libraries throughout their lives. Prerequisites or readiness skills should have been developed in the primary grades and are discussed in another book within this series.

It is the hope of the series editor and author that this book will be useful to elementary library media specialists and teachers in developing their joint instructional programs.

Paula Kay Montgomery

Preface

    Ready for Reference: Media Skills for Intermediate Students suggests practical strategies and activities for establishing a research, study, and information skills program through the joint efforts of library media specialists and classroom teachers. One hopes that it may serve as a sourcebook for both teachers and library media specialists as they integrate library media and content skills instruction for students in the upper elementary grades. Chapters 1-3 include a discussion of essential library media research and study skills, the presentation of an integrated instructional model, and strategies for the implementation of an integrated instructional program. Chapter 4 lists practical activities in the various content subjects involving the application of library media research and study skills. Reproducible activity worksheets appear throughout chapters 2, 3, and 4. The answer keys for worksheets within any chapter are all grouped together at the end of the chapter.

    A note of appreciation is due to those who made it possible for me to write *Ready for Reference.* To my editor and friend, Paula Kay Montgomery, who patiently supplied encouragement, ideas, and editorial assistance, I say a sincere thank-you. To my husband, Fred, thank you for your assistance with the illustrations and your support throughout this endeavor. To the many colleagues and students with whom I have been privileged to work, thank you for your encouragement and enthusiasm.

1   *Library Media Research and Study Skills*

Jack has been assigned to do a mini-report on the history and significance of St. Patrick's Day. He goes to the school library media center to find information on his topic. He intends to ask the library media specialist to help him locate materials about St. Patrick's Day, but she is busy instructing a group about the Dewey decimal system of classification of books. He understands that he can locate information about materials in the card catalog, but he doesn't understand in which drawer to look first.

Sujon is an avid baseball fan of the Boston Red Sox, and his cousin Frank follows the New York Yankees. They are constantly arguing over the statistics of their respective favorite teams. Frank wins most arguments, and Sujon usually loses because he can't keep his team's facts and figures straight. Sujon wishes he could recite his team's statistics as well as Frank can.

Marissa is in a quandry! She has a social studies assignment and her weekly spelling test due tomorrow. She has had two weeks to complete an outline of the material in the chapter on The Industrial Revolution, and she hasn't begun. She hasn't had time to review her spelling words for the week. To make matters worse, Marissa has to appear at a dance recital this evening.

All three students could benefit from knowledge of library media research and study skills. Jack needs independent research skills to help him locate the information for his mini-report on St. Patrick's Day. He requires direction in the use of the card catalog to locate available sources and in the use of call numbers and shelf arrangement to locate specific sources of information. Sujon would be better prepared for his discussions with his cousin Frank if he could use a recent almanac to look up and record his team's statistics. He needs training in locating and interpreting the specific data listed in table format in an almanac. Marissa lacks organizational skills to enable her to adequately complete her assignment and study for her test. She requires guidance in budgeting her time wisely and selecting main ideas and details to complete her outline. Thus, Jack, Sujon, and Marissa need specific instruction in the general area of library media research and study skills.

What are these library media research and study skills? These skills are the subskills included under the educational headings of library media skills, reference skills, information retrieval skills, research skills, organizational skills, and study skills. For our purposes, the term library media research and study skills will mean those skills essential for enabling students to locate, select, interpret, use, and apply information available in print and nonprint sources. Print sources include fiction, nonfiction, and reference books, textbooks, magazines, and newspapers. Nonprint sources are films, filmstrips, television programs, records, audiotapes, videotapes, microcomputer programs, and computer data bases.

Given today's rapidly expanding base of information and knowledge, it is important that students develop useful library media research and study skills in the intermediate grades (grades 3-6) in order to build a strong foundation of proficiencies for locating, selecting, interpreting, using, and applying information from sources. A written sequence of library media research and study skills is necessary for both library media specialists and classroom teachers to implement an instructional program in these areas. It is necessary to understand the arrangement of these library media research and study skills in terms of objectives.

EDUCATIONAL OBJECTIVES

Any instructional program should have educational objectives or goals before planning, implementation, and assessment of learnings are initiated. Such objectives specify behaviors that a student should exhibit to be competent in a particular skill. For planning and implementing instructional programs, educational objectives are classified into three basic categories. They are *program objectives, instructional objectives,* and *performance objectives.*

Program objectives are general educational objectives or goals upon which instructional programs are based. They usually indicate broad categories of behaviors that cannot be directly observed. Some examples of program objectives in library media research and study skills would be

1. Students will locate and use library media sources.
2. Students will interpret graphic aids in library media resources.
3. Students will report information gathered from library media sources.

Instructional objectives are more specific educational objectives that the library media specialist or classroom teacher uses to plan instructional activities. They indicate more specific observable behavior, but they do not indicate the conditions under which the behavior will be observed or how the student will be assessed. Some examples of instructional objectives in library media research and study skills would be

1. Students will use the card catalog to locate sources and information.
2. Students will interpret pictures/diagrams in dictionary entries.
3. Students will summarize information gathered from encyclopedia articles.

Performance objectives are the most specific educational objectives that the library media specialist and classroom teacher design and use directly with students. They indicate a specific observable behavior, the conditions under which performance is observed, and the criteria for assessment.

A performance objective contains three basic component parts. One, it states observable behaviors indicating what knowledge, skill, attitude, or physical performance the student should be capable of upon the completion of the objective. The statement includes an active verb form such as locate, select, recall, predict, list, identify, distinguish, compare, classify, construct, or write.

Two, a performance objective specifies the conditions under which the behavior is observed such as (1) in not more than ten minutes, (2) after viewing a specified filmstrip, (3) upon completion of a microcomputer drill disk program, or (4) upon completion of a specified worksheet.

Three, a performance objective specifies the acceptable performance levels or the other standards by which the student demonstrates proficiency in that particular skill. The library media specialist and/or classroom teacher uses these criteria of acceptable performance to assess the student. Criteria for acceptable performance can be expressed numerically such as (1) in eight out of ten examples or (2) with 100 percent accuracy.

Performance criteria may be omitted if a finished product is the end result of the objective such as (1) prepare a storyboard, (2) write a script, or (3) summarize the paragraph.

Some examples of performance objectives in library media research and study skills would be

1. Given ten sample cards from the card catalog, the student will categorize each as to author, subject, or title card with 100 percent accuracy.

2. Given ten sample pictures/diagrams from dictionary entries, a list of ten dictionary entry words, and a dictionary, the student will use the dictionary to match each picture/diagram with its appropriate entry word in eight out of ten examples.

3. Given a paragraph from a sample encyclopedia article, the student will read the paragraph, take notes, and summarize the paragraph in his/her own words.

CLASSIFYING OBJECTIVES

Educational objectives give direction to instructional planning, provide guidelines for the selection of student activities, and provide a basis upon which to assess students. Benjamin S. Bloom and others provided a structure for classifying educational objectives according to the ways they will change a student's thinking, feelings, and actions. Bloom identified three *domains* or groupings of educational objectives: the cognitive (thinking), affective (feelings), and psychomotor (actions) domains. A well-balanced instructional program will include educational objectives representing all three domains.[1]

The *cognitive domain* concerns educational objectives that deal with recall or recognition of knowledge and the development of intellectual abilities and skills. It is made up of six subcategories of cognition: knowledge, comprehension, application, analysis, synthesis, and evaluation. The *affective domain* involves educational objectives that describe changes in students' interests, attitudes, and values. It also includes the development of personal appreciations and adequate personal adjustment. The *psychomotor domain* concerns behaviors that deal with physical or muscular processes. It involves those physical behaviors and skills necessary for general physical coordination and basic manipulations such as those involved in writing. Many instructional and performance objectives involve cognitive, affective, and psychomotor processes. Therefore, exploration of each domain in more detail with examples of library media research and study skills objectives representing cognitive, affective, and psychomotor components will be insightful.

COGNITIVE DOMAIN

Objectives in the cognitive domain concern behaviors and processes related to intellecutal growth representing six levels of cognition: knowledge, comprehension, application, analysis, synthesis, and evaluation. Cognitive processes are those more readily assessed by educators since they are more easily observable and measurable.

Knowledge

The cognitive area of knowledge includes those processes and skills related to the recall of facts, concepts, and principles, as well as the recall of methods and processes. Traditionally, educators have tested the attainment of knowledge predominantly through memorization; however, although memorization is important, it does not involve higher level thinking processes or long-term memory processes. Some active verb forms often used in knowledge objectives are define, identify, match, list, explain, describe, or name. Library media research and study skills constitutes a specific area of knowledge. Therefore, the demonstration of any skill in the location, selection, and use of library media materials reflects a growth in the cognitive area of knowledge. Some examples of library media instructional objectives in the cognitive area of knowledge are

The student will:

1. Name five examples of reference sources in the library media center.
2. List the sequence of steps to be followed when checking out a book from the library media center.
3. Match selected audiovisual equipment with appropriate nonprint materials.
4. Explain the composition of the call number, given a specific nonfiction book.

Comprehension

Bloom considered the cognitive area of comprehension as the lowest level of understanding in which the individual knows what is being communicated and can use the information or idea being communicated without necessarily relating it to other material or seeing it through to its fullest implications.[2] Comprehension includes the *translation* level of understanding in which the student restates, illustrates, or gives information in his or her own words and the *interpretation* level of understanding in which the student distinguishes, demonstrates, predicts, and infers information from the materials or ideas being presented. Whereas translation involves an objective part-by-part understanding of the material, interpretation involves a re-ordering, rearrangement, or creation of a new view of the material. Educators tend to group all reading-thinking skills related to the understanding of written materials under the broad category of comprehension skills. Bloom's concept of comprehension corresponds to the lowest level of reading-thinking skills that is generally referred to as literal comprehension.[3] Some examples of comprehension instructional objectives related to library media research and study skills are

1. Given a mixed list of ten fiction and nonfiction book titles, the student will distinguish fiction titles from nonfiction titles.
2. Given a bar graph of animal speeds, the student will list the five fastest animals in order of speed.
3. Given a diagram depicting the directions for making a paper airplane, the student will write a time order/sequence paragraph describing the paper-folding process.

Application

The application level of cognition relates to the student's ability to apply knowledge or understandings previously gained to a new situation. Application objectives involve higher level thinking skills, and are best undertaken after a unit of study has been completed. A thorough understanding of concepts and processes is necessary before this knowledge can be applied to a new situation.

Some active verb forms often used in application objectives are transfer, restructure, generalize, or relate. Some examples of application objectives related to library media research and study skills are

1. Upon completion of a unit on tall tales, the student will create a tall tale that includes a unique character and hyperbole (exaggeration).
2. Following instruction in various media production and research methods and when given a topic, the student will research the topic and select media appropriate to express its content.
3. After lessons on the Dewey Decimal Classification system of library books, the student will identify the major categories of at least six out of ten books when given the titles.

Analysis

The analysis level of cognition involves the student's ability to divide a problem into its component parts, its relationships, or its organizational principles. Some active verb forms often used in analysis objectives are deduce, compare and/or contrast, and discriminate between. Analysis skills are necessary in problem-solving activities in mathematics, science, and social studies. Some analysis instructional objectives related to library media research and study skills are

1. When given tables from an almanac listing the average annual rainfall and length of growing season for different parts of the United States, the student will deduce which crops will grow best in five given parts of the country.
2. Given a telephone book time zone chart, the student will determine the time in five given states, assuming it is 6:15 P.M. in New York.
3. The student will observe a political cartoon from a given period of study in history, and list two fact and two opinion statements about it.

Synthesis

The synthesis level of cognition is closely related to the application level of cognition. Synthesis involves the creation of a new product from various elements or pieces after analyzing the parts of structures or ideas. Some active verb forms involved in synthesizing objectives are combine, create, compare, design, or derive. As with application, synthesis level activities are best undertaken after a unit of study has been completed or a number of background-building activities have been experienced. Examples of synthesis instructional objectives that can be applied to library media research and study skills are

1. After conducting research on evidences of "Big Foot" in the United States, the student will create a mystery story concerning an imaginary encounter with "Big Foot."
2. After the study of a given state constitution, the student will propose a set of guidelines for running a library media center club.
3. Upon completion of a unit on musical instrument families, the student will design and create one instrument representative of each of the instrument families.

Evaluation

The evaluation level of cognition concerns the student's ability to make judgments about the value of ideas, works, solutions, methods, and materials based on evidence. Analysis skills are necessary to make quantitive or qualitative judgments based on conclusions reached or generalizations made as the result of the problem-solving processes. Evaluation is closely related to the affective domain's development of feelings, attitudes, and values. It is the highest level of cognition, which educators term *critical reading-thinking skills*. To contrast, appraise, assess, or validate are some active verb forms often used in evaluation objectives. Some examples of evaluation instructional objectives related to library media research and study skills are

1. After using both the Commodore PET and Apple II microcomputers, the student will state two advantages of each.

2. Given a statement of opinion, the student will write three paragraphs: one to tell why the statement is not true, one to tell why he or she thinks it may have become an opinion, and one to tell the consequences of accepting the statement as fact.

3. After studying the Civil War era, the student will write three essays on the causes of the Civil War: one from a Union soldier's point of view, one from a Confederate soldier's point of view, and one from the student's own point of view.

AFFECTIVE DOMAIN

The affective domain of educational objectives involves the development of a student's attitudes, feelings, motives, interests, values, and appreciations. It is generally concerned with three major groupings of objectives: receiving, responding, and valuing. Receiving includes the development of an awareness of and a willingness to give attention to a given area of knowledge being presented in an instructional program. Responding is characterized by a willingness to respond to and actively participate in developmental activities of an instructional program. Valuing involves the internalization of the processes and knowledge of a given instructional program, thereby making such knowledge and processes part of a personal value system.[4]

Because of the individual and personal nature of affective experiences, it is difficult, and probably not advisable, to include formal criteria for evaluating affective instructional objectives. The emphasis instead should be on providing for affective objectives and related activities rather than upon the evaluation of the objectives themselves. It is more important, then, to develop an educational atmosphere conducive to (1) identifying and extending interests, (2) expressing feelings and attitudes, (3) making decisions based on supportable data, (4) clarifying values, (5) taking positions on issues, and (6) developing an appreciation for the processes involved in the pursuit of knowledge.

Some examples of affective instructional objectives as related to library media research and study skills are

1. Following a review of library media center procedures, the student will follow the library media center procedures for the remainder of the school year.

2. The student will develop an appreciation for literature and choose reading as a leisure activity after being exposed to varied literature selections in an instructional program.

3. The student will value library media research and study skills as a means to acquire knowledge.

PSYCHOMOTOR DOMAIN

The psychomotor domain of educational objectives refers to those physical behaviors and skills involving some muscular or motor skill. Psychomotor skills include general physical coordination skills developed in physical education, dance, and drama, as well as those skills needed for basic manipulations such as writing, drawing, arts and crafts, and game playing. The upper elementary student may also be exposed to the psychomotor skills involved in cooking, sewing, woodworking, and the use of manipulative materials in mathematics and science investigations. Library media research and study skills involve psychomotor skills in the operation of audiovisual equipment and in the expression of ideas through media production. Some examples of instructional objectives in library media research and study skills involving psychomotor activities are

1. The student will locate a record with instructions for performing the Virginia reel and a record player on which to play the music.
2. The student will prepare a handmade slide to express his or her interpretation of a given musical selection.
3. The student will preserve a newspaper clipping by applying laminating film.

DEVELOPMENT OF LIBRARY MEDIA RESEARCH AND STUDY SKILLS CHART

The Library Media Research and Study Skills Chart that appears at the end of this chapter (pp. 11-24) was developed to facilitate instructional planning for the library media specialist and the classroom teacher. The chart is the result of the integration of library media skills usually taught by the library media specialist and research and study skills usually taught by the classroom teacher. Library media skills include locating, selecting, interpreting, using, and applying information from library media sources. Research and study skills concern the interpretation, use, and application of information from textbooks, tradebooks, and reference and media sources in reading and language arts and the content area subjects (mathematics, science, social studies, art, music, and physical education). Many skills taught by the library media specialist and the classroom teacher are essentially the same skills. The Library Media Research and Study Skills Chart is an attempt to combine these skills in a unified structure to facilitate instructional planning.

The Library Media Research and Study Skills Chart is arranged into three categories of objectives: Location and Reference Skills, Interpretation Skills, and Organizational Skills. Within this framework, the skills are grouped into clusters. Each skill cluster, in turn, is stratified in order of complexity of objectives.

Each skill listed in the chart is listed in the form of an instructional objective. Next to each instructional objective are grade levels 3 through 6 listed in grid format. Three levels of instruction are indicated for most instructional objectives: Introduction ◪ , Mastery ⊠, and Refinement (or maintenance) ■ . The notation for introduction, ◪, signifies the grade level(s) at which the skill may be introduced. The notation for mastery, ⊠ , indicates the grade level at which most (at least 70 percent) of the students would be proficient at that particular skill. As all students at a certain grade level will not be at the same level of proficiency for any given skill, the expected mastery level indicates where most students should fall within the instructional framework for the intermediate grades. The notation for refinement, ■ , signifies those grades (following the mastery level) in which continued reinforcement and refinement of the particular skills is presented as students use progressively more difficult and complex library media and classroom sources. The determination of introduction, mastery, and refinement levels of instruction is based on the author's fifteen years as an intermediate grade classroom teacher as well as the suggested levels from myriad curriculum guides, graduate level texts, professional sourcebooks, and instructional guides in library media skills, reading language arts, and the content areas of art, music, physical education, mathematics, science, and social studies.

Many skills may appear to overlap. For instance, the assignment of a research report in social studies involves skills in all three categories of objectives. The student must locate information sources; select appropriate sources, interpret, gather, and record data presented in sources; and then organize the data collected into a logical order for presentation in the required report format. Thus, no one skill will be taught in isolation, but instead each skill will be integrated with other requisite skills. What follows is a more detailed description of the objective categories of location and reference skills, interpretation skills, and organizational skills.

LOCATION AND REFERENCE SKILLS

Location and Reference Skills make up the first category of objectives on the skills chart. These skills include those proficiencies students require to locate information sources within the library media center and to find specific information within those sources. Instructional objectives are predominantly in the cognitive domain's subcategories of knowledge and comprehension (the translation level). They involve the recall of specific location skills and the direct use of individual sources. In the affective domain, it is hoped that the student will participate in activities of locating and using reference sources as a valued means to extend knowledge. Psychomotor skill is needed to enable the student to move physically to particular areas for source retrieval, to handle print and nonprint sources properly, and to operate audiovisual equipment without assistance.

Location and Reference Skills are divided into two categories: Location of Sources in the library media center and Use of Sources in the library media center. The Location of Sources category includes cluster objectives involving the organization and location of sources within the library media center, the composition and use of call numbers to locate sources in the library media center, and the established procedures for the checkout and return of sources in the library media center. The Use of Sources category includes cluster objectives concerning the use of the card catalog to locate sources and information about sources, the operation of audiovisual equipment without assistance, the matching of audiovisual equipment with appropriate nonprint materials, the identification and use of parts of materials, and the use of specific sources (dictionaries, encyclopedias, almanacs, atlases, newspapers, magazines, periodical indexes, and other reference sources) to locate information.

Let us refer to Jack, the student who is having difficulty locating information for his mini-report on the history and significance of St. Patrick's Day. Jack is aware that the card catalog can help him find information concerning materials available in the library media center, but he is not familiar enough to look up a subject in the card catalog. Does he look in the *S* drawer for saints, the *P* drawer for Patrick, the *H* drawer for holidays, or the *I* drawer for Ireland? Then, if he happened to find a source listed, would he know the significance of the call number and shelf arrangement in the library media center and thus be able to locate the specific source? Also, is Jack aware that books about holidays can be found in the 300s section of the library collection? Jack could benefit from instruction in the area of location and reference skills.

INTERPRETATION SKILLS

Interpretation Skills make up the second category of objectives on the skills chart. These skills are those competencies students require to comprehend fully the information presented in sources. Instructional objectives are mainly in the cognitive domain of comprehension (interpretation level) and involve the analysis and evaluation of information presented in sources. Many of these skills are referred to as inferential and/or critical reading-thinking skills. Some skills in the affective domain are involved in the recognition of propaganda techniques, the determining of an author's reliability, and in the evaluation of source materials. Interpretation Skills are divided into two major skills clusters: Interpreting Graphic Aids and Interpretive Reading-Thinking Skills.

The Graphic Aids cluster includes the skills necessary for the interpretation of various formats in sources that display data. These graphic displays include pictures, diagrams, indexes, charts, tables, time lines, schedules, graphs, and maps.

The Reading-Thinking Skills cluster includes those skills necessary to increase word knowledge and the higher level cognitive processes involved in comprehending sources and conducting research. This cluster is arranged into three subcategories: Word Knowledge Skills, Interpretive Reading Skills, and Interpretive Research Skills. Word knowledge proficiencies involve using context clues to determine word meaning, decoding compound words, symbols, and abbreviations, identifying base or root words, and interpreting dictionary, thesaurus, and glossary entries. Interpretive reading competencies include interpreting figurative language, determining the main idea of paragraphs and articles, making generalizations about information read, predicting outcomes in narrative selections, following written directions, determining cause and effect relationships, distinguishing fact from opinion, identifying an author's purpose, making analogies, recognizing propaganda techniques, and determining the reliability of an author. Interpretive research skills concern distinguishing fiction from nonfiction sources, distinguishing nonfiction from reference materials, determining the currentness of material by copyright, identifying alternate key words for topic research, determining the most appropriate reference for a specific purpose, determining the validity of a statement by using more than one reference source, and determining the point of view of specific reference material.

Sujon, the avid baseball fan discussed earlier who loses arguments with his cousin because he can't keep his team's facts and figures straight, could benefit from some guidance in locating and interpreting information as presented in an almanac. First, he must determine the appropriate topic to look up in the index of an almanac. Next, he must be able to interpret the information listed in the index entry to locate the specific page where the desired information is listed. After locating the page, he must use headings and captions to find the specific table listing the statistics he needs. Finally, he must interpret the facts and figures listed in the table, some of which may be written as abbreviations, to prepare himself for his next bout with his cousin. Thus, Sujon requires instruction in location, reference, and interpretation skills.

ORGANIZATIONAL SKILLS

Organizational Skills make up the third category of objectives on the skills chart. These skills include those techniques students need to use and apply information gained from sources. The application and synthesis levels of the cognitive domain are used as the student presents understandings gained from sources. Some skills in the affective domain are involved as the student expresses his or her feelings, interests, and values through the writing of opinion paragraphs, reviews of literature selections, and news editorials as well as through creating artistic representations. Psychomotor skills are developed as the student reports information gained through written, graphic, and media production formats. Organizational Skills are arranged in four skills clusters: Data Gathering Skills, Reporting Skills, Media Production Skills, and Study Techniques and Test-Taking Strategies.

Data gathering skills are those techniques students require to gather, organize, and record information from sources. They include using alphabetizing skills, classifying information into categories, sequencing events in time order, following written directions, conducting surveys and interviews, paraphrasing information, taking notes, summarizing information, skimming and scanning for information, and outlining information.

Reporting skills are those techniques students need to report information gathered from sources. Data gathering skills are a necessary prerequisite for reporting skills, as data must be gathered and organized before reporting can take place. Reporting skills include the writing of paragraphs of varied types, the writing of reports and reviews of literature selections, the reporting of information orally or in dramatic form, and the writing of short factual reports, news articles, editorials, and research reports.

Media production skills are those techniques necessary for students to express ideas and learnings gathered from sources via audio and/or visual media formats. They involve the use of audiovisual equipment and nonprint materials to communicate understandings gained. Media production skills include making graphic representations of data through the production of slides, transparencies, filmstrips, storyboards, scripts, audiotapes, photographs, filmloops, and slide/tape, video tape, and microcomputer programs.

Study techniques and test-taking strategies prepare students for optimum levels of achievement on both teacher-made and standardized tests. Study Techniques include finding a place conducive to study, scheduling study time, and reviewing material prior to tests. Reviewing material involves the application of content organizing strategies such as taking notes, outlining, and summarizing as well as the application of studying models using problem-solving strategies and surveying methods such as the SQ3R model (Survey, Question, Read, Recite, Review). Test-taking strategies incorporate the interpreting and following of written test directions, and the application of reading-thinking skills in the analysis of objective and subjective test items.

Refer to Marissa, the student who finds herself in a hopeless situation. In one evening she must perform in a dance recital, complete a social studies outline on the Industrial Revolution, and review for a spelling test. Marissa is not unlike many students. She needs guidance in developing organizational skills to aid her in completing assignments and reviewing for tests. She needs to plan a work/study schedule to enable her to meet required deadlines. She needs instruction in applying data gathering and reading-thinking skills to enable her to select main ideas and details to complete her outline. She also needs to establish a study method to enable her to review her weekly spelling words on a regular basis. Thus, Marissa requires instruction and practice in the development and the application of organizational skills.

(Text continues on page 25.)

LIBRARY MEDIA RESEARCH AND STUDY SKILLS CHART

Level of Skills Instruction

Introduction   /

Mastery   X

Refinement   ■

I. Location and Reference Skills	3	4	5	6
A. Location of sources in the library media center				
1. Student will explain the organization and location of sources within the library media center.				
a) Picture books	■	■	■	■
b) Periodicals	X	■	■	■
c) Fiction	X	■	■	■
d) Vertical file	/	X	■	■
e) Nonfiction	/	/	X	■
f) Nonprint	/	/	X	■
g) Special collections	/	/	X	■
h) Microforms				/
2. Student will explain the composition of call numbers and use call numbers to locate:				
a) Picture books	■	■	■	■
b) Fiction	/	X	■	■
c) Nonfiction	/	/	X	■
d) Nonprint	/	/	X	■
3. Student will check out and return sources to appropriate places according to established procedures.				

Fig. 1.1. Library Media Research and Study Skills Chart.

	3	4	5	6
a) Books				
b) Periodicals				
c) Nonprint materials	X			
d) Overnight materials	X			
e) Equipment	X			
f) Vertical file materials	/	X		
B. Use of sources in the library media center				
1. Student will use the card catalog to locate sources and information.				
a) Use guide letters and guide words	/	X		
b) Use card catalog to find:				
(1) Call number/Media code	/	X		
(2) Author	/	X		
(3) Title	/	X		
(4) Subject	/	X		
(5) Illustrator	/	X		
(6) Publisher/Producer	/	X		
(7) Copyright date	/	X		
(8) Annotation	/	X		
(9) Editor/Compiler	/	/	X	
(10) Collation (number of pages, illustrations, etc.)		/	X	
c) Differentiate author, subject, and title cards.	/	X		
d) Use cross references.	/	/	X	

Fig. 1.1.–*continued*

	3	4	5	6
e) Identify related subjects.	/	/	X	
f) List available materials (given topic or subject).	/	/	X	
2. Student will operate audiovisual equipment without assistance.				
a) Record player				
b) Filmstrip previewer				
c) Overhead projector				
d) Language master				
e) Cassette recorder	X			
f) Filmloop projector	X			
g) Slide previewer	X			
h) Listening station	X			
i) Microcomputer	/	X		
(1) Operate a microcomputer using a simple prepared program.	X			
(2) Select and operate a program independently.	/	X		
(3) Select and operate an online data base for information contained in the data base.		/	X	
(4) Retrieve information from an online data base		/	X	
j) Filmstrip projector	/	/	X	
k) Slide projector	/	/	X	
l) Reel-to-reel recorder	/	/	X	
m) Instamatic camera	/	/	X	
n) Ektagraphic visualmaker	/	/	X	

Fig. 1.1.–*continued*

	3	4	5	6
o) Video tape recorder	/	/	/	/
p) 16-mm projector	/	/	/	X
q) Microform reader			/	/
3. Student will match audiovisual equipment with the appropriate nonprint materials.				
a) Record player with phonodiscs				
b) Filmstrip previewer with filmstrips				
c) Overhead projector with transparencies				
d) Language master with tape cards				
e) Cassette recorder with cassette tapes	X			
f) Filmloop projector with filmloops	X			
g) Slide previewer with slides	X			
h) Listening station with phonodiscs or cassette tapes	X			
i) Microcomputer with disks or cassettes	X			
j) Filmstrip projector with filmstrips	X			
k) Slide projector with slides	/	X		
l) Reel-to-reel recorder with reel tapes	/	X		
m) Instamatic camera with appropriate film	/	X		
n) Ektagraphic visualmaker with appropriate film	/	/	X	
o) Video tape recorder with videotape	/	/	X	
p) 16-mm projector with 16-mm film	/	X		
q) Microform reader with microfiche			/	X
4. Student will identify format characteristics of:				

Fig. 1.1.—*continued*

	3	4	5	6
a) Books	X			
b) Records	X			
c) Charts	X			
d) Study prints	X			
e) Realia	X			
f) Magazines	/	X		
g) Filmstrips	/	X		
h) Filmloops	/	X		
i) Tapes	/	X		
j) Kits	/	X		
k) Newspapers	/	/	X	
1) Transparencies	/	/	X	
m) Slides	/	/	X	
n) Films	/	/	/	X
o) Microcomputer software	/	/	X	
p) Microforms			/	X
5. Student will identify and use parts of materials.				
a) Call number	X			
b) Title page	X			
c) Table of contents	X			
d) Index	/	X		
e) End papers	/	X		
f) Glossary	/	X		
g) Containers for nonprint materials	/	X		

Fig. 1.1.–*continued*

	3	4	5	6
h) Copyright date	/	/	X	
i) Labels on nonprint materials	/	/	/	X
j) Bibliography		/	/	X
k) Appendix		/	/	/
1) Preface/Foreword			/	/
m) List of illustrations				/
6. Student will identify and use dictionaries.				
a) Determine entry word (base word).	/	X		
b) Use guide words to locate entry word.	/	X		
c) Determine correct pronunciation.	/	X		
d) Determine correct part of speech.	/	/	X	
e) Distinguish between abridged/unabridged dictionaries	/	/	X	
f) Distinguish between general/special dictionaries.		/	/	X
7. Student will identify and use encyclopedias.				
a) Locate volume by spine letter/number.				
b) Identify captions, pictures, charts, tables, diagrams, and maps.				
c) Use guide words to locate articles.	/	X		
d) Locate and use index.	/	X		
(1) Locate and use entries/subentries in index.	/	X		
(2) Use cross-references in index.	/	/	X	
e) Invert names of persons.	/	X		
f) Use headings/subheadings to skim articles.	/	/	X	

Fig. 1.1.–*continued*

	3	4	5	6
g) Identify key words to locate topic/subject.	/	/	/	X
h) Use study aids in articles.	/	/	/	X
i) Identify authors of signed articles.		/	/	X
j) Distinguish between and use special encyclopedias.			/	/
8. Student will identify and use almanacs.				
a) Determine frequency of publication.	/	/	X	
b) Use index to locate information.	/	/	X	
c) Determine purpose and content.	/	/	/	X
d) Use headings/subheadings/captions to locate information.	/	/	/	X
9. Student will identify and use atlases.				
a) Use index to locate a specific map.	/	/	X	
(1) Identify page numbers.	/	/	X	
(2) Identify coordinates.	/	/	X	
b) Distinguish between and use general/special atlases.			/	/
10. Student will identify and use newspapers.				
a) Determine and explain frequency of publication.	X			
b) Use index to locate information.	/	X		
c) Identify sections of newspapers.	/	/	X	
d) Compare local/area/national newspapers.			/	/
11. Student will identify and use magazines.				
a) Determine and explain frequency of publication.	X			

Fig. 1.1.–*continued*

	3	4	5	6
b) Locate and use table of contents to locate articles.	/	X	■	
c) Distinguish between types of magazines.	/	/	/	X
12. Student will identify and use periodical indexes.			/	X
a) Locate and decode symbols and abbreviations in entries.			/	X
b) Locate specific articles in:				
(1) Subject Guide to Children's Magazines			/	X
(2) National Geographic index			/	X
(3) Abridged Readers' Guide			/	/
c) Use cumulative supplements.			/	X
13. Student will identify and use other references.				
a) Television guides	/	/	X	■
b) Guinness Book of World Records	/	/	/	X
c) Telephone directories	/	/	/	/
d) Travel guides		/	/	/
e) Catalogs			/	/
f) Quotation books			/	/
II. Interpretation Skills				
A. Interpretation of graphic aids in sources.				
1. Pictures/Diagrams in dictionary entries	X	■		
2. Picture clues and captions	X	■		

Fig. 1.1.–*continued*

	3	4	5	6
3. Encyclopedia indexes	/	/	/	X
4. Magazine subscription information	/	/	/	X
5. Diagrams	/	X		
6. Charts and tables	/	X		
7. Time lines	/	/	X	
8. Schedules	/	/	X	
9. Graphs				
a) Pictographs	X			
b) Bar graphs	X			
c) Circle graphs	/	X		
d) Line graphs	/	/	X	
10. Maps				
a) Determine directionality on a specific map.	X			
b) Use key/legend to decode symbols.	/	X		
c) Use coordinates (longitude/latitude) to locate a specific place on a map.	/	X		
d) Distinguish landforms from waterways.	/	X		
e) Distinguish between physical and political regions or maps.	/	/	X	
f) Identify and use special maps (population, agriculture, precipitation, etc.).	/	/	/	X
B. Interpretive reading-thinking skills				
1. To increase word knowledge skills, the student will:				
a) Use context clues to determine word meaning.	X			
b) Decode compound words.	X			

Fig. 1.1.–*continued*

	3	4	5	6
c) Interpret glossary entries.	/	X		
d) Interpret dictionary entries to determine word meaning.	/	X		
(1) Interpret multiple meanings.	/	X		
(2) Determine etymology (derivation).	/	/	X	
e) Interpret thesaurus entries to distinguish between synonyms and antonyms.	/	X		
f) Identify base words (root words).	/	/	X	
g) Interpret symbols and abbreviations.	/	/	/	X
2. To increase interpretive reading skills, the student will:				
a) Interpret figurative language in the form of:				
(1) Similes	/	X		
(2) Metaphors	/	X		
(3) Idioms	/	/	X	
(4) Personifications		/	/	X
b) Determine the main idea of paragraphs and articles.	X			
c) Make generalizations about information (conclude, infer).	X			
d) Predict outcomes in a narrative selection.	X			
e) Follow written directions.	X			
f) Determine cause and effect relationships.	/	X		
g) Distinguish fact from opinion.	/	X		
h) Identify an author's purpose.	/	/	X	
i) Make analogies.	/	/	/	X

Fig. 1.1.–*continued*

	3	4	5	6
j) Recognize propaganda techniques.	/	/	/	X
k) Determine the reliability of an author.		/	/	/
3. To increase interpretive research skills, the student will:				
a) Distinguish between fiction and nonfiction sources.	/	X		
b) Distinguish between nonfiction and reference sources.	/	/	X	
c) Determine currentness of a material by copyright.	/	/	X	
d) Identify alternate key words for topic or subject being researched.	/	/	/	X
e) Determine the most appropriate reference for a specific purpose.	/	/	/	X
f) Determine the validity of a statement by using more than one reference source.	/	/	/	X
g) Determine the point of view of a specific reference material.		/	/	/
III. Organizational Skills				
A. To gather and record data from sources, the student will:				
1. Use alphabetizing skills.				
a) Alphabetize to the third letter of a word or to author's last name.	X			
b) Alphabetize to the end of a word or to author's last name.	/	X		
c) Alphabetize titles.	/	X		
d) Apply alphabetizing rules used in the card catalog.	/	/	X	
2. Classify information into categories.	X			

Fig. 1.1.—*continued*

	3	4	5	6
3. Identify or sequence events or steps.	X			
4. Follow written directions.	X			
5. Conduct a survey.	/	X		
6. Conduct an interview.	/	X		
7. Paraphrase information.	/	X		
8. Take notes.	/	X		
9. Summarize information.	/	X		
10. Skim and scan material for information.	/	/	X	
11. Outline information.				
a) Distinguish main topics/subtopics.	/	X		
b) Distinguish details under subtopics.	/	/	X	
B. To report information gathered from sources, the student will:				
1. Write paragraphs.				
a) Recognize topic and detail sentences.	X			
b) Write time order/sequence paragraphs.	X			
c) Write descriptive paragraphs.	X			
d) Write factual paragraphs.	/	X		
e) Write opinion paragraphs.	/	X		
f) Write summary paragraphs.	/	X		
2. Write reports and reviews from literature.				
a) Short narratives (experience stories)	X			
b) Play forms	X			
c) Informational articles	/	X		
d) Novels	/	/	X	

Fig. 1.1.–*continued*

	3	4	5	6
e) Fables, myths, legends	/	/	X	
f) Fairy tales, tall tales, folktales	/	/	X	
g) Biographical, historical, and science fiction	/	/	X	
h) Biographies and autobiographies	/	/	X	
i) Narrative poems	/	/	X	
3. Report data orally or in dramatic form.	X			
4. Use correct bibliographic form.	/	/	X	
5. Write factual reports (1-3 sources).	X			
6. Write news articles and editorials.	/	X		
7. Write research reports (several sources).	/	/	X	
C. To express ideas via media production, the student will:				
1. Make a simple map, chart, or graph.	X			
2. Enlarge visuals using an overhead projector.	X			
3. Prepare a handmade slide, transparency, or filmstrip.	/	X		
4. Prepare a storyboard.	/	X		
5. Write a script.	/	X		
6. Select and record musical background or sound effects for an audio production.	/	X		
7. Take a series of pictures with an Instamatic camera.	/	/	X	
8. Represent a sequence of motion (flipbook, zeotrope, animated film).	/	/	/	X
9. Select media appropriate to express content.	/	/	/	/
10. Produce a slide/tape program.	/	/	/	/

Fig. 1.1.–*continued*

	3	4	5	6
11. Produce a super 8-mm film (with sound).		/	/	/
12. Produce a videotape of a presentation or program.		/	/	/
13. Produce a microcomputer program.	/	/	X	
D. To develop skills in studying for and taking tests, the student will:				
1. Practice study methods by:				
a. Finding a place conducive to study	X			
b. Scheduling study time	X			
c. Reviewing material by applying study methods (SQ3R, DRA, etc.)	/	/	/	X
d. Organizing content materials by taking notes, outlining, summarizing, etc.	/	/	X	
2. Practice test-taking techniques by:				
a. Reading and following written test directions	X			
b. Applying reading-thinking skills to interpret test items	X			
c. Developing techniques for objective test items				
(1) Cloze items (Fill-in-the-blank items)	X			
(2) Multiple-choice items	X			
(3) Matching items	X			
(4) True or false items	/	/	X	
d. Developing techniques for subjective test items				
(1) Short answer items (1-2 sentences)	X			
(2) Paragraph answer items (4-6 sentences)	/	/	X	
(3) Essay answer items (several paragraphs)		/	/	/

Fig. 1.1.–*continued*

SUMMARY

Given today's rapidly expanding base of information and knowledge, it is essential that students in grades 3 through 6 receive instruction in library media research and study skills enabling them to locate, select, interpret, use, and apply information available in print and nonprint sources. Instructional programs are planned, implemented, and assessed on the basis of student performance of educational objectives that range from general goals for instruction (program objectives), to delineated concepts, skills, and processes to be taught (instructional objectives), to statements of specific observable student behaviors (performance objectives). A well-balanced instructional program will include educational objectives representing behavioral changes in student thinking (cognitive domain), feelings (affective domain), and actions (psychomotor domain). An effective library media research and study skills program involves the integration of library media skills traditionally taught by the library media specialist with research and study skills usually taught by the classroom teacher. The resultant Library Media Research and Study Skills Chart lists instructional objectives including location and reference skills, which enable students to locate sources within the library media center and find specific information within those sources; interpretation skills, which enable students to comprehend information within sources; and organization skills, which enable students to gather, organize, use, apply, and report information gained from sources.

NOTES

[1] Benjamin S. Bloom, *Taxonomy of Educational Objectives: The Classification of Educational Goals. Handbook I: Cognitive Domain* (New York: Longmans, Green and Co., Inc., 1956), 1-24, 201-7.

[2] Ibid.

[3] Ibid.

[4] D. R. Krathwohl, B. S. Bloom, and B. B. Masia, *Taxonomy of Educational Objectives: The Classification of Educational Goals. Handbook II: Affective Domain* (New York: David McKay Company, Inc., 1964).

2 *Library Media Research and Study Skills Instruction*

NON-INTEGRATED MODEL

The advent of library media instructional programs in elementary schools is a relatively recent phenomenon. It is only in the past two decades that elementary schools have been expected to have library media specialists who take on the role of instructors with teaching responsibilities in addition to their traditional duties in managing library circulation, carding and shelving materials, providing support materials to teachers, and selecting and purchasing appropriate resources to support the curriculum. A cursory survey of curricular documentation indicates that library media skills instruction as a content area is becoming an essential component in more and more school system curriculums. As a result, many library media specialists find themselves suddenly thrust into the role of teacher with little experience and/or background in educational theory and practice. Most school systems now provide curriculum guides in library media skills instruction identifying objectives, skills, and activities appropriate at various grade levels.

The library media specialist must develop an instructional program to meet the needs of the total population of an elementary school and provide learning experiences in library media skills for all students. These skills generally involve library procedure and organization, information location and retrieval, audiovisual equipment operation and use, and the production of media. The library media specialist identifies the library media skills to be taught, develops instructional activities, implements instruction, and evaluates and revises instructional practices.

The classroom teacher teaches many library media skills in the presentation of reference skills, research skills, or study skills in the reading/language arts area of instruction. These skills are often applied in the other content area subjects, especially in social studies and science. Students are taught the processes involved in the location, interpretation, retrieval, and presentation of information gathered from textual, audiovisual, and reference sources. The classroom teacher identifies content objectives, develops instructional activities, and evaluates and revises instructional practices in these skill areas.

The resultant situation is that many processes are taught both by the library media specialist and the classroom teacher. Although at some point the library media specialist and the classroom teacher may relate certain skills identified in each other's domain, generally the library media specialist teaches library media skills and the classroom teacher teaches research and study skills, in isolation at different times. Figure 2.1 represents this process graphically. Thus, in the non-integrated model, there may be considerable overlap between content skills instruction and library media skills instruction.

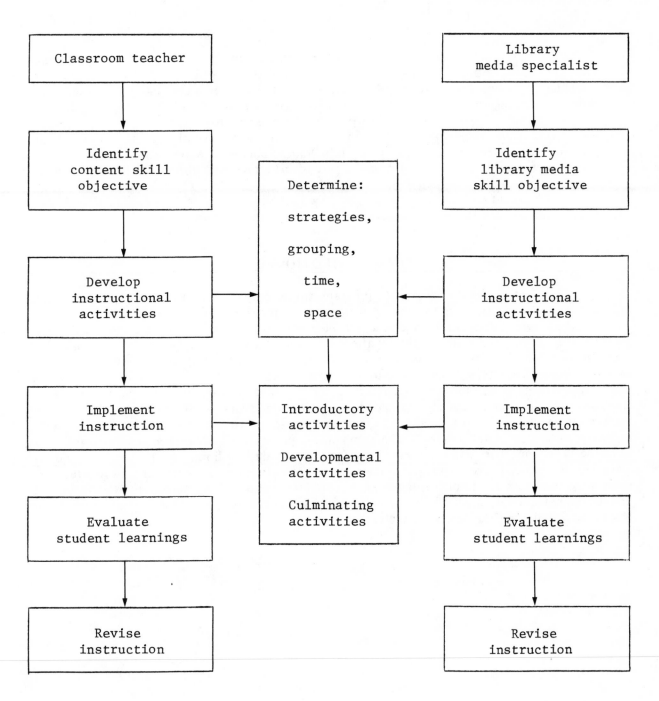

Fig. 2.1. Non-integrated model of library media skills instruction.

EXAMPLE

In January, a sixth-grade classroom teacher began an instructional unit on using reference sources; a research project would be assigned in social studies in February. The teacher chose reference objectives from a reading/language arts unit in a curriculum guide. She developed a series of learning centers in which students had to determine whether an encyclopedia, an almanac, an atlas, or the card catalog would be the most appropriate reference to use, given a series of possible research questions. In April of the same school year, the library media specialist instructed the same group of sixth-grade students in determining the most appropriate reference for a specific purpose—as part of his established library media skills program for sixth grade. Thus, the students received duplicate instruction in the same skill. Although the reinforcement was probably beneficial, it would have been more appropriate if the library media specialist and the classroom teacher had coordinated instruction.

INTEGRATED MODEL

A more effective library media skills program can be developed if the library media specialist and the classroom teacher work together to plan and implement instructional activities.

The Library Media Research and Study Skills Chart (see pages 11-24) is an amalgamation of traditional library media skills taught by the library media specialist and research, reference, and study skills taught by the classroom teacher in the various content areas. It is possible for many of these skills to be taught simultaneously by both staff members. For instance, many of the proficiencies listed under location and reference skills could be introduced by the library media specialist and then reinforced and extended in classroom activities by the teacher. In turn, many interpretation skills and organization skills lend themselves to introduction by the classroom and then extension in the library media center through practice with the varied source materials available. The important point is that through joint planning, the library media specialist and the classroom teacher can develop integrated instructional objectives and activities, and more effectively share responsibilities for implementation of instruction. Figure 2.2 graphically represents an integrated model for library media skills instruction. The actual processes involved in planning strategies will be discussed in greater detail in chapter 3.

(Text continues on page 30.)

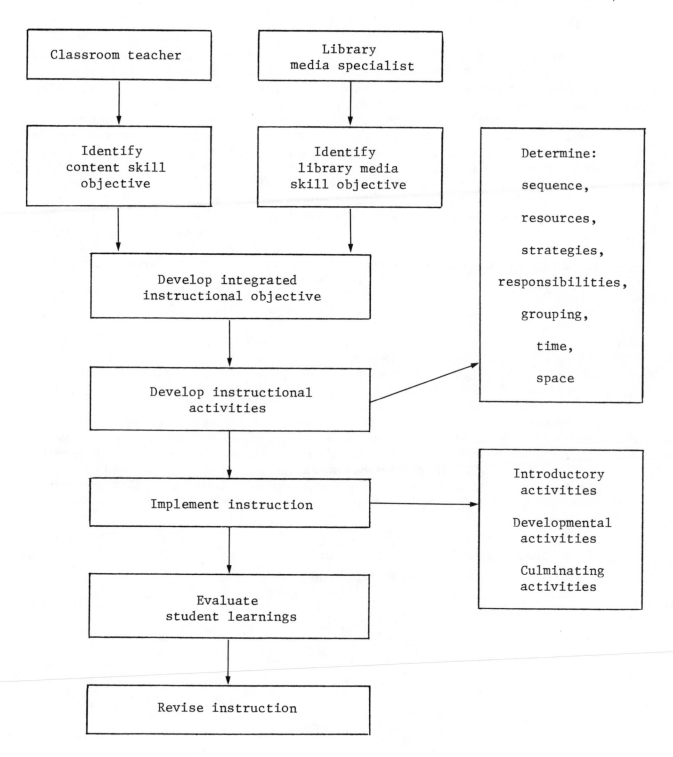

Fig. 2.2 Integrated model of library media skills instruction.

EXAMPLE

Early in the school year, a fourth-grade teacher is planning a reading/language arts unit of study in reference skills entitled "Using the Parts of a Book." The teacher determines that the unit will include activities to enable students to identify, locate, and use the title page, table of contents, glossary, and index of a book.

Next, the classroom teacher meets informally with the library media specialist and they discuss the skills that will be taught in the classroom unit. The library media specialist agrees to support classroom instruction on using a table of contents and an index. The classroom teacher agrees to do all the teaching of the title page and the glossary. They then agree to meet the following day after school to plan their shared instruction.

At this joint planning session, the classroom teacher and the library media specialist decide to concentrate on planning activities for teaching about the table of contents. They schedule another joint planning session in two weeks to plan for instruction about using an index, when they can coordinate it with a unit of study in science on "Light and Color." At this meeting, the library media specialist and the classroom teacher develop the following plan for shared instruction to teach students about the table of contents.

Introductory Activities

Classroom Teacher: Teacher groups students by their reading groups. The teacher meets with each group and has the students answer questions using the table of contents in their reading textbooks. Then, the teacher administers a pretest that he or she has prepared on the use of a table of contents. (See fig. 2.3.)

Library Media Specialist: Students come to the library media center for their weekly scheduled library period as a total class. Students view and discuss a transparency on tables of contents (Polette and Dame, *Using the Library Instructional Materials Center Effectively.* Creative Visuals, 1969). Then, the library media specialist divides the class into pairs. Each pair must select a nonfiction book, bring it back to their seats, locate the table of contents, and report the following information to the library media specialist and the other students:

- The title of the third chapter
- The page on which the second chapter begins.
- The page on which the first chapter ends.

(Text continues on page 32.)

Pretest: Using a Table of Contents

Directions: Read the following table of contents carefully. Then answer
              the questions below it.

```
┌─────────────────────────────────────────────────────────┐
│                   Table of Contents                       │
│                                                           │
│   1.  Care of Indoor Plants . . . . . . . . . . .   7     │
│                                                           │
│   2.  Caring for Seedlings . . . . . . . . . . . .19      │
│                                                           │
│   3.  Winter and Spring Bulbs . . . . . . . . . . 30     │
│                                                           │
│   4.  Special Containers for Plants . . . . . . . 47     │
│                                                           │
│   5.  Plant Pests and Problems . . . . . . . . . .58      │
│                                                           │
└─────────────────────────────────────────────────────────┘
```

1. What is this book about?

2. What does the number before each title represent?

3. What does the number after each chapter title represent?

4. On which page would you begin reading to find out about iris bulbs?
    _____

5. On which page does the chapter on bulbs end? _____

6. Which pages in the book would probably tell about young plants?
    _____

7. On which page would you begin reading to find out how to care for
    houseplants? _____

8. What is the title of the chapter that probably tells about insects
    and diseases that harm plants? _____

9. Which pages probably contain information about bulbs that bloom in
    winter? _____

10. What is the number of the chapter that might contain information about
    clay flower pots? _____

11. On which page would you begin reading about plants that should be
    raised in hanging pots? _____

12. On which page does chapter 4 end? _____

Fig. 2.3. Pretest.

Developmental Activities

Classroom Teacher: Students are assigned written work in their language textbook related to using a table of contents, and the teacher conducts mini-lessons in which students use the table of contents in their mathematics, science, and social studies textbooks.

Library Media Specialist: Students go to the library media center for their weekly library period as a total class. They are introduced to the "Contents Challenge" learning activities package (LAP), which was jointly developed by the library media specialist and the classroom teacher. (The library media specialist contributed the activity sheets related to library books, and the classroom teacher contributed the coversheet and the activity sheets related to textbooks.) The library media specialist and the students do Activity 1—Metric Measure together. Students are sent back to their classrooms to complete the "Contents Challenge" LAP (see figs. 2.4-2.11, pages 33-40).

Classroom Teacher: The teacher meets with students to supervise progress through the "Contents Challenge" learning activities package. The teacher will work through the package with students who displayed difficulty using a table of contents on the pretest and subsequent language book assignments. Other students will complete the package independently. The classroom teacher will meet with all students upon completion of the "Contents Challenge" learning activities package to check answers.

Culminating Activities

Classroom Teacher: Students report to the library media center for their regularly scheduled weekly library period. The library media specialist divides the students into groups of no more than five members each. The library media specialist gives each group a different nonfiction book pertaining to a current social studies classroom unit on Colonial America. Students are directed next on how to play the "Contents Search" game. Each group must choose a chairperson who will be the "teacher" and a scorekeeper who will record the points. The "teacher" asks two questions of each group member. The questions should be similar to those posed in the "Contents Challenge" learning activities package. The scorekeeper will record one point for each correct response. When all groups have completed the task, each scorekeeper will report the total group score to determine the highest scoring group. Appropriate rewards may be given to the winning group.

Classroom Teacher: As the final activity of the jointly planned unit of study, the classroom teacher administers a posttest that he or she has prepared on the use of a table of contents. (See fig. 2.12, page 41.)

(Text continues on page 42.)

CONTENTS

Fig. 2.4. Cover sheet.

Activity 1

METRIC MEASURE

Directions: Read the following table of contents. Then answer the questions below it.

Table of Contents

1. History of the Metric System 4

2. Metric Measures of Length 14

3. Metric Measures of Weight 19

4. Metric Use in the United States 23

5. Metric Use throughout the World 31

---

1. Which pages would you read to find out about the different metric measures of length? _____

2. What is the number of the chapter that tells how the metric system is used in other countries? _____

3. On which page would you begin reading to find out where the metric system was first used? _____

4. What is the number of the chapter that tells the names of metric measures used to weigh things? _____

5. What is the last page that would tell how the metric system is used in the United States? _____

6. What is the title of the chapter that tells who developed the metric system? _____

Fig. 2.5. Worksheet.

Activity 2

SPACE SEARCH RIDDLE

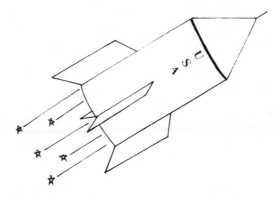

Directions: Study the table of contents below. Read each statement under the table of contents and decide whether it is true or false. For each statement, circle a letter in the True or False column. At the bottom of the page, write the letters you circled to spell out the riddle answer.

Riddle: What keeps the moon in place?

Table of Contents	
1. Planning a Space Trip	1
2. The Planets	.14
3. Stars	.30
4. Our Sun.	61
5. Traveling in Space	77
Index	92

		True	False
1.	There are six chapters in the book.	S	I
2.	This book is probably about space travel.	T	I
3.	Chapter 3 ends on page 60.	S	T
4.	The index ends on page 91.	A	B
5.	Packing foods for the trip would probably be **talked** about in chapter 1.	E	R
6.	The last page in chapter 4 is page 29.	B	A
7.	The space travel chapter begins on page 77.	M	U
8.	The index is a separate chapter.	G	S

Riddle Answer: __ __ __ __ __ __ __ __ .
                  1 2 3   4 5 6 7 8

Fig. 2.6. Worksheet.

Activity 3 -- American History Mix-Up

Directions: The following table of contents has its chapter titles and
page listings out of order! Rewrite the table correctly. You
may use a United States history book to help you.

	The Revolutionary War	150
1.	Early Settlers Meet Native Americans . . .	197
2.	The Nation Divides	105
3.	Explorers Find a New World	239
4.	Westward Movement	52
5.	The Civil War	35
6.	Index	78
7.	Life in the Colonies	5
8.	Reconstruction after the Civil War	126
9.	A New Nation Begins	171
	Contents	

_____

_____

_____

_____

_____

_____

_____

_____

_____

_____

_____

_____

Fig. 2.7. Worksheet.

Activity 4 -- Contents Riddle

Directions: Study the table of contents below. Read each statement under the
              table of contents to decide whether it is true or false. Circle
              a word under <u>True</u> or <u>False</u> for each statement. Use the circled
              words to find the riddle answer.

Riddle: Why is the letter A like twelve o'clock?

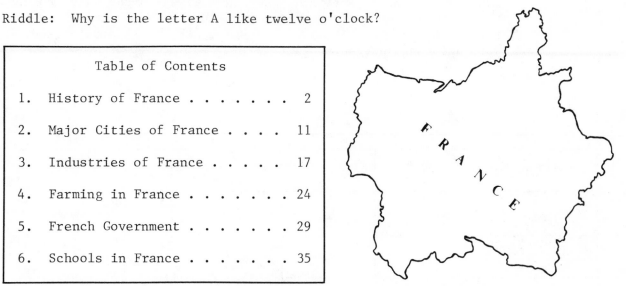

```
┌─────────────────────────────────────────┐
│          Table of Contents                │
│                                           │
│  1.  History of France . . . . . . .   2  │
│                                           │
│  2.  Major Cities of France . . . .  11   │
│                                           │
│  3.  Industries of France . . . . .  17   │
│                                           │
│  4.  Farming in France . . . . . . .  24  │
│                                           │
│  5.  French Government . . . . . . .  29  │
│                                           │
│  6.  Schools in France . . . . . . .  35  │
└─────────────────────────────────────────┘
```

	True	False
1. Pages 17-23 might tell how steel is made.	Because	So
2. This book has seven chapters.	it	it's
3. The first page of the chapter that tells about the education of children in France is page 34.	can	in
4. The title of the chapter that tells about the political system in France is "French Government."	the	play
5. Pages 2-10 would probably tell what happened in France in 1066.	middle	on
6. Chapter 5 would probably tell about the main crops grown in France.	the	of
7. The last page on which you might find out about Paris is page 16.	day	clock

Riddle Answer: ___ _____ _____ _____ _____ _____ _____.
                    1   2   3   4   5   6   7

Fig. 2.8. Worksheet.

Activity 5 -- Contents Contemplation

Directions: Find the message about Ramona Quimby! Go to the library media
center and find a copy of Ramona and Her Father by Beverly
Cleary. Use the table of contents to fill in the "Chapter
Title" column of the chart below. Then locate the message word
in each chapter by following the clues given in the other columns
of the chart. Write the message word in the "Word" column. Rewrite
the message at the bottom of this page. The first chapter and
word are done for you.

Chapter Title	Page #	Paragraph #	Sentence #	Word #	Word
1. "Payday"	14	3	1	1	Ramona
2.	38	2	2	6	
3.	62	1	2	5	
4.	87	8	1	6	
5.	120	1	4	6	
6.	144	2	2	21	
7.	179	2	6	14	

Message: Ramona _____ _____ _____ _____ _____ _____.
            1   2   3   4   5   6   7

Fig. 2.9. Worksheet.

Activity 6 -- Focus on Science

Directions: Read the following table of contents
carefully. Then read each topic below
the table of contents. Write the
beginning page number of the chapter
you would read to find information on
that topic.

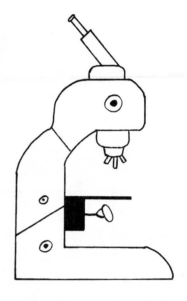

_____ 1. Oil used as a lubricant

_____ 2. How canyons are formed

_____ 3. Saltwater environments

_____ 4. Chlorophyll in plant cells

_____ 5. Cool air contracts

_____ 6. Larva stage of a butterfly

_____ 7. Colors of stars

_____ 8. Electricity conduction

_____ 9. Frequency of sounds

_____ 10. Star constellations

_____ 11. Friction creates heat

_____ 12. Soil conservation

_____ 13. Life in a pond

_____ 14. Bone tissue

_____ 15. Low-pitched sounds

_____ 16. Plants growing from buds

_____ 17. Warm air rises

_____ 18. How a flashlight works

_____ 19. The muscular system

_____ 20. How we hear sounds

_____ 21. Series and parallel wiring

_____ 22. Life stages of a frog

_____ 23. The sun as a star

_____ 24. Life in rapid streams

_____ 25. The formation of caves

_____ 26. Barometers measure air pressure

Fig. 2.10. Worksheet.

Activity 7 -- Contents Query Quiz

M
E
X
I
C
O

Directions: Pretend that
you are a teacher or a library
library media specialist.
Using the table of contents
below, make up at least five
questions for a quiz. (Your
quiz may be in the form of a riddle
or a puzzle.) Try your "Contents
Query Quiz" out on your classmates!

Table of Contents

1.   The Land and Climate of Mexico   5

2.   Mexico's History 21

3.   The Government of Mexico 40

4.   The People and Their Customs 51

5.   Earning a Living in Mexico 95

     Glossary 120

     Index. 127

_____

_____

_____

_____

_____

_____

_____

_____

_____

_____

Fig. 2.11. Worksheet.

Posttest: Using a Table of Contents

Directions: Read the following table of contents carefully. Then answer each question below it. Circle the best answer.

Table of Contents

1. The table of contents of a book is found near (a) the beginning (b) the middle (c) the end

2. The table of contents is arranged (a) alphabetically (b) by page sequence (c) by topic

3. The book above is probably about (a) animals (b) pets (c) cats

4. The title of chapter 3 is (a) "Other Pets" (b) "Dogs as Pets" (c) "Birds as Pets"

5. In this book there are (a) five (b) six (c) four chapters

6. The index begins on page (a) 68 (b) 81 (c) 80

7. (a) The index (b) The first chapter (c) The introduction is found on page 3

8. The longest chapter is (a) chpater 5 (b) chapter 1 (c) chapter 2.

9. The shortest chapter is (a) **chapter** 5 (b) chapter 4 (c) chapter 3.

10. This book would most likely have (a) 95 (b) 80 (c) 68 pages

Fig. 2.12. Posttest.

WHO TEACHES LIBRARY MEDIA RESEARCH AND STUDY SKILLS?

In the proposed model for the teaching of library media research and study skills (integrating them with content area instruction), the responsibilities for teaching are jointly shared by the library specialist and the classroom teacher. The library media specialist, with his or her unique qualifications as a process specialist, and the classroom teacher, with his or her expertise as a content specialist, work together to develop appropriate learning alternatives for students.

The library media specialist contributes to library media research and study skills instruction by:

- Working with the classroom teacher to determine which library media skills will be integrated into a unit of instruction, which instructional strategies will be used to teach the identified skills, and who will do the actual teaching—library media specialist, classroom teacher, or both.

- Coordinating with the classroom teacher to establish assessment procedures to be sure that skills are learned effectively and at the appropriate time.

- Teaching some of the library media research and study skills that are mutually agreed upon.

- Developing student objectives, activities, and assessments as they are needed during the implementation of a given unit of study.

- Providing assistance to individual students using the library media center.

- Selecting and purchasing appropriate library media resources, with the classroom teacher's input, for the implementation of instructional units of study.

- Providing resources to students and teachers as they are needed.

- Evaluating and revising instructional activities on the basis of assessment of student learnings.

The classroom teacher contributes to library media research and study skills instruction by:

- Working with the library media specialist to determine how library media skills will be integrated with content learnings for a unit of study, what instructional strategies will be used to teach the skills, and who will do the actual teaching—classroom teacher, library media specialist, or both.

- Coordinating with the library media specialist to establish assessment procedures to be sure that skills are learned effectively and at the appropriate time.

- Teaching some of the library media research and study skills that are mutually agreed upon.

- Integrating library media research and study skills into the various content area subjects.

- Developing student objectives, activities, and assessments as they are needed during the implementation of a given unit of study.

- Developing activities and assignments in all subject areas that involve student use of the library media research center and application of library media research and study skills.

- Providing support to the library media specialist in selecting and purchasing appropriate library media resources for the implementation of instructional units of study.

- Evaluating and revising instructional activities on the basis of assessment of student learnings.

INSTRUCTIONAL VARIABLES

There are many variables that must be considered before initiating an integrated library media research and study skills program. Characterisitics of the community, school facility, curriculum design, and instructional staff must be reviewed and understood before beginning any such program. The proposed model attempts to provide a method for establishing an integrated program under ideal conditions. Realistically speaking, educational settings often vary from the ideal situation despite the best efforts of individuals to transcend deficiencies. A school that lacks the ideal setting can still use many of the processes inherent in integrated library media instruction. Many of the processes involved can be adapted to meet the needs of students, teachers, and library media specialists despite differences in community, facility, curriculum, and staffing.

THE COMMUNITY

There are a number of characteristics of a school community to be considered before implementing an integrated library media skills instructional program. These characteristics include rural, suburban, or urban location; the educational, occupational, and economic levels of the members; the cultural and ethnic backgrounds of the population; the influence of the civic, social, and religious groups; the role of the local Parent Teachers Association; and cultural and recreational opportunities available to members. Although some of these community characteristics may be perceived as impediments to integrated library media instruction, some of the processes involved in integrating library media instruction may be adapted to compensate for community limitations.

Location

The location of a school—rural, suburban, or urban—can have some bearing on the development of an integrated library media research and study skills program. School system structure may be dependent upon community location. In some states, school system organization is based upon political boundaries, with each town, city, or county funding and maintaining its own schools. Often rural schools are part of a school system that covers a large geographical area. This may limit the sharing of resources, access to central library media centers, and contact with other library media specialists and teachers.

In times of declining enrollment, budgetary considerations are necessary in all locations. Suburban and urban schools may be faced with budgetary problems but may have the advantages of access to central school system library media centers and public libraries, the sharing of resources between schools, and contact with other library media specialists and classroom teachers.

EXAMPLE

The library media specialist of Acton County Consolidated Elementary School has relocated and is faced with providing a library media program in a rural school that is part of a school system that is geographically large but generally low in student population. She was formerly a library media specialist at a suburban elementary school in another county with relatively unrestricted access to school system resources and monies for program implementation. Physical distance precludes the sharing of materials and contact with school system and public libraries: her school is twenty-five miles from the Acton County Public School's Central Library Media Resource Center, twenty miles from the nearest public library, and seventeen miles from the closest elementary school. She wishes to establish an integrated library media instructional program, but after assessing the library media resources available at Acton Consolidated School and the funding limitations for elementary school libraries in Acton County Schools, she realizes that she will have to develop her integrated program slowly. She decides to spend her first year assessing student strengths and needs, teaching library media skills appropriate at particular grade levels in a non-integrated manner, and familiarizing herself with curriculum standards and practices in order to work with the principal and staff to develop means of integrating instruction with available resources, funding, and curricular design.

Educational, Occupational, and Economic Levels

Other community characteristics that may be pertinent to the development and implementation of integrated library media instructional programs include the general educational, occupational, and economic levels of community members. The prevalent educational level of a school community may determine the amount of parental involvement in and support of instructional programs and procedures. Parental participation in the actual selection of instructional materials, although sometimes helpful, may result in the censorship of and restrictions upon the use of materials available for curricular support. The availability and successful use of volunteers for library media center and classroom clerical duties and instructional support is in part related to general educational, occupational, and economic factors. School system budgetary considerations are indirectly made on the basis of occupational and/or economic levels of the community, as most school system budgets are dependent on federal income taxes and state and local property taxes for a large portion of the funds needed to finance the schools.

EXAMPLE

The library media specialist at Mark Twain Elementary School, an "open" school in a middle-class suburban community, has developed a highly successful library media skills program supporting classroom instruction in the content subject areas over the past five years. She has effectively used parent volunteers as library media center aides to help with the clerical duties in the library media center and the record keeping involved with the individualization of instruction. During the past year, she has been faced with an increasing number of volunteers who have ceased their duties as library media center aides, as they have acquired paying jobs elsewhere in the community. Upon closer inspection, the library media specialist discovered that in many cases, the volunteers had been forced to go to work because their spouses were victims of the "riffing" of hundreds of workers at a local corporation dependent upon federal contract grants. Although the loss of the majority of her volunteer force did impede the individualized instruction somewhat, the library media specialist instituted a Library Aides Club in which responsible fifth and sixth grade students were trained to perform some of the clerical duties formerly handled by parent volunteers.

Cultural and Ethnic Backgrounds

Another community characteristic that may influence the integration of library media research and study skills instruction and content skills instruction is the cultural and ethnic backgrounds of community members. Varying cultural and ethnic origins may alter the institution of library media programs as library media specialists and classroom teachers develop strategies and activities that reflect the educational priorities and attitudes of community constituents. Although some accommodations for bilingual instruction may have to be made, this situation presents a perfect opportunity for students to become involved in cross-cultural peer teaching or peer tutoring situations. Communities in which varying cultural and ethnic groups are represented provide unique opportunities for the development of educational activities that enhance multicultural and multi-ethnic exchange, respect, and understanding.

EXAMPLE

The library media specialist and the fourth-grade teaching team at Sonorama Elementary School, a rural school in an agrarian community in the southwestern United States, have developed a unique form of integrated library media and content area instruction to accommodate the needs of a largely transient student population. Approximately 45 percent of the students are of Mexican-American origin. These students generally attend Sonorama School from early December until early April each year. Since their parents are migrant workers, the students follow them to wherever the work becomes available as crops become ready for harvesting. The fourth-grade teachers and the library media specialist have adapted the curriculum to build upon the experiences of the migrant students. During the months when the migrant students are present, two units of study are jointly taught by the library media specialist and the fourth-grade team. A social studies unit on State Geography and History highlights the settlement of the state by Mexican-Americans and their subsequent contributions to the history of the state. A science unit on Plant Cycles and Agriculture capitalizes on experiences of all students in this agrarian community. The library media specialist and the teachers have carefully planned activities in which students use library media materials and apply library media research and study skills in both units of study. This program is also enhanced by pairing transient and permanent students for instruction in a manner that is conducive to intercultural exchange and respect.

Civic, Social, and Religious Groups

Another community characteristic that may greatly influence the planning and implementing of instructional programs is the role played by civic, social, and religious groups in the community. The setting of educational policy has become a national, state, and local political issue. Civic and religious leaders and groups increasingly have become involved in political movements related to education. In most school systems, the board of education is responsive to community representatives who voice educational priorities at meetings and work sessions open to the general public. Local school system policy on controversial topics such as sex education, prayer in the school, censorship, teacher competency, and merit pay reflect national and local community opinion. Political movements such as the "back to basics" movement and the "trim" taxation measures have greatly influenced educational funding in many communities. Even informal social gatherings such as neighborhood coffees or cocktail parties and conversations at the community swimming pool may be antecedents to educational policy change, which, in turn, may influence instructional programming at the local school level. Thus, the opinions and actions of community civic, social, and religious groups are often felt at the local school level, and they can indirectly determine to some degree the community acceptance of new instructional programs such as an integrated library media research and study skills program.

EXAMPLE

Two years ago, the constituency of a middle-class suburban community voted for "slim" taxation measures in order to lower local property taxes. They were influenced by a national media bombardment campaign espousing unfair taxation policies and spending excesses at national, state, and local government levels. As a result, the local school system had to make drastic budgetary cuts in the educational appropriations for the following year. Unfortunately, the spending cuts were devastating at the local school level. The number of elementary library media specialists for the entire school system was cut in half. Those elementary library media specialists who were still employed at the end of the first year after the "slim" measures took effect, found themselves assigned to two and sometimes three elementary schools. Library media specialists who had formerly been involved in integrated library media and content skills instructional programs found the process too taxing, as time limitations precluded such instructional practices. The library media specialists had to spend more time in outlining cooperative efforts with classroom teachers so that precious time with students could be given to meaningful experiences. Fortunately, at the next local election, the "slim" measures were not reinstated by the voters.

Parent Teacher Association

The local school Parent Teacher Association is perhaps the most influential community group involved in the establishment, implementation, and maintenance of effective educational programs. In schools where there is supportive participation of Parent Teacher Association leaders and members, positive rapport between parents, teaching staff, and students develops. This positive atmosphere is conducive to promoting the success of instructional programs. Parent Teacher Association leaders and members who support staff-determined educational needs are an invaluable source of ideas and experiences for generating, funding, and maintaining existing and prospective educational programs. The local school Parent Teacher Association may be a source of funds for needs that cannot be met by school system budgetary allotments and a source of volunteers for clerical and instructional support roles. The amount of participation in and support of instructional programs by Parent Teacher Association members is determined by (1) the number of parents actively involved; (2) the role of the principal and the teaching staff; (3) the educational, occupational, and economic levels of the parents; and (4) the degree of involvement in regional and national Parent Teacher Associations. Although in some communities the Parent Teacher Association may take on an almost dictatorial role in determining school policies and programming, most are an inimitable asset to instructional support.

EXAMPLE

The school board of a large, affluent, progressive school system passed a resolution that "computer literacy" be integrated into instructional programs at all levels of the curriculum. The board advocated intensive exposure to microcomputers and hands-on experiences with computer hardware and software beginning with kindergarten students. Each elementary school was allotted one microcomputer and several pieces of introductory software. The library media specialist in each school was designated coordinator of computer literacy instruction as "information disseminator" of each school.

The library media specialist at Brookstone Elementary School was already coordinating computer literacy instruction at his school with two existing microcomputers and a bank of ten program tapes previously purchased through school funds. The program was limited, however, by scarcity of materials, lack of teacher training, and inequitable use of computer time by all students. The library media specialist and a teacher representative, with the support of the principal, petitioned to the Parent Teacher Association for financial and volunteer assistance. Over the next few months, the Parent Teacher Association organized several fundraising events to raise money to support the computer literacy program. As a result, the Parent Teacher Association purchased two additional microprocessors as well as several software packages. The library media specialist set up a computer lab with the five microcomputers accommodating groups of up to fifteen students at a time. The Parent Teacher Association also set up a network of parent volunteers familiar with microprocessors to assist students in the computer lab.

Cultural and Recreational Opportunities

Another community characteristic that may influence instructional programming is the existence of cultural and recreational opportunities in the community. Although closely related to location, the proximity and availability of cultural sites enhances instructional programming by providing access to museums, theaters, and government and publication offices that may offer tours, resource persons, loans, and printed materials to extend curricular learnings. Individual members of the community with expertise in art, drama, dance, and music may offer extracurricular opportunities for students to foster artistic appreciation and expression. Recreational options in the form of organized sports and exercise classes enable students to extend psychomotor skills and practice good sportsmanship and fair play. Students practice social skills and peer interaction through community-sponsored clubs such as Boy Scouts, Indian Guides and Princesses, Camp Fire Girls, and Girl Scouts. In many communities, recreational clubs and organizations coordinate with the local elementary schools to share materials and space for meetings and to plan activities that support the curriculum. Thus, cultural and recreational opportunities may extend educational programs and student learnings.

EXAMPLE

The library media specialist and the fifth grade teachers at Readville Elementary School coordinated a unit of study on Colonial Life. The library media specialist contacted a representative of the Reading County Historical Society and made arrangements for a field trip to a reconstructed eighteenth century home that had been converted into a colonial museum. The Historical Society representative offered the loan of a "colonial package" prior to the visit to the museum. The library media specialist set up a "Colonial Corner" of the library media center to which teachers brought students to prepare them for their subsequent field trip. Students were then directed to locate information concerning the various realia on display in print and nonprint materials. After conducting research, the students reported the information gained by producing a slide/tape presentation of their learnings. Later, at the colonial museum, the students were taken on a tour led by guides dressed in authentic colonial-style clothing. They observed and participated in special demonstrations of colonial crafts such as broom making, weaving, spinning, blacksmithing, quilting, and tinsmithing. The student response to this unit of study was tremendous. The opportunities experienced as a result of the arrangements made through the Reading County Historical Society certainly enhanced the instruction of this unit of study.

THE SCHOOL FACILITY

The structure of a school building may determine, to some degree, the logistics involved in providing an integrated library media instructional program. The location of the library media center varies from one elementary school to another. The inclusion of a library media center as an integral part of an elementary school is a relatively recent occurrence. Schools built before the 1960s may house the library media center in a converted classroom, an all-purpose room, or, in some cases, a basement or hallway. The accessibility of the library media center to students, in part, affects its use by students. In some older elementary schools that have two or more stories, movement to and from the library media center may be restricted by distance and safety precautions. In some newer open space schools, the library media center may be a central focal point from which classroom suites radiate. Although ideally this type of structure physically integrates the library media center as part of every classroom, problems in traffic management and noise control may impede the provision of an atmosphere conducive to student concentration and study.

The provision of special areas and facilities, in addition to the library media center, may extend library media instruction by furnishing additional spaces for instruction and use and storage of instructional materials. The inclusion of specified areas or rooms designated as art, music, or drama centers or reading, math, or science laboratories can expedite joint planning for instructional implementation by library media specialists, classroom teachers, and educational specialists in the content areas.

The availability of designated areas for large group activities may restrict instructional practices by limiting space for such activities. The *ideal* elementary school has, as separate facilities, an auditorium, a cafeteria, and a gymnasium. In many elementary schools, however, an all-purpose room serves to incorporate the functions of cafeteria, auditorium, and gymnasium, which places restraints on the scheduling and use of such large-space instructional areas.

The structure and location of an elementary school facility may also determine the use of outdoor areas for instructional purposes, especially for student experiences involving outdoor observations of scientific phenomena. Urban schools often have little space for outdoor activities other than a small blacktop area designated as playground. Suburban and rural schools may have the advantage of large grassy areas for outdoor instruction.

The characteristics of an elementary school facility may limit student access to the library media center and space for instructional extension, but library media specialists and teachers dedicated to integrated library media research and study skills instruction will find ways to overcome these limitations. Accommodations can be made readily to compensate for physical space restrictions. The key to a successful integrated library media research and study skills program is the interactive processes between students, teaching staff members, and instructional materials, rather than the physical setting of such a program.

EXAMPLE

Public school #24, commonly referred to as Central Street Elementary School, is housed in a three-story building in a large metropolitan city in the northeastern United States. The library media center is located in a converted classroom on the third floor. There are no areas or facilities available for special instruction other than a remedial reading room located on the second floor, and an all-purpose room on the basement level adjacent to the boiler room.

Space for instruction in the library media center is very limited, as it can accommodate only fifteen students at a time. All classes are scheduled for two twenty-minute "Library Skills" periods per week; half of the class comes to the library media center at a time.

Within this framework, the library media specialist created a plan that provided fifth- and sixth-grade classroom teachers with a weekly forty-minute planning period during their students' scheduled "Library Skills" time. As part of the plan, the library media specialist created a "Mini-Library Media Center" in one classroom of each grade level. On a bimonthly basis, the library media specialist selected fiction, nonfiction, and/or reference materials from the library media center that supported a content area unit of study in reading/language arts, science, or social studies and placed these materials in the Mini-Library Media Center. She developed instructional strategies and activities for library media skills instruction based on the use of the selected materials. During the scheduled "Library Skills" periods, the library media specialist came to the Mini-Library Media Center, thus, freeing the classroom teacher.

At first some teachers resisted the idea of sharing their rooms and materials with students other than their own; but, after the first few months, teachers became more enthusiastic and the instructional program began to run more smoothly. Some teachers began to consult with the library media specialist to plan follow-up activities to lessons initiated by the library media specialist, as teachers noted changes in student motivation and interest. At the end of the year, the sixth-grade teachers asked the library media specialist to help them organize and manage a departmentalized instructional plan for the following year as well as a more flexible scheduling pattern for "Library Skills" instruction.

CURRICULUM DESIGN

Most school systems today publish and distribute curricular documents designating the subjects and skills to be taught at appropriate grade levels. Most local school system documents incorporate state standards for student learnings at particular grade levels. In fact, many states are now identifying minimal competency skills in such areas as functional reading, functional math, and survival and are designing and distributing criterion reference tests to be administered at certain grade levels to ensure minimal standards for student advancement from grade to grade.

Most curriculum documents list basic program and instructional objectives for a particular grade level and content subject. Many also give suggested unit topics and listings of suggested resources and activities to ensure adequate student exposure to the concepts, skills, and processes entailed in each subject area. In many school systems, the teaching staff may select topics within the general framework set up in the curriculum guide that are appropriate to the needs and interests of their students. Therefore, in school systems in which the teaching staff is allowed more flexibility in adhering to curricular standards, staff members select student objectives, develop learning activities, choose instructional strategies, procure or create instructional materials, implement instructional practices, and evaluate student learnings in an atmosphere conducive to creative teaching and learning.

Unfortunately, in some school systems, this flexible pattern of teaching is not encouraged. Students must progress through a school system-determined set of instructional objectives sequentially organized for each subject at each grade level. Teachers may be observed and evaluated on the basis of adherence to the school system curricular plan. When this occurs, the spontaneity and creativity of the teacher is thwarted, and student needs and interests are neglected rather than developed. When too rigid adherence to curricular scope and sequence documents is expected, teachers expend their energies attempting to cover material rather than trying to teach it.

An integrated library media research and study skills program would flourish in the more flexible school system. Activities in the various curriculum areas would be coordinated to eliminate unnecessary overlap between content areas and to enable studies in the diverse subjects to reinforce one another.

EXAMPLE

The library media specialist at an elementary school in a large progressive school system has observed much frustration among the teaching staff members of her school during the past three years. The school system has been revising its curriculum in the major content areas of reading, mathematics, science, and social studies. Curricular documents have been revised, reissued, and redistributed to schools. Each time a "new" document has arrived, the staff has become involved in a series of workshops to survey curricular documents, practice techniques suggested in the documents, write long-range plans including the new instructional objectives, and become familiar with new testing and record-keeping practices. In addition, each revised curriculum has a series of system-created criterion reference tests that must be administered twice per school year in grades three through six.

Classroom teachers have become increasingly frustrated, because their involvement in various stages of curricular implementation has included much time preparing students for criterion reference testing, administering the tests, and recording test data on the new record-keeping documents provided for each major content area. The library media specialist has been responsible for the same processes in implementing the revised program in library media skills, however, she has realized that this was concentrated on one content area, whereas classroom teachers have been responsible for implementing instructional programs in four revised content areas. One fifth grade teacher pointed out that during the school year, nine weeks had been involved in preparing students for and administering system-derived tests. Since nine weeks is equivalent to one marking period, other teachers began to wonder—"When do I teach the material covered by these tests?"

The library media specialist and the classroom teachers in this school had previously worked closely together integrating content area and library media skills instruction, but the classroom teachers now had less time to devote to planning with the library media specialist. After consulting with the principal, the library media specialist made a proposal to the teaching staff. The library media specialist would meet with one representative for each content subject from each grade level to identify common content and library media skills tested. Then, after this survey was complete, the library media specialist would meet with the total staff to discuss commonly tested skills, and suggest ways she and the classroom teachers could plan together to coordinate instruction to eliminate unnecessary overlap between content areas and to expedite implementation of new curricular standards. At this meeting, the library media specialist would share a learning activities package that she had developed in "using tables to locate information," which she had previously identified as a skill common to reading, mathematics, science, and social studies instruction in grades three through six (see figs. 3.16-3.25 on pages 91-100).

THE INSTRUCTIONAL STAFF

Successful implementation of an integrated library media research and study skills program is dependent upon the cooperative efforts of all staff members. Variations exist among different elementary schools as to staff allocation, the role of the principal, preferred instructional practices, and interaction among staff members. As with differing characteristics of the community, school facility, and curriculum design, instructional staff variables that are not ideal need not preclude integrative instruction. Instead, accommodations can be made to compensate for limitations in the instructional staff.

Allocation of Staff

The establishment, implementation, and maintenance of an integrated library media research and study skills program may be subject to variations because of allocation of staff at a particular school. School staff assignments may often be made on the basis of budgetary or declining enrollment considerations. The total number of classroom teachers and the organization of students into straight-grade or combination-grade classes may affect the strategies involved to integrate library media research and study skills instruction. Whether the school is allotted a full-time or a part-time library media specialist is of utmost importance in determining the teaching responsibilities of the library media specialist. The inclusion of library media aides and their apportionment on a full-time or part-time basis is another staff allocation variable that can be quite pertinent to an integrated library media research and study skills program. Library media aides are often given responsibility for many of the clerical duties involved in managing library circulation and the carding and shelving of materials, thus supplying the library media specialist with more time to plan instruction with classroom teachers and teach students essential information skills.

EXAMPLE

Valley Acres Elementary School, located in an affluent suburban community, was subjected to drastic staff allocation changes as a result of declining enrollment. The total number of classroom teachers was reduced from eighteen to fourteen, resulting in four combination-grade classes. Although Valley Acres was still allotted a full-time library media specialist, the library media aide position was cut to half-time. The library media specialist had always worked closely with classroom teachers to coordinate library media skills instruction with current classroom units in social studies and science, and the former full-time library media aide had essentially handled most of the clerical duties associated with circulation management. The library media specialist wanted to continue her teaching duties, as she enjoyed working directly with students in an instructional capacity. Scheduling was difficult, as she could only meet with instructional groups on the days when her library media aide was present. She had to change from a flexible schedule to a fixed one in order to accommodate all classes, which included the four combination-grade classes that required two sessions each. Although it meant that the library media specialist would have two and one half days per week that would be spent in nonstop instruction, she felt that the other two and one half could be devoted to circulation management and planning for instruction with classroom teachers. In addition, the library media specialist contacted a local senior citizen organization, which referred two former librarians who were willing to function as volunteer aides two mornings per week.

Role of the Principal

An important factor in the development, implementation, and maintenance of an effective integrated library media research and study skills program is the role played by the administrator of a particular school. The principal's support of and attitude toward the instructional strategies and methods can ultimately determine the teaching staff's attitude toward and support of such a program. If the administrator values integrated instruction, communicates a positive view toward its implementation, and expects cooperation from staff members, the probability of a successful integrated library media research and study skills program is increased. If classroom teachers feel that the principal is in full support of an instructional program, they are much more likely to cooperate in its implementation. On the other hand, if an administrator shows disinterest or responds negatively toward the establishment of an integrated instructional program, staff members will be less likely to support it. Although the backing of the school principal is important, integrative programs are still possible without it, as long as the library media specialist and many of the classroom teachers are committed to content and library media skills integration.

EXAMPLE

The library media specialist of Farnsworth Elementary School, a large school in a rural area, was interested in expanding content-integrated library media skills instruction. She was already working cooperatively with the fifth-grade teaching team, and they had jointly developed and successfully implemented several instructional units correlating library media skills with reading/language arts and social studies activities. The library media specialist approached the school's principal proposing expansion of the integrated instruction. Although he was not actively supportive, he told the library media specialist that as long as the students' achievement test scores remained at their present high level, he really didn't mind if she expanded her program. It would not, however, become *school policy*. He did agree, nevertheless, to allow her to address the staff about her proposed integration of instruction at the next faculty meeting. At first, only two teachers, in addition to the fifth-grade team, were interested in implementing integrative practices, so the library media specialist continued traditional library media skills instruction with the rest, relating instruction to grade level social studies materials whenever possible. The following year, the third-grade teaching team approached the library media specialist for support in the teaching of a science unit on "Animal Habitats." Other teaching staff members began to coordinate some instructional units in varied content areas with the library media specialist. Although the formal support of the principal was lacking, the library media specialist was able to extend integrated instruction, albeit gradually, as classroom teachers observed the results of cooperative planning and integrative strategies.

Preferred Instructional Practices and Staff Interaction

Other instructional staff variables that can affect the implementation and day-to-day operation of an integrative library media research and study skills program are the preferred instructional practices and modes of interaction between staff members. These teaching methods and interactive patterns may characterize a school staff, a particular grade level or teaching team, or an individual staff member.

Instructional styles and methods vary in the amount of structure involved. Many educators prefer more structured learning situations in which the instructor directs and controls student participation and learnings. Some examples of commonly used structured instructional strategies are lectures, teacher demonstrations, directed reading and discussion activities, and drill and practice exercises. Other teachers prefer less structured learning activities in which the student "discovers" learnings through interaction with materials, teachers, peers, and ideas. Some examples of commonly used instructional strategies involving less structure and teacher control are brainstorming techniques, role-playing and dramatization, student demonstrations, and student-derived learning contracts. Although both general approaches have their merits and drawbacks, a well-balanced instructional program would incorporate both structured and unstructured learning activities to accommodate the varied learning rates and styles of students.

Teaching styles and instructional methods most commonly used in a school—by a team or grade level, or by individual instructors—may at times limit change in instructional practices. Although it would be ideal if all educators were open to new methods of instruction, realistically, the word *change* induces insecurities in those who assume that suggestions for change are criticisms of their teaching strategies. Such paranoia is not uncommon to educators, who are often subjected to intense criticism by parents, community members, the news media, and local, state, and national civic leaders.

Since successful student learnings in any instructional program involve effective interactions between students, instructional materials, and teaching staff members, an atmosphere of mutual cooperation and understanding among instructional facilitators should prevail. Collective cooperation among staff members may be dependent upon the formal and informal hierarchy of instructional leadership in the school. In some schools, the administrator is the formal instructional leader, and any decisions concerning programming must be sanctioned, organized, and implemented by him or her. In other schools, the principal delegates responsibility to certain staff members, who then take on the leadership role in determining program implementation. In reality, however, designated leaders and actual leaders may differ. Often staff members may informally align themselves with certain other staff members on the basis of instructional, social, or philosophical similarities. They form cliques that may sometimes function in a manner subversive to delegated authority figures. Often these are the real school leaders, and the success or failure of instructional programming may actually depend upon their acceptance or rejection.

The differences in willingness to share instructional materials and students and the diversity of patterns for grouping and scheduling students for instruction may require certain concessions to be made by either the library media specialist or the classroom teacher. Inflexibilities among staff members may become minor limitations to program operation for which adjustments can be made, as illustrated in the examples that follow.

EXAMPLE

Each time Ms. Hoarder began a new unit in social studies or science, she would come to the library media center and check out every trade book, filmstrip, audiovisual kit, poster set, and vertical file material that she could find in support of the unit. The library media specialist assumed that she was checking out the materials for the entire grade level. She was surprised to find out from the other two fourth-grade teachers that Ms. Hoarder refused to share the materials with them. The other teachers said that whenever they asked to borrow any of the support materials, Ms. Hoarder responded with some excuse as to why it was impossible to give them the materials at that time. At the next grade level meeting for integrated library media skills planning, the library media specialist proposed that for the next jointly taught science unit on "Energy Sources," all support materials would be divided into four equal sets—one to remain in the library media center, and the other three to be equally distributed among the three classrooms. Since the unit would take approximately six weeks, the support materials would be rotated at the end of each two-week period. The library media specialist asked Ms. Hoarder to be "rotation facilitator." Ms. Hoarder agreed and for that unit everyone had equal access to the support materials.

EXAMPLE

Ms. Freewheeling has been teaching third grade for twenty years. Her basic philosophy of education includes the ideas that students will learn when they are ready, that it is the teacher's role to provide experiences and materials from which students will select meaningful learnings, and that students thrive in an atmosphere of free expression. Every available space in her classroom is filled with posters, books, learning games, and learning centers. Students are assigned "cubbies" for their personal belongings, and desks are arranged in groups of four to facilitate student interaction. Each morning students select the learning centers in which they will participate for that day, and they are free to change if another activity is more appealing. Ms. Orderly, the library media specialist, is having a difficult time managing Ms. Freewheeling's class each Tuesday morning when they come to the library media center for their weekly library media skills lesson. Ms. Orderly prefers structured sequential learning activities that she directs with total class groups. She expects students to enter and leave the library media center quietly, and she assigns seats for students when they come to the library media center for instruction. After three months of Tuesday morning headaches, Ms. Orderly arranges a planning meeting with Ms. Freewheeling. Ms. Orderly suggests an alternate plan for joint instruction. Since the students are experienced with learning centers, Ms. Orderly offers to coordinate with Ms. Freewheeling to create learning centers involving integration of library media skills into the content areas being studied in the classroom. Each Tuesday morning, instead of the students' coming to the library media center, Ms. Orderly will come to the classroom and provide a follow-up activity. Ms. Freewheeling is delighted and immediately begins planning a series of learning centers for a science unit on "The Solar System."

EXAMPLE

The fifth-grade teachers at one elementary school have departmentalized for instruction in the four major subject areas of the curriculum. The library media specialist has repeatedly attempted to get Mr. Reading, Ms. Math, Mr. Science, and Ms. Social Studies to discuss joint planning strategies for integrating library media skills instruction with their various subject disciplines but to no avail. Each has no desire to jointly plan for integrated instruction. They each feel that they are responsible for delivering one subject area to over one hundred students and that the library media specialist should be totally responsible for her subject area. The library media specialist decides to teach traditional library media skills to the fifth graders, using related curricular materials when she is able, until different staff are responsible.

EXAMPLE

Mr. Flex recently joined the staff of a traditional elementary school after serving five years as library media specialist at an open space school. Although the classroom teachers were accustomed to weekly library skills periods scheduled on a fixed basis, Mr. Flex convinced the classroom teachers that a flexible schedule would work better. Mr. Flex promised that he would be available each Monday to meet with classroom teachers to plan and schedule instructional activities. One sixth-grade teacher made arrangements with Mr. Flex to bring his class to the library media center on Tuesday morning for instructional support in teaching his students how to use the *Abridged Readers' Guide* to enable them to use periodicals for a current events project. The teacher arrived to find Mr. Flex working with another class of students, and was quite agitated by the situation. Later that day, Mr. Flex and the sixth-grade teacher had a heated discussion. Mr. Flex still refused to institute a fixed schedule for each class, but he did agree to post a written weekly schedule that would be filled in as teachers met with him on Mondays.

EXAMPLE

The third- and fourth-grade teachers in one small elementary school were teaming for instruction. There were three classes—one third, one fourth, and one combination third/fourth. They had scheduled library and physical education periods back-to-back, and they used an instructional aide to cover one class, which provided the teachers with a weekly team planning session. The problem arose when the teachers started a rotating schedule for the order in which the classes came to the library media center. The library media specialist was never quite sure which group of students would arrive, because sometimes they came as homeroom groups and sometimes they came as mixed groups from their reading and/or math classes. To facilitate instruction, the library media specialist instituted an individualized program in library media skills that would span the essential library media skills covered in both grades. Each student would then progress at his or her own rate, and the library media specialist would be available to help those students who were having difficulty. The groupings of students sent to the library media center would not interfere with the implementation of the individualized instructional program.

SUMMARY

Library media research and study skills instruction can follow a *non-integrated* pattern: library media specialists provide experiences in library procedure and organization, information retrieval, audiovisual equipment operation and use, and the production of media; and classroom teachers duplicate instruction in some areas of library media skills in the presentation of reference, research, or study skills instruction as applied to content area instruction. Both library media specialists and classroom teachers identify objectives, develop instructional activities, implement instruction, evaluate student learnings, and revise instruction—but they do it in isolation of one another.

Library media research and study skills instruction can follow an *integrated* pattern in which library media specialists and classroom teachers identify library media and content objectives, develop instructional activities, implement instruction, evaluate student learnings, and revise instruction—as a joint venture. Library media research and study skills are then jointly taught by the library media specialist and the classroom teacher.

There are many instructional variables that should be considered before initiating an integrated library media research and study skills program. They are generally based upon differences in community characteristics, curriculum design, school facility, and instructional staff. Community characteristics include its location; its educational, occupational, and economic levels; its cultural and ethnic backgrounds; its civic, social, and religious groups; the role of the Parent Teacher Association; and its cultural and recreational opportunities. Characteristics of the school facility include its structural design and the available space for instruction. Curriculum design may vary as to rigidity of curricular standards and the amount of deviation from these standards that is allowed. Characteristics of the instructional staff include differences in staff allocation, the role played by the principal, preferred instructional practices, and staff interaction. Although some adaptations of an integrated instructional program may be needed to accommodate instructional variables based on community, school facility, curriculum design, and instructional staff, most can be readily compensated for by library media specialists and classroom teachers who are committed to content and library media skills integration.

(Answer keys for Chapter 2 are on pages 56-57.)

ANSWER KEYS FOR CHAPTER 2

Figure Number	Title and Answers
2.3	**Pretest: Using a Table of Contents** 1. houseplants, indoor gardening, or something similar; 2. chapter number; 3. page the chapter begins on; 4. page 30; 5. page 46; 6. pages 19-29; 7. page 7; 8. "Plant Pests and Problems"; 9. pages 30-46; 10. chapter 4; 11. page 47; 12. page 57.
2.5	**Activity 1 -- Metric Measures** 1. pages 14-18; 2. chapter 5; 3. page 4; 4. chapter 3; 5. page 30; 6. "History of the Metric System."
2.6	**Activity 2 -- Space Search Riddle** $\underset{1}{I}\ \underset{2}{T}\ \underset{3}{S}\quad \underset{4}{B}\ \underset{5}{E}\ \underset{6}{A}\ \underset{7}{M}\ \underset{8}{S}$.
2.7	**Activity 3 -- American History Mix-Up** **Contents** 1. Explorers Find a New World . . . . 5 2. Early Settlers Meet Native Americans . . . . 35 3. Life in the Colonies . . . . 52 4. The Revolutionary War . . . . 78 5. A New Nation Begins . . . . 105 6. Westward Movement . . . . 126 7. The Nation Divides . . . . 150 8. The Civil War . . . . 171 9. Reconstruction after the Civil War . . . . 197 Index 239
2.8	**Activity 4 -- Contents Riddle** $\underset{1}{\text{Because}}\ \underset{2}{\text{it's}}\ \underset{3}{\text{in}}\ \underset{4}{\text{the}}\ \underset{5}{\text{middle}}\ \underset{6}{\text{of}}\ \underset{7}{\text{day}}.$

Figure Number	Title and Answers
2.9	Activity 5 -- Contents Contemplation 1. "Payday," Ramona; 2. "Ramona and the Million Dollars," and; 3. "The Night of the Jack-O'-Lantern," her; 4. "Ramona to the Rescue," father; 5. "Beezus's Creative Writing," helped; 6. "The Sheep Suit," one; 7. "Ramona and the Three Wise Persons," another. Ramona and her father helped one another. 1 2 3 4 5 6 7
2.10	Activity 6 -- Focus in on Science 1. 120; 2. 30; 3. 246; 4. 94; 5. 154; 6. 4; 7. 182; 8. 64; 9. 212; 10. 182; 11. 120; 12. 30; 13. 246; 14. 94; 15. 212; 16. 4; 17. 154; 18. 64; 19. 94; 20. 212; 21. 64; 22. 4; 23. 182; 24. 246; 25. 30; 26. 154.
2.11	Activity 7 -- Contents Query Quiz (Answers will vary.)
2.12	Posttest: Using a Table of Contents 1. a; 2. b; 3. b; 4. c; 5. a; 6. b; 7. c; 8. b; 9. c; 10. a.

3 Strategies for an Integrated Curriculum Approach to Library Media Research and Study Skills Instruction

Successful library media specialists and classroom teachers establish and use strategies that will enable students to locate and use informational sources independently and effectively to enhance their performance in individual content area subjects. Classroom teachers and library media specialists must develop subject-integrated instructional plans that involve educational activities designed to promote interactions between students, informational sources, and the teaching staff. This instructional plan is most easily integrated in the form of instructional units planned for a specified content area unit of study. Library media research and study skills are infused with the content skills to establish an integrated unit of study. The instructional unit is developed prior to actual instruction to provide direction and suggested resources for planned learning activities for the students.

PLANNING AN INSTRUCTIONAL UNIT

An instructional unit may be short-term or long-term, depending upon the complexity of the subject matter and the library media research and study skills included. An instructional unit may be composed of one activity or a series of activities, depending upon the depth of the unit of study. The design for a specific instructional unit includes strategies for identifying instructional objectives, determining the ways students will learn in the form of planned instructional activities, and determining the means of assessing student learnings in the form of observations, pretests, posttests, or products. Instructional unit planning must also include provisions for evaluating and revising unit objectives, activities, and assessments upon completion of the unit of study.

The preparation of units of study in which content area skills and concepts and library media research and study skills processes are integrated involves joint planning techniques to be adopted by library media specialists and classroom teachers. Some basic assumptions concerning the integration of content skills and library media research and study skills processes are in order.

1. Library media specialists and classroom teachers must develop alternative techniques for planning, implementing, and evaluating instructional units.

2. The integration of content skills and library media research and study skills processes facilitates integrated instruction at appropriate times for students.

3. Developmental instructional activities should assist students in their cognitive, affective, and psychomotor growth.

4. Students should be exposed to a variety of instructional resources and informational sources in developmental activities.

5. Instructional activities should employ a variety of instructional strategies or methods to increase student motivation.

6. Students should be grouped for instruction in a variety of ways to accommodate their diverse learning rates, styles, and interests.

7. Time and space for instruction should accommodate differences in group size, access to instructional resources, and availability of informational sources.

8. There is no single best way to integrate library media research and study skills and content teaching. Instead, it is a multifaceted process involving the expertise of library media specialists and classroom teachers, content area skills, and library media research and study skills processes.

The proposed instructional model offered in chapter 2 is presented as a means by which library media specialists and classroom teachers can successfully integrate content area skills and library media research and study skills into an integrated instructional unit. It includes strategies for planning, implementing, and evaluating an instructional unit on the table of contents. As seen in figure 2.2, integrating library media research and study skills instruction involves the following procedural steps:

1. Identification of content skill objectives
2. Identification of library media research and study skills objectives
3. Development of integrated objectives
4. Development of instructional activities through the determination of:
    a. Sequence of instruction
    b. Instructional resources
    c. Instructional strategies
    d. Teaching responsibilities
    e. Grouping of students for instruction
    f. Time for instruction
    g. Space for instruction
5. Implementation of instruction through:
    a. Introductory activities
    b. Developmental activities
    c. Culminating activities
6. Evaluation of student learnings
7. Revision of instructional unit and activities

The remainder of this chapter will discuss each step of the instructional model in greater detail. Examples of joint planning techniques and teaching strategies and practices will provide a structural framework upon which to develop integrated learning activities within a specified teaching unit. Examples of assessment techniques for individual instructional activities and evaluation procedures for instructional units as a whole will be provided within the model framework.

IDENTIFICATION OF CONTENT SKILLS OBJECTIVES

Integration of content area skills and library media research and study skills begins with the selection of general instructional objectives for a unit of study within a specific content subject area to be taught for a specific time period, grade level, and group of students. A clear delineation of content to be taught must occur before any instruction takes place. Instructional activities must be planned on the basis of instructional objectives that determine the expected behavioral learnings of students upon completion of the unit of study. The classroom teacher must also select appropriate instructional materials to support the objectives as well as determine the most suitable means of communicating expected outcomes.

In many elementary schools, classroom teachers are asked to develop a yearly plan for the sequence of units to be taught in each subject area. This yearly plan is usually made at the beginning of the school year to facilitate long-range planning, to ensure a proper balance among content areas of instruction, and to assure the optimal use of instructional materials and resources. A yearly plan provides a useful planning resource for classroom teachers and library media specialists. Figure 3.1 shows a sample yearly plan for a third-grade class.

Subject	September	October	November	December	January
Art	Care of materials	Line	Shape and form		Color and Light
Math	Numeration place value	Addition/Subtraction		Money	Fractions
Music	Group singing		Rhythm	Music appreciation	
Reading (Literature)	Short narratives (Realistic fiction)				(Fantasy)
Science	Habitats		Forms of energy		Solar system
Social Studies	Maps and globes		Tundra region (Alaska)		

Subject	February	March	April	May	June
Art	Color and light	Space	Design and composition		
Math	Multiplication and division		Measurement	Geometry	Graphs and tables
Music	Reading music		Melody/Harmony/Rhythm		
Reading (Literature)	(Fantasy)	Fables	Fairy tales/Folktales		
Science	Solar system		Populations (Animals)		
Social Studies	Desert/Grasslands/Forest region (Mexico)		Island/Mountain region (Japan)		

Fig. 3.1. Sample yearly plan for a third-grade class.

The classroom teacher, as designated content specialist, identifies content objectives for a specific unit of study. Content objectives can be derived from numerous sources. Curriculum guides developed by state and local school districts and/or by the staff of an individual school can serve as a basis for instructional planning. Commercially prepared curriculum materials, such as textbooks and programmed learning kits, contain teacher's guides that identify topics, concepts, skills, and processes involved in various units of study. The curriculum source from which the classroom teacher identifies content objectives depends upon local school goals, staff attitudes toward curricular planning, and the nature of the content area to be taught. Figure 3.2 is a blank form that the classroom teacher can use to itemize the content objectives for a unit of study.

EXAMPLE

A fourth-grade teacher is planning a six-week science unit about "Sound Energy" to be taught in October and November. In mid-September, she begins planning the unit, which will be taught in conjunction with the library media specialist. Figure 3.3 (see page 64) provides the information identified by the classroom teacher.

(Text continues on page 65.)

Content Objectives for a Unit of Study

Grade level: _____	Class group: _____
Content area: _____	Unit of study: _____
Estimated time: _____	When: _____

Concepts or vocabulary to be developed:

Skills or processes to be developed:

Content objectives:

Text resources:	Supplemental resources:

Related curriculum ideas for activities

Art	Careers	Computer Lit.	Dance/Drama	Math
Music	P.E.	Reading/L.A.	Science	Social Studies

Other:

Fig. 3.2. Blank form.

Content Objectives for a Unit of Study

Grade level: _____4_____	Class group: _____Ms. Bradley_____
Content area: _____Science_____	Unit of study: _____Sound Energy_____
Estimated time: _____6 weeks_____	When: _____mid-Oct.-Nov._____

Concepts or vocabulary to be developed:

vibrations, pitch, frequency, source, outer ears, ear canal, eardrum, inner ear, noise

Skills or processes to be developed:

Problem solving: observation skills
                   recording and interpreting experimental data

Content objectives:

The student will:
1. Observe and demonstrate that sounds are produced by vibrations, that vibrations affect loudness or softness of sounds, and that vibration frequency relates to the pitch of a sound.
2. Observe and demonstrate how sound travels in waves through various materials.
3. Describe the human ear and the function of its various parts.
4. Explain how sounds affect different living things.

Text resources:	Supplemental resources:

<u>Science 4</u> (Addison-Wesley, 1980)
 	
chapter 8, pp. 211-245.
	Sound investigations for center,
	   (teacher-made)
	
	Duplicating masters #21-25
	   (Milliken-Sound)

Related curriculum ideas for activities

Art	Careers	Computer Lit.	Dance/Drama	Math
illustrate sounds (see Art teacher)	audiologist	look for simulation software	square dance (follow caller's direct.)	graphs tables

Music	P.E.	Reading/L.A.	Science	Social Studies
instruments (see Music teacher)		listening (identify and discriminate)		noise pollution (implications)

Other:

Check with library media specialist about kits and sound effects recordings.

Fig. 3.3. Sample completed form.

IDENTIFICATION OF LIBRARY MEDIA RESEARCH AND STUDY SKILLS OBJECTIVES

After the classroom teacher has identified the concepts, processes, and objectives that will be taught in a specific content area unit of study, the library media specialist must identify the library media research and study skills that can most effectively be used for the unit of study. The library media specialist, as designated library media skills expert, selects certain library media research and study skills and processes to be integrated into the content area unit. Those library media research and study skills most appropriate to grade level and subject content are identified by the library media specialist to be assimilated within the framework of school system objectives. These skills, processes, and objectives can be derived from state and local curriculum guides and/or commerically prepared curricular and programmed instruction materials. Figure 3.4 (see page 66) is a blank form that the library media specialist can use to itemize the library media research and study skills objectives for a unit of study.

EXAMPLE

Using the content objectives previously developed by the fourth-grade classroom teacher, the library media specialist identifies library media research and study skills to be integrated into the content unit on "Sound Energy." The classroom teacher shares the information (from fig. 3.3) specifying content objectives for the unit with the library media specialist. After reviewing the content objectives, the library media specialist identifies the library media research and study skills to be included in the unit (see fig. 3.5, page 67).

(Text continues on page 68.)

Library Media Research and Study Skills Objectives for a Unit of Study

Grade level: _____	Class group: _____
Content area: _____	Unit of study: _____
Estimated time: _____	When: _____

Skills or processes to be developed:

Location and reference	Interpretation	Organization

Library media research and study skills objectives:

Print resources	Nonprint resources	Audiovisual equipment

Fig. 3.4. Blank form.

Library Media Research and Study Skills Objectives for a Unit of Study

Grade level: 4	Class group: Ms. Bradley
Content area: Science	Unit of study: Sound Energy
Estimated time: 6 weeks	When: mid-Oct.-Nov.

Skills or processes to be developed:

Location and reference	Interpretation	Organization
Locate and use record player and sound effect records. Use cassette recorder to record sounds. Locate books by Dewey decimal system.	Make generalizations about experimental data. Determine cause and effect relationships. Interpret diagram of human ear.	Classify sounds. Use problem-solving techniques to organize information. Enlarge visuals using overhead projector.

Library media research and study skills objectives:

The student will:

1. Use a record player and a cassette recorder to identify and classify sounds.
2. Use problem-solving techniques to recognize cause and effect relationships and make generalizations about experimental data.
3. Enlarge a visual using an overhead projector.

Print resources	Nonprint resources	Audiovisual equipment
Cosgrove. Messages and Voices: The Communication of Animals. 1974. Davis. Musical Insects. 1971. Elgin. Human Body: The Ear. 1967. Jacobs. Sounds in the Sea. 1977. Podendorf. Sounds All About. 1970. Silverstein. The Story of Your Ear. 1981.	FS – Finding Out about Sound. SVE. FS – About Sound. Eye-Gate. FS – The Ears. McGraw-Hill. KIT – Sound and Noise. Encore. RD – Sounds of Animals. Folkways. RD – Environments. Atlantic Records. TRA – Eye & Ear. Milton Bradley.	Record player Cassette recorder Overhead projector Filmstrip projector Filmstrip previewer Film projector Filmloop projector

Fig. 3.5. Sample completed form.

DEVELOPMENT OF INTEGRATED OBJECTIVES

Once the classroom teacher has identified content objectives for a unit of study and the library media specialist has identified library media research and study skills objectives to be integrated into the unit of study, the classroom teacher and the library media specialist make up one set of combined instructional objectives to be used jointly as a basis for planning teaching activities. This combined set of objectives gives direction to both day-to-day and long-range instructional planning and implementation. It is at this point that integration of content skills and library media research and study skills instruction is initiated. Figure 3.6 is a blank form that the classroom teacher and the library media specialist can use to itemize the integrated objectives for the unit.

EXAMPLE

The classroom teacher, using the information from the completed form for content objectives for the unit (fig. 3.3), and the library media specialist, using the information from the completed form for library media research and study skills objectives for the unit (fig. 3.5), review the identified objectives and select compatible objectives for joint teaching. Figure 3.7 (see page 70) represents the information developed by the library media specialist and the classroom teacher at their joint planning session.

(Text continues on page 71.)

INTEGRATED OBJECTIVE(S) FOR A UNIT OF STUDY

Grade level: _____	Class group: _____
Content Area: _____	Unit of study: _____
Estimated time: _____	When: _____

Integrated content and library media research and study skills
objective(s):

Preliminary plan for instruction

Facilitator	Proposed activity

Fig. 3.6. Blank form.

INTEGRATED OBJECTIVE(S) FOR A UNIT OF STUDY

Grade level: ___4___		Class group: Ms. Bradley	
Content Area: Science		Unit of study: Sound energy	
Estimated time: 6 weeks		When: mid-Oct. - Nov.	

Integrated content and library media research and study skills objective(s):

The student will:

1. Describe the human ear and the function of its various parts.

2. Enlarge a diagram of the human ear using an overhead projector.

Preliminary plan for instruction

Facilitator	Proposed activity
Classroom teacher	Read/Discuss and perform investigations related to textbook pp. 235-241, "Sounds and Hearing," Science 4.
Library media specialist	Group Project (5-7 member groups) Each group will locate 2 diagrams of human ear using an encyclopedia and a nonfiction book. Enlarge one diagram using opaque projector.

Fig. 3.7. Sample completed form.

DEVELOPMENT OF INSTRUCTIONAL ACTIVITIES

Once the library media specialist and the classroom teacher have identified an integrated set of instructional objectives upon which to base the unit of study, decisions must be made concerning instructional procedures that will help students accomplish these objectives. The development of a unit plan of purposeful educational activities includes procedures to determine what a student is to do, how he or she is to do it, and what can be done with the results or products. Learning activities should be designed to (1) meet instructional objectives; (2) reflect a balance of the cognitive, affective, and psychomotor areas of learning; and (3) accommodate the varied learning rates, interests, and styles of individual members of the instructional group. The development of learning activities is a multifaceted process that involves the following steps (not necessarily in this order):

1. Determination of the sequence of instruction
2. Selection of instructional resources
3. Selection of instructional strategies
4. Designation of teaching responsibilities
5. Determination of grouping students for instruction
6. Designation of time for instruction
7. Designation of space for instruction

DETERMINATION OF THE SEQUENCE OF INSTRUCTION

After identifying the integrated content and library media research and study skills objectives, the classroom teacher and the library media specialist must determine the order in which the objectives are to be presented to the students. If a textbook or some other programmed material is to be used as the primary means of communicating the content objectives of the instructional unit, the sequence of content objectives has probably already been organized for concept development. Since the library media specialist and the classroom teacher have identified and infused library media research and study skills objectives into the unit of study, these objectives must be reexamined to determine if they require any prerequisite skills not already listed in the integrated objectives.

Assessment

This stage of planning an instructional unit also involves the determination of assessment procedures to be used in the unit. It is necessary to determine the means by which library media specialists and classroom teachers will measure student achievement of specified unit objectives; however, the assessment means need not be elaborated in great detail at this time. The library media specialist and classroom teacher must determine whether assessments will be formal pretests and/or posttests; informal observation of performance in introductory, developmental, and culminating activities; or evaluation of a student project such as a worksheet, center, report, project, or demonstration.

Preassessment

If the library media specialist and the classroom teacher have identified content and/or library media research and study skills objectives that require prerequisite skills not included in the integrated unit objectives, preassessment may be needed throughout the implementation of introductory and developmental unit activities. The preassessment will help determine which teaching strategies and student groupings are most appropriate for students—based on student abilities, interests, and styles of learning.

EXAMPLE

Referring to the completed form for integrated objective(s) for the unit (fig. 3.7), the library media specialist notes a proposed activity in which students enlarge a diagram of the human ear by using an opaque projector. She determines that students needed exposure to the operation of an opaque projector before being expected to use the equipment to enlarge a diagram.

The library media specialist schedules an instructional session with the total class involved in the "Sound Energy" unit. She demonstrates the operation, care, and use of the opaque projector and then administers a pretest she devised to determine which students would be able to come to the library media center during their free time to use the opaque projector independently and which students would require guided use of the opaque projector. Figure 3.8 is the pretest she used.

Postassessment

After a student or group of students has engaged in an instructional activity or a series of instructional activities, postassessment measures must be used to measure student achievement of objectives. Postassessments can help determine whether students need to engage in further developmental activities or progress to a new objective or area of study. Postassessments can be formal or informal, can measure the learnings from one activity or a series of activities, and can be part of introductory, developmental, or culminating activities.

EXAMPLE

The library media specialist determines that the postassessment measures to evaluate the student learnings about the operation of the opaque projector will be twofold. She will observe students as they use the opaque projector to enlarge a diagram of the human ear, and she will evaluate the finished product of this learning activity—the actual diagrammatic enlargement of the human ear made by the student. The classroom teacher will also use the enlarged diagram as one component in grading students.

SELECTION OF INSTRUCTIONAL RESOURCES

The library media specialist and the classroom teacher must survey available resources for materials pertinent to the unit of study being developed. During the initial stages of unit planning, the classroom teacher, when identifying content objectives, and the library media specialist, when identifying library media research and study skills objectives, choose textual and supplementary resources to support instructional objectives. When the library media specialist and the classroom teacher are ready to begin the formulation of learning activities, they may specify additional instructional resources that they have found since the preliminary survey made while identifying instructional objectives. They may also wish to specify materials to be made for instructional activities, such as learning centers and/or contracts, worksheets, bulletin boards, pretests and/or posttests.

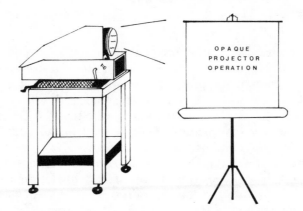

Part A

Directions: Number the following steps in the order in which they would be performed in the operation of an opaque projector.

_____ Center and focus the image on the screen or wall.

_____ Unplug machine.

_____ Insert material to be projected.

_____ Turn off lamp.

_____ Plug in machine.

_____ Cool the lamp.

_____ Turn on lamp.

Part B

Directions: Read each statement carefully to determine the best answer. Write the letter of your answer in the blank.

1. An opaque projector is used to show _____.

   (a) overhead transparencies   (b) filmstrips and slides   (c) something in a book or magazine

2. The bulb of an opaque projector is _____ watts.

   (a) 60   (b) 1000   (c) 100

3. Opaque projectors have a _____ focus.

   (a) long   (b) short   (c) transparent

4. Care must be taken not to <u>scorch</u> materials used in an opaque projector. <u>Scorch</u> means _____.

   (a) scratch the surface of   (b) burn the surface of   (c) burn a hole through

5. If the lamp is not cooled after the opaque projector is turned off, _____.

   (a) the focused material may burn   (b) the on/off switch may get stuck
   (c) the lamp may blow out

Fig. 3.8. Pretest.

EXAMPLE

The classroom teacher listed preliminary textual and supplementary materials when she identified the content objectives for the instructional unit in science (fig. 3.3), and the library media specialist listed preliminary print sources, nonprint resources, and audiovisual equipment when she identified the library media research and study skills objectives to be integrated into the "Sound" unit (fig. 3.5). While planning specific activities to support the unit, the library media specialist and/or classroom teacher may locate additional textual, print, and nonprint resources. At this point, the classroom teacher has several worksheets to make supporting the textbook presentation of "Sound Energy" content, including a unit test. The library media specialist has already made the pretest to determine independent use of an opaque projector and may need to make additional worksheets, learning centers, pretests, and posttests as implementation of the integrated unit proceeds.

SELECTION OF INSTRUCTIONAL STRATEGIES

The selection of instructional strategies or teaching methods is one of the most important parts of any unit plan. Instructional methods serve as the basis for the presentation of unit objectives to students. Teaching strategies also serve as the basis for implementing the ongoing instructional activities involving the interaction of students, resources, and instructional staff. Library media specialists and classroom teachers choose from a variety of instructional methods to include many alternative strategies to maximize opportunities for content and library media research and study skills integration. The selection of alternative teaching processes also provides for optimal development of student knowledge, skills, interests, values, learning styles, and achievements. Various instructional strategies are often combined with different methods within an instructional unit, or even within a specific lesson activity. Alternative processes are simply selected during initial planning stages and are further developed when planning specific instructional activities. Figure 3.9 is a blank form that the classroom teacher and library media specialist can use when they select instructional strategies.

EXAMPLE

Figure 3.10 (see p. 76) represents the instructional strategies selected by the library media specialist (LMS) and the classroom teacher (CT) to be employed in instructional activities with students in the classroom (CR) and the library media center (LMC) for the science unit on "Sound Energy."

The alternative instructional strategies listed in figures 3.9 and 3.10 are discussed individually in the following section of this chapter. Examples are provided of activities in which content and library media research and study skills are integrated. The examples span the content and library media skills curricular spectrum for grades three through six. Specification of instructional strategies and activities for the sample unit on "Sound Energy" will resume later in this chapter in the section entitled "Implementation of Instruction."

(Text continues on page 77.)

Alternative Instructional Strategies

- ☐ Audiovisual Presentation
    - ☐ Films   ☐ Slides   ☐ Filmstrips   ☐ Filmloops
    - ☐ Audiotapes   ☐ Videotapes   ☐ Televised productions
    - ☐ Other _____
- ☐ Brainstorming _____
- ☐ Computer-assisted Instruction
    - ☐ Game/Simulation _____
    - ☐ Drill/Practice _____
- ☐ Demonstrations
    - ☐ Instructor _____
    - ☐ Student _____
- ☐ Directed Reading Activity _____
- ☐ Discussion
    - ☐ Group discussion _____
    - ☐ Panel discussion _____
    - ☐ Debates _____
- ☐ Drill-Practice
    - ☐ Flashcards _____   ☐ Games _____
    - ☐ Worksheets _____
    - ☐ Other _____
- ☐ Field Trips _____
- ☐ Games
    - ☐ Matrix _____   ☐ Board _____
    - ☐ Card _____   ☐ Other _____
- ☐ Learning Activity Packages
      _____
- ☐ Learning Centers
    - ☐ Subject _____   ☐ Skill _____
    - ☐ Interest _____   ☐ Other _____
- ☐ Lectures _____
- ☐ Peer Teaching/Peer Tutoring
    - ☐ Same age _____   ☐ Cross age _____
    - ☐ Cross-cultural_____
- ☐ Problem Solving _____
- ☐ Programmed Instruction _____
- ☐ Projects
    - ☐ Group _____
    - ☐ Individual _____
- ☐ Role Playing/Dramatization _____
- ☐ Simulations _____
- ☐ Structured Overviews _____
- ☐ Student-Teacher Contracts _____
- ☐ Study Strategies _____

Fig. 3.9. Blank form.

Alternative Instructional Strategies

☒ Audiovisual Presentation
    ☒ Films   ☐ Slides   ☒ Filmstrips   ☒ Filmloops
    ☒ Audiotapes   ☐ Videotapes   ☐ Televised productions
    ☒ Other   _phonodiscs -- LMS_

☒ Brainstorming   _CT -- noise pollution_

☒ Computer-assisted Instruction
    ☒ Game/Simulation   _if appropriate software available -- LMS and CT_
    ☐ Drill/Practice

☒ Demonstrations
    ☒ Instructor   _CT -- investigations, LMS -- audiovisual equipment_
    ☒ Student   _CR -- investigations, LMC -- A-V equipment operation_

☒ Directed Reading Activity   _CT -- textbook readings_

☒ Discussion
    ☒ Group discussion   _CT and LMS -- part of most activities_
    ☒ Panel discussion   _CT -- effects of noise pollution_
    ☐ Debates

☒ Drill-Practice
    ☐ Flashcards   ☐ Games
    ☒ Worksheets   _CT and LMS_
    ☒ Other   _CT and LMS as needed_

☒ Field Trips   _Science Center Museum if scheduling possible_

☒ Games
    ☐ Matrix   ☐ Board
    ☐ Card   ☒ Other   _CAI simulation ?_

☐ Learning Activity Packages

☒ Learning Centers
    ☐ Subject   ☒ Skill   _CT -- investigations_
    ☐ Interest   ☐ Other

☒ Lectures   _LMS and CT -- as appropriate accompanying demonstrations_

☒ Peer Teaching/Peer Tutoring
    ☒ Same age   _LMS and CT_   ☐ Cross age
    ☒ Cross-cultural   _LMS and CT -- ESOL student_

☒ Problem Solving   _CT -- investigations and brainstorming activity_

☒ Programmed Instruction   _CT -- textbook and learning centers_

☒ Projects
    ☒ Group   _LMS -- enlarge diagram of human ear using opaque projector_
    ☒ Individual   _CT -- create demonstration or written report_

☐ Role Playing/Dramatization

☒ Simulations   _CAI, if appropriate software available -- CT and LMS_

☒ Structured Overviews   _CT -- introduce textbook unit_

☒ Student-Teacher Contracts   _CT -- with two gifted students_

☒ Study Strategies   _CT -- use SQ3R to review for unit test_

Fig. 3.10. Sample completed form.

Audiovisual Presentation

Audiovisual presentation is a method of communicating information to students in the form of films, slides, filmstrips, audiotapes, or televised productions. It is not an instructional strategy per se; however, it involves the teaching methodologies of lectures, demonstrations, resource persons, and field trips. It is not a primary method of instruction and therefore it is often used as part of an introduction to or follow-up for other learning activities. Integration of audiovisual presentations with other teaching strategies is necessary to enable students to interpret the information presented meaningfully. Audiovisual presentation also provides motivation to students by animating and enlivening material that may seem dry and lifeless to some students.

EXAMPLE

A fifth-grade classroom teacher begins an instructional unit in social studies entitled "Explorers Who Found a New World." As a culminating activity, she plans to have the students conduct research and write reports on particular explorers. The library media specialist agrees to support classroom instruction by reviewing with students the processes involved in the selection of reference sources for research on a particular topic. He will also teach students the use of indexes, cross-references, and bibliographies to lead them to other information sources. As an introductory activity, the library media specialist shows the filmstrip *Using Reference Materials* (Troll Associates, 1970). During the discussion period following the presentation of the filmstrip, the students are asked to locate specific reference sources in the library media center.

Brainstorming

Brainstorming is an instructional technique used to develop the creative thinking processes of students. It is a relatively simple strategy in which students are asked to generate as many ideas as possible on a given concept, topic, skill, or problem in a given amount of time. Brainstorming encourages nonthreatening participation of all students by stressing the quantity and originality of responses rather than the quality of the ideas generated. Although it may involve higher level cognitive processes of application, analysis, and synthesis, brainstorming is applicable to all subject areas and grade levels of students. Brainstorming activities can be used effectively to introduce or reinforce learnings, to enrich integration of content and skills, to encourage creative expression, and to develop classification and problem-solving skills.

Library media specialists and classroom teachers may use brainstorming techniques to generate student motivation and interest. There may be management difficulties, however, as some students may become overly enthusiastic during a brainstorming session. Guidelines for student participation should be established before beginning a brainstorming activity. Careful structuring of brainstorming sessions will increase student responses and ease group management.

EXAMPLE

A third-grade classroom teacher is involved in preparing students for standardized testing. An important skill tested in the verbal subtests is the high-level thinking skill of making analogies. She has initiated several introductory lessons in which students have matched word sets based on relationships (for example, chair is to sit as bed is to sleep). The library media specialist, who works closely with classroom teachers in all areas of the curriculum, supports the teaching of test-taking skills. The library media specialist and the classroom teacher plan together a brainstorming activity to reinforce and extend student skills in word relationship patterns. Students are put in groups of two or three. The library media specialist and/or classroom teacher gives each group five minutes to generate as many examples of the given relationship pattern as they can. At the end of five minutes, each student group reports the patterns to the total group and points are awarded. Then the process is repeated with other word relationship patterns. Some examples of relationship patterns are

1. Antonym relationship—black:white :: day:night
2. Place relationship—glove:hand :: shoe:foot
3. Synonym relationship—small:tiny :: story:tale
4. Purpose relationship—chair:sit :: pencil:write
5. Cause and effect relationship—heat:furnace :: seed:tree
6. Degree relationship—infant:adult :: home:mansion
7. Object to action relationship—car:drive :: gun:shoot
8. Part to whole relationship—arm:body :: leaf:plant
9. Part to part relationship—hand:elbow :: index:glossary
10. Action to object relationship—write:author :: wiggle:worm
11. Grammatical relationship—win:won :: make:made

Computer-assisted Instruction

Computer-assisted instruction (CAI) is an automated form of programmed learning in which instructions and activities provided for students are performed by a computer. Commercially prepared software programs in the form of drill/practice exercises and simulations or role-playing games are becoming increasingly available to schools, educators, and students. These programs serve as supplemental teaching aids in the same way as films or videotaped programs—to add variety to lessons within a unit of study. The skills necessary for the use of microcomputer programs are being integrated into content area and library media instructional objectives in many school systems. The presence of microcomputers in elementary schools and the availability of prepared software will determine the degree to which computer-assisted instruction will be used as an instructional alternative.

Although computer-assisted instruction is a highly motivating instructional activity, the cost of computer hardware and software may limit its widespread use. In many cases, computer software, especially drill/practice programs, is merely the programming of textual or workbook exercises onto a tape or disk. Like a textbook, a workbook, a duplicating master set, a film, or a television program, a computer program is an excellent means for reinforcing and extending student learnings in any content area. It should not, however, become the primary means of instruction in any content area.

EXAMPLE

A library media specialist ascertains that several students in grades three through six are having difficulty in alphabetizing—a requisite skill for locating materials in the library media center and locating information by using dictionaries, encyclopedias, indexes, and bibliographies. Since there are two Apple II computers housed in the library media center, she refers students who are having difficulty in alphabetizing to "Alphabet: Sequencing and Alphabetizing," a drill/practice/game program (Random House; also available for TRS-80). She prescribes the level at which each student should begin the program. The library media specialist communicates to the classroom teachers of students needing the additional alphabetizing drill, and together they schedule students to come to the library media center to work through the program.

Demonstrations

Demonstrations are commonly used instructional techniques in which a classroom teacher and/or library media specialist shows or demonstrates an object, process, or procedure to students. Demonstrations range from a simple instructor demonstration (e.g., filling out a library loan card) to a complex demonstration of a laboratory experiment (e.g., displaying the construction of and operation of a sling psychrometer to measure and calculate relative humidity). Demonstrations by teachers are often used as introductory or developmental activities within an instructional unit.

Students are often asked to demonstrate evidence of knowledge gained in a unit of study by demonstration of a specific concept, skill, or process. Since most educational programs are based on behavioral objectives in which student growth is measured by changes in student behavior, demonstrations by students provide a basis upon which educators observe student behavior and evaluate student performance. Many affective and psychomotor learnings may be observed only through the teacher's observation of student-presented demonstrations. Student-presented demonstrations can range from a simple demonstration of how to operate a record player to the creation of a laboratory investigation to show the physical properties of air. Student-presented demonstrations are often assigned after several introductory or developmental unit activities have taken place, enabling students the time required to assimilate the varied cognitive, affective, and psychomotor processes involved.

EXAMPLE

A fourth-grade teacher is beginning a unit in reading/language arts on fictional novels. An important objective of the unit involves having students identify and explain character traits of fictional characters. The library media specialist agrees to support this classroom instructional unit, and the following activities are planned:

1. The classroom teacher guides the students' reading of fictional narratives from their basal readers, discussion of *character traits*, and writing of *character sketches* as exemplified in the stories they read.

2. The library media specialist demonstrates, while students observe and review, the step-by-step operational processes for using a reel-to-reel tape recorder. The library media specialist has dry mounted the procedural steps (see fig. 3.11, p. 80).

(Text continues on page 81.)

REEL-TO-REEL TAPE RECORDER OPERATION

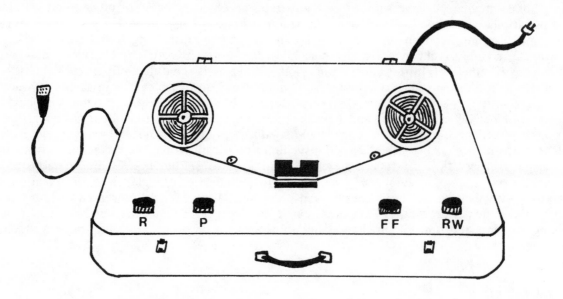

a. Open the tape recorder and remove the top.

b. Remove the tape reel from its box, and install the tape reel.

c. Locate the unrecorded portion of the tape by using the play (P) and fast forward (FF) buttons.

d. Install the microphone.

e. Record your material on the tape. Be sure the record (R) button is engaged.

f. Disengage the microphone.

g. Use the rewind (RW) and the play (P) buttons to listen to the portion of the tape that you recorded.

h. Rewind (RW) the entire tape reel, and remove it from the machine.

i. Return the microphone and the top for proper storage.

j. Insert the tape reel into its box.

Fig. 3.11. Procedural steps for reel-to-reel tape recorder operation.

3. The classroom teacher assigns students to go to the library media center to select and check out a fiction novel to be used for activities on character traits.

4. The library media specialist assists students in the selection of appropriate novels for use in the character traits activities.

5. The classroom teacher assigns students to read their selected novels and identify a character on which to base their character traits activities.

6. The library media specialist observes and evaluates as students demonstrate the operation of a reel-to-reel tape recorder.

7. The classroom teacher assigns students to select a scene from the novel, involving the previously chosen character, to illustrate a poster depicting the scene. Figure 3.12 (see p. 82) is a sample poster made by the classroom teacher.

8. The classroom teacher assigns students to write a character sketch in which they tell, from the point of view of the character, the background scene depicted in their poster.

9. The library media specialist is available as students record their character sketches on the class tape on the reel-to-reel tape recorder in the library media center.

10. The classroom teacher and the library media specialist are both present for the final activity. When all posters are made and all character sketches have been written and recorded, each student plays his or her portion of the class tape and displays his or her poster to the entire class. The classroom teacher and the library media specialist evaluate each student's operation of the reel-to-reel tape recorder, identification and explanation of character traits as exemplified by his or her posters, and taped character sketches.

THE BULLY OF BARKHAM STREET

by Mary Stolz

Character: Martin Hastings

Fig. 3.12. Teacher-made sample poster depicting a scene from a book.

Directed Reading Activity

A teaching strategy that can be applied to all content area instruction is the directed reading activity (DRA) or guided reading lesson. DRAs are structured procedures to enable students to read and comprehend the content information presented in print format within a unit of study. Most DRAs are based on Stauffer's five-step "directed reading-thinking activity" (DRTA).[1] Burmeister's five-step "directed reading activity,"[2] Herber's three-step "instructional framework,"[3] Singer and Donlan's "directed reading activity,"[4] and the Cheeks' six-step "directed learning activity,"[5] are all variations of the directed reading activity. Although the DRA may vary as to what the process is called and the number of steps involved, the function remains the same. The purpose of a DRA is to provide students with an introduction to and follow-up to material they must read. The processes involved are especially helpful when students must read silently complex expository material such as that in science and social studies textbooks and nonfiction sourcebooks.

EXAMPLE

A group of sixth-grade students was ready to begin a unit of study in social studies on Ancient Greece. The teacher, recognizing the difficulty of the concepts and vocabulary introduced in the textbook chapter on Ancient Greece, decides to apply Directed Reading Activity strategies to guide the students through the material. Since the chapter is divided into six major sections, the teacher applies the following steps as the students read each section.

1. *Orientation to selection.* The teacher identifies the concepts and vocabulary presented in the selection and exposes the students to the major concepts and vocabulary they will encounter in their reading. A structured overview of the material is often helpful to orient students to the concepts and vocabulary of the section. (Structured overviews are discussed later in this chapter.)

2. *Survey and preview material.* The teacher helps students to set purposes for reading the selection. Students survey the organization of the material to be read by applying the steps of the SQ3R study model. (The SQ3R study model is discussed later in this chapter.)

3. *Read silently.* Students read the material silently. The amount of reading assigned will vary as to the independent reading levels of the student group involved.

4. *Discuss information presented.* The teacher checks the students' comprehension of the concepts, vocabulary, and main ideas presented in the selection. The teacher guides the discussion in order to lead students to apply their experiences to the information given.

5. *Follow-up activities.* The teacher provides workbook or worksheet practice for specific skill development or assigns appropriate follow-up activities such as creative writing, art projects, and library media research.

Discussion

Since some form of discussion is involved in most instructional activities, this instructional strategy is often chosen as a method of teaching. Discussion is a strategy frequently used to encourage students to develop and share learnings orally. It may be used as a motivational experience for students before other instructional methods are employed, or it may be used in conjunction with other teaching methods such as demonstration or directed reading activity after students have read, heard, or viewed information pertaining to the content of a lesson within an instructional unit. Discussions may range from informal question-and-answer sessions during a particular lesson to structured activities such as small group discussions, panel discussions, or formalized debates.

As discussion is an integral part of most instructional lessons, it is important that the classroom teacher and/or library media specialist structure questioning sessions so that questions will range from literal to inferential levels. Literal level questions (Who?, What?, Where?, When?) lead to translation level student answers. Though recall of facts is important to most content teaching, literal questioning does not develop higher level cognitive processes. Inferential level questions (How?, Why?) lead to higher level cognitive processes as students search for answers. Questioning approaches should be varied to enable students to practice high-level thinking skills involving the interpretation, analysis, application, synthesis, and evaluation of information presented as well as the literal translation of such information.

Careful monitoring of discussion sessions can also lead to the extension of students' listening and oral speaking skills. As students engage in more small and large group discussions, their participation increases. Students develop the skill and habit of listening to others, and they learn to express themselves more effectively as they gain confidence through successful discussion sessions.

EXAMPLE

A sixth-grade class is completing a science unit on "Energy Sources." The classroom teacher and the library media specialist plan a series of discussions as culminating activities. Students have been engaged in extensive experimentation and research during the developmental activities of the unit. The library media specialist will divide students into groups of four to six pupils. Each group will select a discussion leader and a recorder. Students will discuss the advantages and disadvantages of currently used energy resources. Figure 3.13 is a worksheet that can be used by the recorder of each discussion group.

The classroom teacher holds a follow-up session to the small group discussions coordinated by the library media specialist. Student recorders report their small group findings. A large group discussion of the advantages and disadvantages of currently used energy sources ensues in which students summarize their small group discussions.

Drill-Practice

Drill and/or practice activities may be used as a teaching strategy in itself or a follow-up to some other method of instruction. Drill or practice activities occur most often after introductory or developmental activities. They are appropriate for instruction in any subject area. The purpose of drill and/or practice activities is to provide reinforcement or extension of the concepts, skills, or processes that have already been introduced. Oral drill exercises, through the use of flashcards and reinforcement games, provide strategies to aid students in reviewing or memorizing content information. Written practice worksheets can provide opportunities for students to review, apply, or synthesize knowledge already gained. Microcomputer programs, in the form of drill-practice exercises and games, furnish an automated form of drill-practice reinforcement activities. Drill-practice is one of the most commonly used teaching strategies in an elementary school. Students require practice using and applying the various concepts, skills, and processes introduced in instructional activities.

Advantages	ENERGY SOURCES	Disadvantages
	ATOM	
	COAL	
	NATURAL GAS	
	OIL	
	SUN	
	WATER	
	WIND	

Fig. 3.13. Worksheet.

EXAMPLE

A library media specialist has been working with his third and fourth graders on distinguishing between fiction and nonfiction books. He provides a practice exercise in which students must decide whether a book is fiction or nonfiction by reading and interpreting its title. Figure 3.14 is the practice worksheet provided by the library media specialist.

Field Trips

Field trips are a supplemental teaching strategy to extend learning activities in a unit of study by bringing students to realistic situations and places and resource people. When field trips are a form of introductory instruction to be followed up by classroom experiences, they provide an exciting stimulus to learning. Field trips taken when a unit of study is fairly well advanced give students a sense of realism and reinforce the information, skills, and processes being developed in the classroom. Field trips provide direct experiences in which students observe the real world. Visits to museums, business concerns, newspaper offices, and government buildings often offer guided tours, loans of materials, and printed matter to further extend the learning experiences of students.

EXAMPLE

A fifth-grade classroom teacher and the library media specialist at one school have been jointly teaching a reading/language arts unit entitled "The Newspaper as an Information Source." As a culminating activity, the classroom teacher and the library media specialist plan to take the students on a field trip to a local newspaper office. The students will tour the newspaper's printing facilities. After the field trip, follow-up activities will be provided by the classroom teacher and the library media specialist in which students will "publish" a school newspaper.

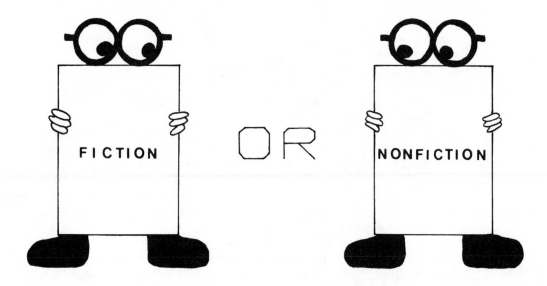

Directions: Read each title below. Decide whether it would be found in the fiction or nonfiction section of the library media center. Write <u>Fiction</u> or <u>Nonfiction</u> on the line next to the title.

1. Colonial Crafts for You to Make _____

2. Sweeney's Ghost _____

3. Wonders of the Cactus World _____

4. Tiger's Bones, and Other Plays for Children _____

5. Ben and Me _____

6. Cities, Old and New _____

7. The Great Brain at the Academy _____

8. Langston Hughes, American Poet _____

9. The Bully of Barkham Street _____

10. Tales of a Fourth Grade Nothing _____

11. Careers in a Medical Center _____

12. Davy Crockett -- Frontier Adventurer _____

13. Ramona and Her Father _____

14. Let's Find Out about Bees _____

15. Charlie and the Chocolate Factory _____

16. Me and the Terrible Two _____

17. The Phantom Tollbooth _____

18. How to Play Soccer _____

19. How to Eat Fried Worms _____

20. Album of the Civil War _____

Fig. 3.14. Worksheet.

Games

The use of educational games is a supplemental instructional strategy that reinforces or extends the knowledge, concepts, skills, or processes involved in a unit of study. Instructional games may be developed to practice skills appropriate to any subject area of the curriculum or to any age or grade level of students.

Learning games provide activities in which students exercise cognitive, affective, and psychomotor areas of development. Varied cognitive processes are applied as students review, apply, or synthesize knowledge previously gained in introductory or developmental unit activities. Psychomotor skills are often important to manipulative and muscular activities involved in the playing of the game. Games also provide opportunities for affective growth when students augment positive self-images through successful playing strategies. Competition can be destructive, however, if game-playing activities are not carefully controlled. Classroom teachers and/or library media specialists must be careful to structure learning game activities that emphasize the acquisition, retention, reinforcement, and extension of skills. Students should win or lose on the basis of knowledge of a particular skill rather than on the basis of game-playing strategies.

Instructional games can take the form of informal drill and practice exercises, formal learning games based on matrix board games (Checkers, Bingo, Tic Tac Toe), playing board games (Clue, Candy Land, Race), or card games (Fish, Concentration, Rummy). The advent of numerous microcomputer drill and practice and simulation games available to students and educators has extended the use of games as an instructional strategy.

A successful follow-up, review, or culminating activity for students is to have them design and construct an instructional game to teach others the content or skills learned in a unit of study. Students must apply and synthesize information gained in the instructional unit in order to communicate this knowledge to others in the form of a learning game.

EXAMPLE

A third-grade class has been involved in a science unit on Animal Classification. Students have done several developmental activities on animal groupings in the classroom and encyclopedia usage in the library media center. The library media specialist and the classroom teacher have developed the following relay game to practice encyclopedia skills and to precede a research project in which students will locate information about a particular animal of a species. This game activity should take place in the library media center with a group of no more than fifteen students. The student group is divided into three teams of about five students each. Each team is provided with one set of encyclopedias, an "Animal Search Activity" checklist (see fig. 3.15), one 3" x 5" index card, and a table or surface on which to work. Each team is assigned one list from the "Animal Search Activity" checklist and one set of encyclopedias with which to work. Using the encyclopedias, each team must locate an article about each animal on the list. Team members use a relay method of alternating turns. Team members must stay seated away from the worktable, and only one team member is allowed out of his or her seat at a time. Once a player locates an encyclopedia article about one animal on the team's list, he or she must put the index card in the encyclopedia volume, and bring the volume and the checklist to the library media specialist. The library media specialist checks off the appropriate animal on the checklist. The player returns the encyclopedia volume, and hands the checklist and the index card to the next player on the team. This procedure continues until the allotted time runs out (about 25 minutes). The library media specialist collects the "Animal Search Activity" checklist from each team, tallies team points scored for number of animals found, and provides appropriate awards for winning team members.

ANIMAL SEARCH ACTIVITY

List 1	List 2	List 3	List 4
amoeba	alligator	albatross	ant
barnacle	bird	bear	butterfly
clam	coral	crab	coyote
deer	dog	duck	dolphin
eagle	emu	earthworm	elephant
fish	frog	fox	flamingo
gorilla	goat	gnu	grasshopper
hamster	horse	hippopotamus	hummingbird
iguana	insect	ibex	ibis
jaguar	jellyfish	jackrabbit	jackal
koala	ladybug	katydid	kangaroo
leopard	lobster	lizard	lion
mouse	mosquito	moth	monkey
nightingale	newt	nautilus	nighthawk
ostrich	owl	orangutan	opossum
prairie dog	pigeon	plankton	penguin
quahog	quarter horse	quail	queen bee
rhinoceros	rabbit	raccoon	rat
salamander	sea urchin	starfish	snail
tiger	turtle	toad	tortoise
whale	worm	walrus	vulture
zebra	yak	wombat	wolf

Fig. 3.15. Checklist.

Learning Activity Packages

Learning Activity Packages (LAP packs), a form of programmed learning, are self-contained instructional units developed by a classroom teacher and/or library media specialist and are organized around a specific content area topic, skill, or process. They are usually in the form of a printed packet that includes objectives, assessments, and alternative activities to enable students to gain the knowledge, skills, and processes to be developed in the instructional unit. Parallel activities are alternatives from which students may choose during the completion of the package. These parallel activities permit students to develop and pursue interests and to progress at their own learning rates.

Since individual students may progress through the LAP pack at different rates and sequences, the use of LAP packs helps to maximize the use of instructional resources such as textbooks, trade books, reference sources, and audiovisual sources and equipment. The incorporation of other instructional strategies such as learning centers and individual and/or group projects and/or demonstrations makes using LAP packs an eclectic teaching approach.

LAP packs are closely related to student-teacher contracts. The main differences are that with contracts students generate and select activities to determine how they will meet the objectives of a unit *before instruction is begun*; with LAP packs students independently choose among parallel activities from a predetermined set of alternatives *as instruction is taking place*.

The library media specialist or classroom teacher using a given LAP pack may select individual worksheets to use independently with particular students or groups of students if he or she so chooses. The entire package may be reproduced, bound, and laminated to make it more durable, especially if paper consumption at a particular school is limited.

EXAMPLE

In chapter 2, a library media specialist created a LAP pack to demonstrate to classroom teachers an example of integrated content and library media skills instruction. She had previously identified using tables to locate information as a skill common to reading, mathematics, science, social studies, and library media instruction. Based on this one common skill, she produced the "Table Tackle" LAP pack (figs. 3.16-3.25, pp. 91-100) that includes a pretest, a posttest, and several activity worksheets in which students apply the skill in the major content areas of reading, mathematics, science, and social studies.

(Text continues on page 101.)

Fig. 3.16. Cover sheet.

Table Tackle Pretest

Directions: Use the table to answer the questions below. Write the answers
in the blanks.

Continents by Size		
Continent	Area (sq. mi.)	Percentage of earth's land
Asia	16,999,000	27.9
Africa	11,688,000	20.4
North America	9,366,000	16.3
South America	6,881,000	12.0
Antarctica	5,100,000	8.9
Europe	4,017,000	7.0
Australia	2,966,000	5.2

Source: <u>World Almanac</u>, 1983

1. The **continent** with the largest land area is _____.

2. _____ is the continent with the smallest land area.

3. North America's area is _____ square miles.

4. Europe's area is _____ square miles.

5. Asia occupies _____% of the earth's land.

6. South America occupies _____% of the earth's land.

7. The area of _____ is approximately seventeen million
square miles.

8. The area of _____ is approximately five million square
miles.

9. The information listed in this table came from _____.

10. The sum of the areas of Europe and Asia is _____.

11. The difference between the areas of North America and South America
is _____.

12. _____ occupies approximately one-fifth of the earth's
land.

13. _____ occupies approximately three million square miles.

Fig. 3.17. Pretest.

Activity 1 -- Wind Chill Factor

Directions: Read the paragraph and study the table to answer the questions below. **Underline your answers.**

Wind Chill Factor

The wind chill factor has a strong impact on how cold it feels outside. A strong wind combined with temperatures below freezing can have the same effect as a temperature nearly fifty degrees lower with no wind! For example, if the outside temperature is twenty degrees Fahrenheit (20°F) and the air is calm, the wind chill factor is the same as the temperature: twenty degrees above zero. However, with the same temperature and a 40 MPH wind, the effect on you is **the** same as if the temperature was twenty-one degrees below zero (-21°F)!

Temperature	Wind Velocity		
	10 MPH	25 MPH	40 MPH
30°F	16°F	1°F	-5°F
20°F	3°F	-15°F	-21°F
10°F	-9°F	-29°F	-37°F
0°F	-22°F	-44°F	-53°F

Source: <u>World Almanac</u>, 1983

1. Wind velocity means wind: (a) temperature (b) speed (c) factor

2. The symbol $^{\circ}$ means: (a) Fahrenheit (b) minus (c) degree

3. The abbreviation MPH means: (a) miles per hour (b) minutes per hour (c) minus per hour

4. The temperatures above were measured on a (a) Celsius thermometer (b) Fahrenheit thermometer (c) Centigrade thermometer

5. A minus before a number means: (a) minus zero (b) below Fahrenheit (c) below zero

6. If the temperature is 10° and the wind is blowing at 25 MPH, the wind chill factor is: (a) -29° (b) -37° (c) -9°

7. If the temperature is 0° and the wind is blowing at 10 MPH, the wind chill factor is: (a) -44° (b) 16° (c) -22°

8. At a wind speed of 40 MPH and a temperature of 20°, the wind chill factor is: (a) -29° (b) -21° (c) -22°

9. At a wind velocity of 25 MPH and a temperature of 30°, the wind chill factor is: (a) -9° (b) 16° (c) 1°

Fig. 3.18. Worksheet.

Activity 2 -- Metric Measurements

Directions: As the United States changes over to the metric system, most occupations will be affected. Fill in the "Metric Measurements" column in the table below. Find the information you need in a math book, an encyclopedia, or another reference source.

Occupation	Current Measurements	Metric Measurements
1. Shipping clerk	pound, ton	
2. Forester	mile, acre	
3. Meteorologist	mi./hr., ^{O}F, inch	
4. Electrician	inch, horsepower	
5. Meat cutter	ounce, pound	
6. Cook	teaspoon, cup	
7. Painter (house)	gal., sq. ft.	
8. Clothing salesperson	whole sizes	
9. Plumber	inch, gallon	
10. Taxi driver	mile	
11. Carpenter	inch, foot	
12. Geologist	^{O}F, sq. ft.	
13. Engineer	ft., lb., horsepower	
14. Fire fighter	mi., sq. ft., ^{O}F	
15. Shoemaker	inch, sq. in.	
16. Real estate salesperson	acre, mile	
17. Gasoline station attendant	gallon	

Fig. 3.19. Worksheet.

Activity 3 -- Calendar Caper

Directions: Fill in the calendar for the fifth month of the year. Let
               the first date be on the seventh day of the first week. Fill
               in the name of the month. Then use the calendar to answer the
               questions below. Write your answers in the blanks.

Month						
S	M	T	W	T	F	S

1. The first day of the month is on a _____ .

2. The date of the third Friday is the _____ .

3. The seventeenth is on a _____ .

4. The last day of the month is on a _____ .

5. The date of the second Thursday is the _____ .

6. The twenty-sixth is on a _____ .

7. There are _____ days in this month.

8. Using abbreviations, list the months of the year in order. _____,

   _____, _____, _____, _____, _____,

   _____, _____, _____, _____, _____,

   _____.

9. There are _____ days in one year.

10. Using abbreviations, list the days of the week in order. _____,

    _____, _____, _____, _____, _____,

    _____.

11. There are _____ weeks in a year.

12. A leap year occurs every _____ years. The month of
    _____ gains a day in a leap year.

Fig. 3.20. Worksheet.

Activity 4 -- Science TV Guide

Directions: Read through a television guide for programs related to science. Find three documentary and three science fiction programs. List only those programs that you would be able to view outside of school time. Fill in the information in the table below. Television guides are available in the library media center, or you may use one at home. Two examples have been provided below.

Program Title	Date	Time	Channel	Type	Description
"Time of the Grizzly"	Apr. 4 Thurs.	8:30 P.M.	20	Documen-tary	Life of grizzly bears in the wild.
"The Green Slime"	Apr. 6 Sat.	3:00 P.M.	5	Science fiction	Asteroid plant life attacks U.S. space station.

Fig. 3.21. Worksheet.

Activity 5 -- Astro Airlines

Directions: One word, number, or time in each sentence below is incorrect.
Use the Astro Airlines schedules to correct the errors. Cross
out each mistake and write the correct word, number, or time
above it.

Departures				Arrivals			
Flight	Destination	Time	Gate	Flight	Origin	Time	Gate
136	St. Louis	7:20	26	146	Houston	8:00	25
208	Chicago	7:30	22	130	Miami	9:20	35
413	Dallas	8:05	30	123	Baltimore	9:30	27

1. Flight 208 leaves at 7:30 from Gate 26.

2. Flight 123 arrives at 9:20 at Gate 27.

3. Flight 136 goes to Chicago at 7:20.

4. Flight 146 arrives from Houston at 9:30.

5. The flight to Dallas leaves from Gate 22.

6. The flight from Miami arrives at Gate 25.

7. The flight to St. Louis arrives at 7:20.

8. The flight from Baltimore leaves at 9:30.

9. Gates 25, 26, 27 handle only arriving planes.

10. Gates 22, 26, and 35 handle only departing planes.

11. Flight 413 leaves for St. Louis at 7:20.

12. Flight 130 arrives from Houston at 8:00.

13. **Origin** means the place a flight is going to.

14. There are three flights arriving after 9:00.

15. Destination means the place a flight is coming from.

16. There are two flights arriving after 7:25 from Gates 22 and 30.

17. If someone were standing at Gate 35 at 9:20, he or she would meet people
    coming off the plane from Houston.

18. You would go to Gate 413 to catch the next plane to Chicago, which leaves
    at 7:30.

Fig. 3.22. Worksheet.

Activity 6 -- Store Directory

Directions: Study the Store Directory. Fill in the floor numbers for each of the items listed below the directory.

First Floor	Second Floor	Third Floor
Ladies' Fashions	Garden Shop	Children's Wear
Men's Wear	Hardware	Photo Department
Shoes	Sporting Goods	Toys

Fourth Floor	Fifth Floor	Sixth Floor
Appliances	Curtains	Credit Office
Furniture	Linens	Restaurant
TV & Stereo	Sewing Goods	Restrooms

_____ 1. sleeping bag

_____ 2. restroom

_____ 3. boys' shirts

_____ 4. stove

_____ 5. bath towels

_____ 6. fabric

_____ 7. ladies' blouses

_____ 8. last month's bill

_____ 9. photographer

_____ 10. speakers for stereo

_____ 11. fishing pole

_____ 12. garden hose

_____ 13. leather boots

_____ 14. bedroom curtains

_____ 15. video recorder

_____ 16. film

_____ 17. dolls

_____ 18. a hamburger platter

_____ 19. ladies' shoes

_____ 20. plant fertilizer

_____ 21. refrigerator

_____ 22. coffee table

_____ 23. tennis racket

_____ 24. a cup of coffee

_____ 25. Monopoly game

_____ 26. girls' dresses

_____ 27. men's slacks

_____ 28. pillows

_____ 29. couch

_____ 30. dining room table

_____ 31. living room drapes

_____ 32. a screwdriver

_____ 33. golf clubs

_____ 34. thread and yarn

Fig. 3.23. Worksheet.

Activity 7 -- Precipitation Table

Directions: Complete the table to show the difference between the highest and lowest precipitation levels for each city. Then use the completed table to fill in the blanks.

Monthly Normal Precipitation

City	Jan.	Apr.	July	Oct.	Difference
Atlanta	4.3	4.6	4.9	2.5	2.4
Baltimore	2.9	3.1	4.1	2.8	1.3
Boston	3.7	3.5	2.7	3.0	—
Chicago	1.9	3.8	4.1	2.6	—
Los Angeles	3.0	1.3	.05	0.3	—
New York	2.7	3.3	3.7	2.9	—
Reno	1.2	0.5	0.3	0.4	—

Source: The World Almanac, 1983

1. _____ has the most precipitation in January.

2. Reno has its highest precipitation in _____.

3. _____ has the greatest difference between highest and lowest precipitation levels.

4. _____ has the least precipitation in April.

5. New York has its lowest precipitation in _____.

6. _____ has the least difference between highest and lowest precipitation levels.

7. _____ has the most precipitation in July.

8. Los Angeles has its least precipitation in _____.

9. _____ and _____ have a difference of 1.0 inch between highest and lowest precipitation levels.

10. _____ has its lowest precipitation in October.

11. Chicago has its most precipitation in _____.

12. The least amount of precipitation listed in the table is _____ inches.

13. _____ has the lowest precipitation listed in January.

14. Boston has the least precipitation in _____.

15. The greatest amount of precipiation listed in the table is _____ inches.

16. The amount of precipitation listed for New York in April is _____ inches.

Fig. 3.24. Worksheet.

16,575

Table Tackle Posttest

Directions: Use the tables to fill in the blanks below.

Weight in Grams

Ball	Weight
Baseball	150
Basketball	600
Football	400
Soccer ball	500
Tennis ball	60

1. A _____ is the heaviest ball listed.

2. A _____ is the lightest ball listed.

3. The difference between the weights of a basketball and a football is _____ grams.

4. A baseball weighs _____ grams more than a tennis ball.

5. Together, a basketball, a soccer ball, and a baseball weigh _____ grams.

Areas of Oceans

Ocean	Area (sq. mi.)	Percentage of earth's water
Arctic	5,105,700	3.9
Atlantic	33,420,000	22.9
Indian	28,350,500	20.3
Pacific	64,186,300	46.0

Source: The World Almanac, 1983.

1. The ocean with the largest area is the _____ Ocean.

2. The _____ Ocean has the smallest area.

3. The area of the Indian Ocean is _____ square miles.

4. The Atlantic Ocean's area is _____ % of the earth's water.

5. The information listed in the table "Areas of Oceans" came from _____.

6. The _____ Ocean occupies approximately 23% of the earth's water.

7. The area of the _____ Ocean is approximately five million square miles.

8. The difference between the areas of the Atlantic and Pacific Oceans is _____ square miles.

9. The sum of the areas of the Atlantic and Indian Oceans is _____ square miles.

Fig. 3.25. Posttest.

Learning Centers

Learning centers are a form of programmed instruction that may be used as a primary instructional method or a supplemental teaching strategy to introduce, diagnose, reinforce, or extend the concepts, skills, or processes involved in a unit of study. Learning centers are specified areas in the library media center and/or classroom designed by the library media specialist and/or classroom teacher that contain varied instructional materials and activities to be used by individuals or small groups of students to meet unit objectives. Learning centers are generally of three types: subject, skill, and interest centers.

Subject centers are designed to be used by students following the introductory activities for a subject area unit of study. They provide activities and materials to extend learnings in a single subject or a multisubject format. Although subject centers may involve the use of commercially prepared programmed instructional kits and/or laboratories, most employ teacher-made practice, problem-solving, or research activities related to the content unit being studied. Subject centers may be set up as permanent learning centers with activities and materials changing to accommodate current units of study in that particular subject area.

Skill centers are designed to be used by students after initial instruction in the skill. Students may take part in activities using manipulatives (often games) and media resources to practice and extend the particular skill or skills being developed. Skill centers may also include activities in which students apply interrelated subject skills and materials. Classroom teachers and/or library media specialists may also use skill centers to diagnose student learnings, in the form of pretests and posttests, and to identify student knowledge of prerequisite skills that may be necessary for successful completion of the current skill being developed by the skill center.

Interest centers are designed to encourage students to develop interests in subject matter that is not a part of designated educational curriculum. Hobbies, sports, photography, sewing, arts and crafts, and career explorations are examples of topics that can be used. Interest centers allow students to independently investigate and take part in extension activities not directly related to curricular units of study. Interest centers provide highly motivational learning activities in which students apply the concepts, skills, and processes introduced by other instructional strategies.

Library media specialists and/or classroom teachers may use a combination of subject, skill, and interest centers when integrating content and library media research and study skills instruction. Learning centers provide a medium through which such integration may take place as students use library media print and nonprint sources and audiovisual materials provided at a learning center.

EXAMPLE

The library media specialist and the classroom teachers of one elementary school determined that functional reading skills were of utmost importance in the upper elementary grades (3-6) to prepare students for state-mandated functional reading tests to be administered in grades seven and nine. The library media specialist set up a permanent functional reading center (see fig. 3.26, p. 102) to be used by students in grades three through six. Classroom teachers agreed to provide activities for the center on a rotating basis. Each center would remain posted for a three-week period to ensure maximum use by students. One third-grade teacher provided an "Emergency!" activity (fig. 3.27, p. 103) to help students practice using a pay telephone in case of an emergency. The functional reading center (fig. 3.26) includes a worksheet to be used by students at the center or in the classroom. The classroom teacher prepared the worksheet, and the library media specialists provided several copies, which were laminated to economize paper consumption.

(Text continues on page 104.)

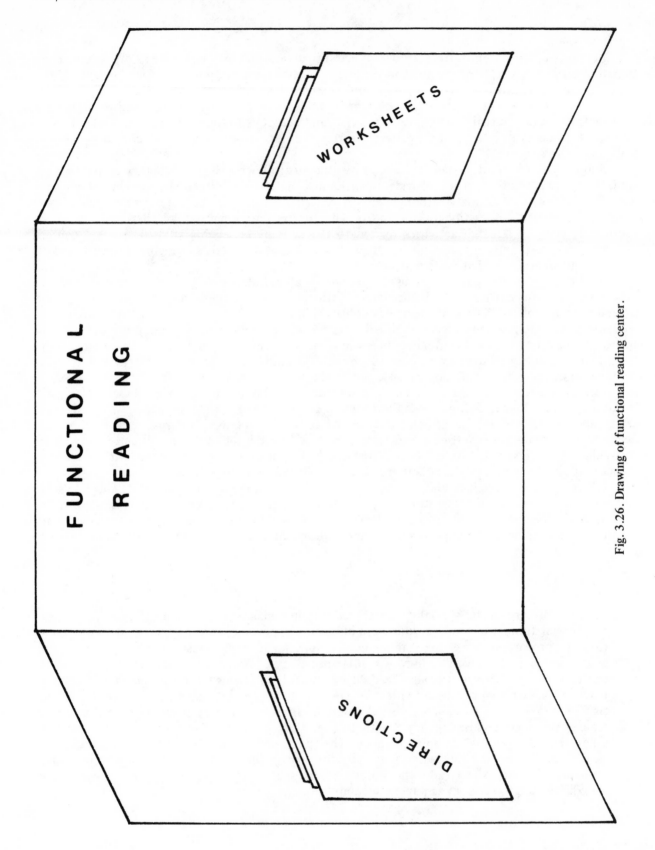

Fig. 3.26. Drawing of functional reading center.

Emergency!

Directions: Use the information listed on the pay telephone to fill in the blanks below.

1. You are walking through a parking lot and observe a fire in an abandoned building across the street! You dial _____ .

2. You witness an automobile accident in which someone is injured! You dial _____ .

3. You need local directory assistance right away. You dial _____ .

4. You see a robbery taking place at a store in a shopping center! You dial _____ .

5. No one is answering your emergency call. Have you dialed all _____ digits that are in every local number?

6. On a long distance emergency call, you must tell the operator the AREA CODE listed on the pay telephone. You say _____ .

7. You need to tell the Rescue Squad switchboard operator the pay telephone's number! You say _____ .

8. Your sister has just slipped on the ice in front of a telephone booth and she has hurt her leg! You dial _____ .

9. You enter an office building and smell the strong odor of smoke! You dial _____ .

10. You witness a purse snatcher at work while walking down the main street of town! You dial _____ .

COINS 25 5 10

INFORMATION .... Dial 411
OPERATOR .... Dial "0"

301
555-1234

EMERGENCY

FIRE   555-4422

RESCUE   555-0178

POLICE   555-9634

Fig. 3.27. Worksheet.

EXAMPLE

The library media specialist and a sixth-grade classroom teacher designed a learning center to review reference skills with students prior to a research assignment that would involve the use of reference sources. The library media objectives identified by the library media specialist were:

1. The student will determine the most appropriate reference for a specific purpose.
2. The student will locate specific information within a given reference source.

This learning center would follow lessons presented by the library media specialist and the classroom teacher on the use of almanacs, atlases, the card catalog, and encyclopedias. The library media specialist would present the center to the total class, and students would work independently to complete the "Source Search" learning center (see fig. 3.28). Figure 3.29 (see p. 106) is a list of directions for the center and figure 3.30 (see p. 107) is an answer sheet for the center.

Suggested research questions for the question cards are

1. How many people live in Nevada today? (almanac)
2. When was construction of the Washington Monument in Washington, D.C., begun? (encyclopedia)
3. Which continents border the Indian Ocean? (atlas)
4. Who illustrated the book *Rattlesnake Cave* by Evelyn Lampman? (card catalog)
5. What is the world's tallest building? (almanac)
6. How long is the Panama Canal? (encyclopedia)
7. What is the area of New Mexico in square miles? (atlas)
8. Which author wrote *How to Eat Fried Worms*? (card catalog)
9. Who was governor of Alabama in 1975? (almanac)
10. What does a koala bear usually eat? (encyclopedia)
11. At what latitude is London, England? (atlas)
12. Who is the author of the book *Sweeney's Ghost*? (card catalog)
13. What city has the largest population in the world today? (almanac)
14. How long do whales usually live? (encyclopedia)
15. Through which states does the Mississippi River flow? (atlas)
16. What is the title and who is the author of one book about Mexico? (card catalog)

(Text continues on page 108.)

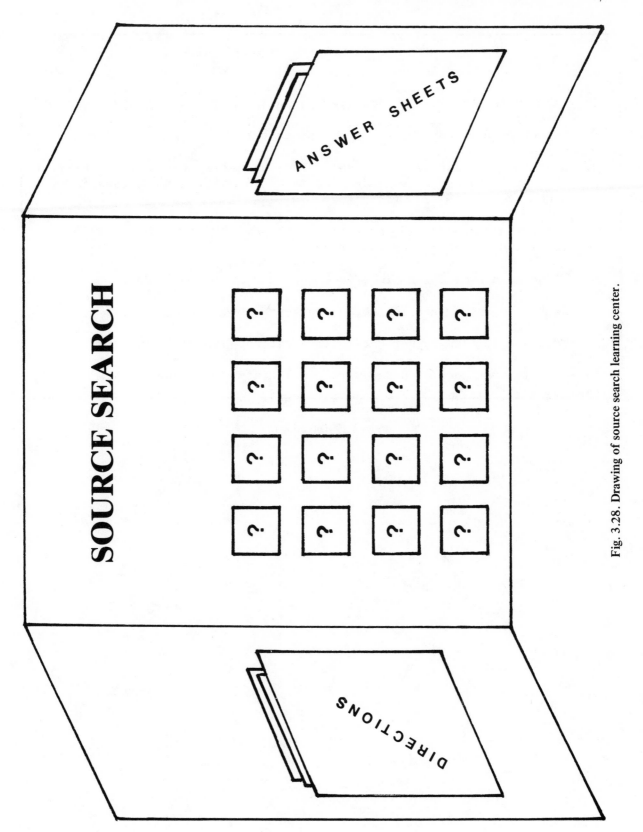

Fig. 3.28. Drawing of source search learning center.

Directions for Source Search

1. Take an answer sheet and put your name in the top right-hand corner.

2. Select a question card ⟦ ? ⟧ from the center.

3. Read the question carefully to decide whether an almanac, an atlas, the card catalog, or an encyclopedia would be the best reference source to use to find the answer.

4. Write the number of the question in the small box in the upper left-hand corner of the answer box.

5. Find the answer in the reference source that you selected.

6. Write the answer and the source on your answer sheet.

7. Continue in this manner until all questions have been answered.

8. Turn in your completed paper to the library media specialist.

Fig. 3.29. Directions.

Source Search

Sample Question

21	
	What is the most common food of an armadillo?

Sample Answer

21	
	Answer: small insects
Source:	World Book v. 1 p. 79

Almanac	Atlas	Card Catalog	Encyclopedia
Answer: Source:	Answer: Source:	Answer: Source:	Answer Source:
Answer: Source:	Answer: Source:	Answer: Source:	Answer: Source:
Answer: Source:	Answer: Source:	Answer: Source:	Answer: Source:
Answer: Source:	Answer: Source:	Answer: Source:	Answer: Source:

Fig. 3.30. Answer sheet.

EXAMPLE

A fifth-grade classroom teacher designed "TV Center" (see fig. 3.31) to be used as a permanent interest center in her classroom. Every two weeks, she replaces the student activity at the "TV Center." The particular activity detailed here, which involves student monitoring of television commercials, is to be completed at home. Each student is provided with a directions list (see fig. 3.32, p. 110) and a "TV Commercials Monitoring Form" (see fig. 3.33, p. 111).

(Text continues on page 112.)

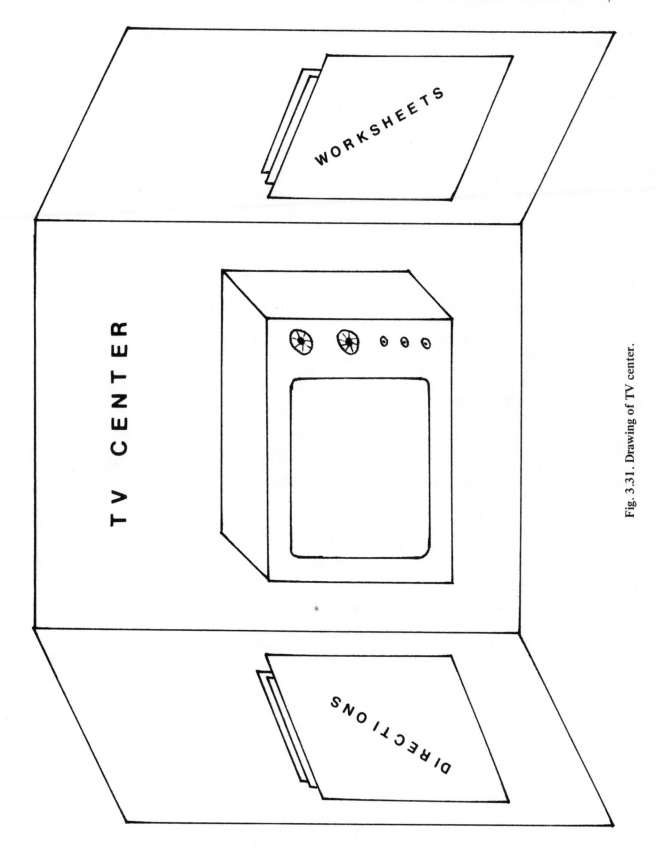

Fig. 3.31. Drawing of TV center.

Directions for Monitoring TV Commercials

1. You are to monitor one hour of commercial television broadcasting between the hours of seven and nine in the evening, or between the hours of nine and eleven in the morning on either Saturday or Sunday.

2. At least one day in advance, select a television program to be monitored. (Try to select a program that is one hour in length.)

3. Have these materials handy at least ten minutes before the program begins: a monitoring form, several pieces of scratch paper, two pencils, and a clock or watch with a second hand.

4. Tune in the television set to the channel you will be watching at least five minutes before the program is scheduled to begin.

5. Do all recording on scratch paper while you are actually watching the television program.

6. Time the program from its actual beginning to the beginning of the program that follows it.

7. Time each commercial accurately in minutes and/or seconds.

8. Record the starting time, the sponsor, the product, a brief description of the commercial, and the ending time for each commercial.

9. When the program is over, neatly copy your data on the "TV Commercials Monitoring Form."

10. Return completed monitoring forms to your classroom teacher.

Fig. 3.32. Directions.

TV Commericals Monitoring Form

Program: _____   Viewer: _____

Station: _____   Date: _____

Time: _____   Type of program: _____

Start	Sponsor	Product	Description of Commercial	End

Fig. 3.33. Worksheet.

Lectures

Lectures are a commonly used instructional strategy in which a classroom teacher and/or a library media specialist presents an oral exposition on a given subject to a student or a group of students. This presentation of information in a clear, precise form enables educators to inform students of the terms, facts, processes, and skills involved in a unit of study. Lectures are often used in conjunction with the instructional methods of demonstration and discussion and may be accompanied by the use of audiovisual aids. Lectures are an efficient means of communicating the objectives of a unit of study; all that is needed is an instructor and an attentive group of students. In the upper elementary grades, lectures are an especially successful means for developing listening techniques and note-taking strategies.

Because the attention spans of students in grades three through six are quite varied, lectures may need to be limited in frequency and duration. If lectures are the primary mode of communicating the objectives, terms, facts, and processes involved in a unit of study, some students may be turned off to the information presented. Also, if lectures are too long, some students will lose interest, and their attention will wane. If, however, lectures are used in conjunction with another instructional strategy, such as discussion, demonstration, or audiovisual presentation, students will become more actively involved, and their attention will be less likely to wander.

EXAMPLE

The third graders at one elementary school are studying about the solar system. The classroom teachers are basing classroom experiences on a chapter in the textbook *Concepts in Science, Green* (Harcourt Brace Jovanovich, 1980). The library media specialist develops a series of lectures about the nine planets of the solar system. Students must apply listening skills in order to take notes on a chart (fig. 3.34) that is provided for them. The series of three lectures takes place over a three-week period, and each lecture covers three planets. The information presented in the lectures is based on the book *The Solar System* by Isaac Asimov (Follett, 1975), with updated information provided by *The World Almanac* (1983 edition). Figure 3.35 (see p. 114) is a sample of a completed chart.

(Text continues on page 115.)

Planet	Nickname	Distance from Sun	Diameter (Size)	Revolution Period (Year)	Rotation Period (Day)	Moons
Mercury						
Venus						
Earth						
Mars						
Jupiter						
Saturn						
Uranus						
Neptune						
Pluto						

Fig. 3.34. Chart: Planetary Facts.

Planet	Nickname	Distance from Sun	Diameter (Size)	Revolution Period (Year)	Rotation Period (Day)	Moons
Mercury	smallest hottest	closest 36 million mi.	3,100 mi.	88 days	59 days	0
Venus	veiled planet	2nd 67 million mi.	7,700 mi.	225 days	243 days	0
Earth	our living planet	3rd 93 million mi.	7,918 mi.	365¼ days	24 hours	1
Mars	red planet	4th 141 million mi.	4,200 mi.	687 days	24 hours	2
Jupiter	giant planet	5th 480 million mi.	largest 88,000 mi.	12 years	10 hours	16+
Saturn	ringed planet	6th 886 million mi.	2nd largest 71,000 mi.	30 years	10 hours	at least 22
Uranus	contrary tipped ringed planet	7th almost 2 billion mi.	32,000 mi.	84 years	16 hours	5 known
Neptune	last of the greater ringed planet	8th almost 3 billion mi.	31,000 mi.	164 years	18 hours	3 known
Pluto	youngest planet ?	9th? between 3 & 4 billion mi.	1,500 mi.	248 years	6 days	1 known

Fig. 3.35. Sample of a completed chart on planetary facts.

Peer Teaching/Peer Tutoring

Peer teaching/peer tutoring is an instructional strategy in which students are given the role of instructor and teach other students the concepts, terms, skills, and/or processes involved in a unit of study. A basic assumption concerning this teaching method is that students must fully understand an educational concept, skill, or process in order to teach it to someone else. Through peer teaching/peer tutoring, students may gain knowledge about the process of learning, and, in turn, apply this knowledge to their own future learning endeavors. Peer teaching/peer tutoring promotes the improvement of self-concept of both the student who is teaching and the student who is being taught. In addition, it conveys the feeling that the education of all students is important. There are three basic types of peer teaching/peer tutoring: same-age, cross-age, and cross-cultural.

Same-age peer teaching/peer tutoring is an informal process in which a student who has mastered certain knowledge, skills, or processes is assigned to or volunteers to help another student in his or her class or grade level to learn these mastered concepts, skills, or processes. The classroom teacher and/or library media specialist uses assessment measures to determine those students who have mastered certain learnings and then assigns or asks for volunteers to assist others in meeting instructional objectives.

Cross-age peer teaching/peer tutoring is a process in which students volunteer or are assigned to assist younger students in learning the objectives of a previous grade level. It is more formalized, since it involves cooperation among school staff members and scheduling at appropriate times for both the older and younger students. It is usually beneficial to all students involved. Older students practice adult roles and reinforce previous learnings, and younger students learn new concepts, skills, and processes from older role models.

Cross-cultural peer teaching/peer tutoring may be either an informal or a formal process depending on the students involved. A student of a culturally different background and/or language is matched with another student to facilitate communication and instruction. It may involve either same-age or cross-age peer teaching/peer tutoring. Cross-cultural peer teaching/peer tutoring increases contact with culturally diverse students and develops understanding of, tolerance toward, and appreciation of cultural differences among students.

EXAMPLE

A classroom teacher indicates to the library media specialist that several students in her third/fourth grade combination class are having difficulty using guide words to locate dictionary entries. The library media specialist has just completed a series of lessons in which most students have been able to successfully differentiate author, title, and subject cards in the card catalog. Since the library media specialist feels that the processes involved in using guide letters on drawers of the card catalog to locate catalog cards are essentially the same as those involved in using guide letters to locate dictionary entries, he creates an activity involving the use of card catalog guide letters. Students are paired off on the basis of their skill proficiency in using dictionary guide words, as assessed by the classroom teacher. Since it is a combination grade class, cross-age and same-age peer teaching/peer tutoring is involved. After the library media specialist demonstrates a few examples, the student pairs complete the worksheet on page 116 (fig. 3.36).

Card Catalog Guide Letters

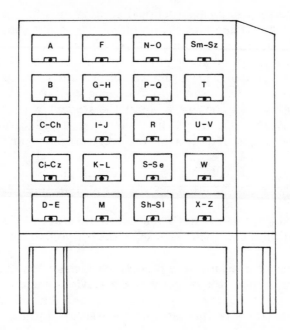

Directions: Write the guide letters for the drawer in which you would find
a catalog card for each of these.

_____ 1. A book by Laurence Pringle

_____ 2. The Story of Soil

_____ 3. Measurement

_____ 4. Deserts

_____ 5. Animals in Winter

_____ 6. A book by Franklyn Branley

_____ 7. A book by Munro Leaf

_____ 8. Pond Life

_____ 9. Projects With Air

_____ 10. Solar system

_____ 11. A book by Jeanne Bendick

_____ 12. Air

_____ 13. Bones and Skeletons

_____ 14. Shadows and More Shadows

_____ 15. A book by Seymour Simon

_____ 16. Heat All Around

_____ 17. Light

_____ 18. China

_____ 19. A book by Rocco V. Feravolo

_____ 20. The Sun

_____ 21. Seashores

_____ 22. A book by Sylvia Johnson

_____ 23. Worms

_____ 24. A book by Carol Carrick

_____ 25. A Closer Look at Deserts

_____ 26. Satellites

_____ 27. A book by Howard Smith

_____ 28. The Soil That Feeds Us

_____ 29. Chemistry

_____ 30. A book by Millicent Selsam

Fig. 3.36. Worksheet.

Problem Solving

Problem-solving strategies involve instruction in the processes and skills necessary to enable students to solve problems in the various content areas and to apply the solutions to everyday situations. Methods of problem solving include the use of many higher level cognitive and affective skills in which students apply critical and creative thinking processes to produce solutions to problems. Problem-solving techniques constitute a sort of knowledge that involves the use of higher level cognitive processes when interpreting, analyzing, synthesizing, applying, and evaluating information to find solutions. Effective problem-solving skills and/or processes must be developed over many years from varied experiences in which students determine desirable methods and practice these methods until they become habits. Although the steps in problem-solving strategies may vary from one subject area to another, the basic steps involved in problem-solving techniques are

- Examining and defining the problem
- Interpreting and analyzing the information given
- Forming a tentative hypothesis and/or synthesizing information to find a solution
- Testing the hypothesis and/or performing the processes necessary to solve the problem (experimenting, computing, researching, etc.)
- Evaluating the solution

The teaching of problem-solving strategies is perhaps one of the most difficult instructional areas that classroom teachers and library media specialists face. Since higher level cognitive processes are involved in most problem-solving activities, classroom teachers and library media specialists must ensure that students get adequate practice in prerequisite skills through varied experiences using the steps of the problem-solving process. For instance, if students have difficulty forming a tentative hypothesis in order to find a solution to a problem, it may be that they need more practice in interpretive thinking skills, such as drawing conclusions, making inferences, predicting outcomes, or determining cause and effect relationships. Student exposure to instructional activities that involve the prerequisite skills that are part of the problem-solving processes is essential if students are to apply problem-solving strategies.

Classroom teachers and library media specialists must carefully monitor student activities related to problem-solving skills and processes to be sure that the frustration level of students does not impede the thinking processes involved. Problem-solving activities are best introduced through concrete examples using the practical experiences of students rather than abstract situations for which students have limited experiential referents. A nonthreatening technique such as brainstorming may provide activities in which students can exercise the creative and critical thinking skills involved in problem-solving processes.

EXAMPLE

A library media specialist and a third-grade classroom teacher were jointly teaching a reading/language arts unit on Fairy Tales. After reading several fairy tales in the classroom and engaging in follow-up activities in the library media center, the library media specialist created an activity in which students would practice two important skills requisite for the development of problem-solving strategies. Students would practice determining the main idea and identifying cause and effect relationships of fairy tales with which all students were familiar. The "Fabulous Fairy Tales" worksheet (fig. 3.37, see p. 118) is the activity the library media specialist created.

Fabulous Fairy Tales

a. "Cinderella"
b. "Hansel and Gretel"
c. "Jack and the Beanstalk"
d. "Little Red Riding Hood"
e. "Sleeping Beauty"
f. "Snow White and the Seven Dwarfs"
g. "The Ugly Duckling"

Part A

Read each main idea sentence below. Match each sentence to one of the fairy tales listed above.
Write the letter of the fairy tale in the blank before the sentence.

____ 1. Two lost children are captured by a witch, but they use their wits to escape.

____ 2. An unattractive young animal grows up to be a handsome adult.

____ 3. A girl, living with several small men, is bewitched, but she is saved by a prince.

____ 4. A young woman goes to a ball and wins her prince.

____ 5. A princess is awakened, after a very long rest, by a prince's kiss.

____ 6. One little girl's visit to her grandmother ends up in disaster.

____ 7. A young boy escapes from a giant and gains a kingdom.

Part B

Read each sentence pair below. Match each pair with a fairy tale as you did in Part A. Then, on the blank following each sentence of each pair, write C for Cause or E for Effect.

____ 1. The princess slept for 100 years. ____
She pricked her finger. ____

____ 2. He was hungry. ____
The wolf found himself a delicious meal. ____

____ 3. Everyone made fun of him. ____
He was so unattractive. ____

____ 4. The shoe fit her foot. ____
The prince knew that she was the one he had danced with at the ball. ____

____ 5. He arrived home safely and cut down the beanstalk. ____
He was able to outrun the giant. ____

____ 6. The witch decided to wait for a while before she ate him. ____
He was not quite fat enough to make a tasty meal. ____

____ 7. The apple stuck in her throat. ____
The little men were not able to wake her up. ____

Fig. 3.37. Worksheet.

Programmed Instruction

Although several examples of programmed instruction are discussed as separate instructional strategies (i.e., computer-assisted instruction, student-teacher contracts, learning centers, LAP packs, and commercially prepared simulations), it is necessary to list programmed instruction as a separate category because of its widespread use and the availability of commercially prepared programmed materials. Programmed instruction is most often used today as a supplemental instructional strategy to extend student understandings of classroom instruction.

Programmed learning materials are produced when a subject is analyzed by its component parts and the parts are arranged into a sequential order. Students perform these parts or tasks in order and reinforcement and assessment components are often provided. Branching activities are those in which students who easily attain instructional objectives skip some tasks and proceed to more difficult tasks, or students who need more instructional reinforcement on a particular concept or skill perform additional tasks.

Programmed instruction is based on the assumption that a student will fully understand one component concept, skill, or process before proceeding to the next, and that in the end he or she will understand all the component ideas that contribute to a general conclusion or body of knowledge. Since programmed instruction is designed so that a student can proceed in steps, it is well suited for independent instruction. Each student can proceed at his or her own rate. It is important, therefore, to enable students of differing abilities to learn material that all students are expected to learn in the same form.

Programmed learning materials are available commercially. They can also be made by classroom teachers and library media specialists to supplement instructional programs. Commercially prepared programmed materials may take the form of computer programs and simulations, learning kits or laboratories, textbooks, workbooks, or series of worksheets. Teacher-prepared programmed materials may be developed in the form of student-teacher contracts, learning centers, LAP packs, task cards, or worksheets. Classroom teachers and library media specialists may incorporate the use of both commercially made and teacher-made programmed materials into a unit of study to reinforce concepts, skills, or processes.

EXAMPLE

A fifth-grade teaching team and the library media specialist at one school share instructional responsibilities for teaching outlining skills through the use of a programmed learning kit. The "Outline Building Kit" (Curriculum Associates, Inc., 1977) contains a series of manipulative activities that introduce, provide practice, and assess student performance in basic organization and outlining skills.

Classroom teachers provide several introductory lessons. Then students take a pretest, which is included in the "Outline Building Kit." Students are placed at a starting level for the kit activities on the basis of their performance on the pretest, and they are given a record sheet with a notation indicating their starting level in the kit.

The library media specialist sets up an "Outline Building" center in the library media center. Students are sent by the classroom teachers in pairs to work independently through the activities in the kit. The library media specialist monitors student advancement through the sequential activities of the kit. Students check their own answers and update their record sheets. When a student completes all activities, the library media specialist administers a posttest (which is included in the kit), checks the posttest, and returns it to the classroom teacher for evaluation.

Projects: Individual or Group Study

Individual or group study projects give students opportunities to pursue their own study of topics related to classroom learnings in any given subject area or unit of instruction. They are often used in conjunction with other methods within an instructional unit. Students use problem-solving skills, organizational skills, and a variety of materials to pursue their project. Students may use highly sequenced programmed materials, complete a student-teacher contract, participate in a learning center, or work through a LAP pack as they complete their projects. Often a student or a group of students use independent or guided research skills to develop a background for their topic of study by using textbooks, tradebooks, reference sources, and audiovisual materials.

Individual or group study projects provide for more active participation of individual students and allow for differences in learning rates and styles. Projects are usually assigned to or derived by students as culminating activities in a unit of study. Students are asked to present evidence of information gained from study projects in the form of a product that represents their learnings. These products may take many forms—written or oral reports, demonstrations or investigations, posters, dioramas, scrapbooks, notebooks, bulletin boards, filmstrips, movies, dramatizations, puppet shows, displays, murals, diagrams, and models.

EXAMPLE

A sixth-grade class is completing a science unit on "Light Energy." As a culminating activity, students are assigned an individual project. Each student must create an investigation to demonstrate some principle or concept about light energy. The classroom teacher distributes a list of questions to generate student involvement (see fig. 3.38). From these guide questions each student must choose one question as a starting point of his or her investigation. Once students have chosen a guide question to stimulate the formulation of their investigation, they must go to the library media center to research the topic area they have chosen. The library media specialist has agreed to aid students in their search for information upon which to base their investigation. Students must first determine a hypothesis for their investigation. They must list the materials and/or equipment used for the investigation. Then, they must conduct the investigation and record the results. Next, they must either support or refute their original hypothesis on the basis of their experimentation. Finally, they must report to the whole class their findings in the form of a demonstration or a visual display. Figure 3.39 (see p. 122) is a worksheet for the science project that each student must complete. Figure 3.40 (see p. 123) is a sample of a completed worksheet.

(Text continues on page 124.)

Light Energy Questions

1. What are optical illusions?

2. How can light be bent?

3. How are two eyes more helpful than one in judging the distances of objects?

4. How does the pupil of the eye react to different brightnesses of light?

5. How does a telescope work?

6. How does a camera work?

7. How do the eyes of insects differ from ours?

8. How does a magnifying glass produce enlarged images?

9. What is the difference between concave and convex lenses?

10. How does a film projector work?

11. How does a mirror reflect an image?

12. How can lenses in eyeglasses improve vision?

13. How does a microscope work?

14. What is a kaleidoscope and how does it work?

15. Why is writing that is reflected in a mirror reversed?

16. What is the difference between transparent, translucent, and opaque materials?

17. How does a curved mirror form an image?

18. **How can water bend light?**

19. How is a rainbow formed?

20. What are the colors of light?

21. How can a prism bend light to produce colors?

22. How can you create an illusion using water and a light source?

23. Why does the moon "shine?"

24. How does a lightning bug "glow?"

25. How do binoculars work?

26. Why do stars appear to twinkle?

27. Do your left eye and your right eye see the same thing?

28. Why do we see lightning before we hear thunder?

29. How can mirrors be used for sending messages?

30. How can we make still pictures appear to move?

31. How does a pin hole camera work?

32. What colors absorb radiant heat most?

33. How can you show that sound is produced by vibrating objects?

34. How do we produce sounds of different pitch?

35. What causes an eclipse of the sun?

36. What causes an eclipse of the moon?

Fig. 3.38. List of questions.

Science Project Worksheet

Investigative question: _____

_____

Hypothesis: I think that if I _____

_____

  then, _____

_____

Equipment and/or materials:_____

_____

_____

Procedure: _____

_____

_____

_____

Results: _____

_____

_____

Conclusion: _____

_____

_____

Reporting on the investigation:

  ☐ I will demonstrate the actual investigation to the class.

  ☐ I will create a visual display. (Specify: poster, diorama,
     bulletin board, diagram, model, written report, etc.) _____

_____

Fig. 3.39. Worksheet.

Science Project Worksheet

Investigative question: __What happens when light passes through__

__different substances?__

Hypothesis: I think that if I __put a pencil in a glass that is__

__half-filled with water,__

then, __the pencil will appear to bend or break.__

Equipment and/or materials: __Pencil, clear glass, water__

Procedure: __Fill the glass about half-full with water. Place the__

__pencil in the glass so that it is resting against the side of__

__the glass. Look directly at the spot where the pencil sticks out__

__of the water.__

Results: __The pencil looked as if it was broken or cracked at the__

__spot where it stuck out of the water.__

Conclusion: __My hypothesis was right! When light passes through__

__water, the light rays are bent, and that made the pencil appear__

__to be broken or cracked.__

Reporting on the investigation:

☒ I will demonstrate the actual investigation to the class.

☐ I will create a visual display. (Specify: poster, diorama,
   bulletin board, diagram, model, written report, etc.) _____

Fig. 3.40. Sample of a completed science project worksheet.

Role-playing/Dramatization

Role-playing is a short dramatization in which students assume a role and act out experiences related to a specified topic, situation, or problem. Dramatization of curricular content is an alternative instructional strategy to help students understand the concepts, information, and skills of a given content area unit of study. Role-playing and/or dramatization are instructional strategies appropriate to any age or ability level and to any subject area or unit of study. Cognitive, affective, and psychomotor processes are involved as students use their creative and expressive abilities to extend and apply the concepts and skills of any content subject area.

Role-playing also provides a unique opportunity for students to apply problem-solving methods and skills. Students may dramatize problems and alternative solutions to problems. Situations may be derived from curriculum materials, real-life situations, current or historical events, or, student concerns, problems, and interests. After alternate solutions have been presented through role-playing and/or dramatization, discussions may be held to evaluate the effectiveness of the solutions in relation to the problems depicted. In any role-playing or dramatization situation, the evaluative components are related to student interpretations and solutions rather than to the quality of the acting itself. Thus, role interpretation may be used to discuss and evaluate student-derived alternative solutions to problems.

EXAMPLE

A fifth-grade class is involved in reading realistic fiction novels as part of a reading/language arts classroom unit. The students are divided into groups of four to six members. Each small group selects or is assigned to read a novel. Each member of the group is given a copy of the novel by the library media specialist. After reading the book, the students of each small group design a bulletin board display depicting the main characters in a favorite scene or episode from the novel. Each group also plans, practices, and presents a dramatization of the content of the bulletin board. The dramatization is shared with other students from the class and grade level of the students involved. The bulletin boards are displayed in the library media center to motivate other students to read the novels represented.

Simulations

Simulations, often in the form of learning games, represent situations in which students experience an event, process, or problem found in the real world. They provide a means for students to apply problem-solving skills by making decisions, acting upon those decisions, and studying the consequences of those decisions. Simulated situations can be used to supplement and extend the learnings of any content area unit of study. Through simulation activities, students experience the relationship between real-life situations, content learnings, and problem-solving techniques.

Simulations range from simple role-playing situations to highly complex games in which computer programming may be required. Optimal use of simulation activities occurs after the introduction of a unit of study. When students have a background of concepts from which to draw, they can make more judicious decisions. Simulations provide highly motivational developmental or culminating activities within a unit of study. They can also provide an incentive for further examination of the content area topic.

EXAMPLE

A classroom group of fifth graders is involved in a social studies unit on "Westward Expansion." They are currently studying the gold rush period with classroom lessons and library media center research. The classroom teacher and the library media specialist derive the following simulation activity that takes place in the library media center with the classroom teacher and the library media specialist present.

1. The classroom teacher collects small pebbles and covers them with gold spray paint.

2. The library media specialist prepares a large map of the library media center with "landmarks" (the Fiction, Reference, and Nonfiction sections) clearly marked.

3. Shortly before the simulation activity is to begin, the library media specialist hides the "gold" on about twelve shelves within the landmarked sections.

4. The classroom teacher brings the class to the library media center, and the students are divided into groups of no more than six members.

5. Each group designs a sign with a group insignia to identify their "claim."

6. Student groups are given a few minutes to "survey" the Fiction, Nonfiction, and Reference sections in order to select a shelf to stake as its claim. (Students do not actually search shelves at this time. The "survey" is only to identify and "claim" a shelf.)

7. Each group stakes its claim by placing its sign on the selected shelf.

8. Once the claim is staked, each group must file its claim. In order to do this, the group must go to the "assaying and claims office" (the circulation desk), identify their claim (shelf) by section (Fiction, Reference, Nonfiction) and call numbers (range from first to last book on the shelf).

9. The library media specialist then "registers" the claim on the large map.

10. Finally, the groups "work their claims." All found gold must be brought to the claims office (the circulation desk) to be weighed on a scale and noted by the claims officer (classroom teacher).

At the end of the activity, the group with the most gold has staked the best claim! Students must be cautioned about "claims jumping," as any unregistered gold becomes the property of the assay office. Student groups that wish to change their claims must do so only after proper filing at the assaying and claims office.

Structured Overviews

Structured overviews, sometimes referred to as graphic organizers, are teaching strategies in which students are exposed to the new concepts and vocabulary of a unit of study prior to the actual implementation of the teaching unit. A structured overview is a graphic technique identifying the vocabulary and concepts that are essential to the understanding and use of content area materials. Based on research by Richard Barron,[6] and closely related in theory to Ausubel's "advanced organizers,"[7] structured overviews are most useful in the upper elementary grades as introductory classroom lessons to prepare students for readings and activities of a unit of study by exposing them to the conceptual framework and terms of that particular unit of study. Structured overviews provide students with a background of concepts and vocabulary with which to better understand the information presented in textbooks, tradebooks, and reference sources. Such information sources are often written in a complex expository manner, and may be confusing to students lacking the skills and background experiences needed to fully comprehend the materials. The concepts and vocabulary presented in a structured overview are introduced, whenever possible, in a diagrammatic manner that shows the relationships among the concepts being studied. Structured overviews are a very useful instructional strategy used to prepare students for a new content area unit of study.

EXAMPLE

A fifth-grade classroom teacher is ready to begin a science unit on "The Human Body" that concentrates on the structure and function of six major body systems. The classroom teacher designs a structured overview of the instructional unit (fig. 3.41) to introduce students to the most important concepts and vocabulary involved in the unit. Copies are provided for each student during an initiating activity to introduce the "Body Systems" unit of study. A classroom period is spent discussing the structured overview to furnish students with background concepts and terms requisite for comprehension of unit objectives.

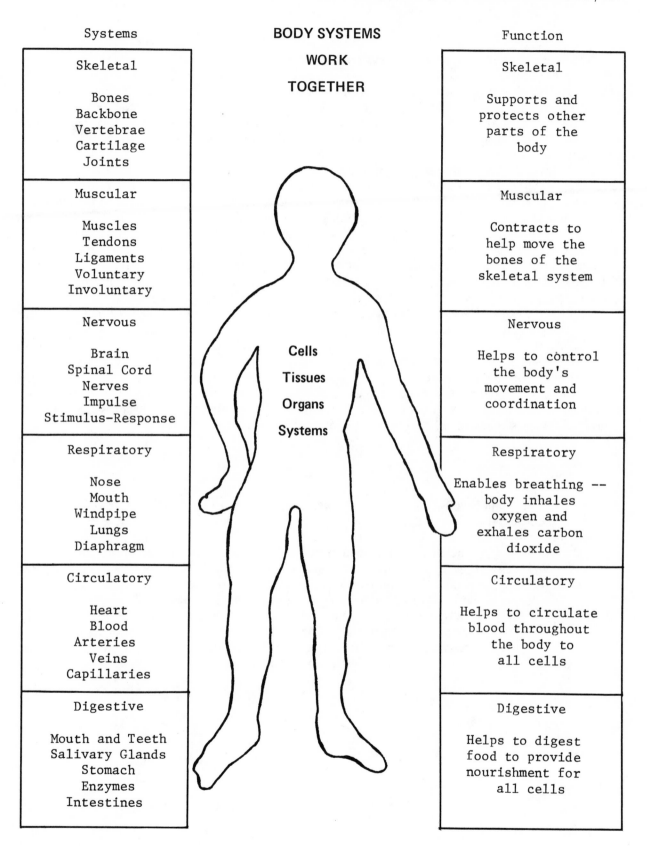

Fig. 3.41. Structured overview of body systems unit.

Student-Teacher Contracts

The student-teacher contract is a method of individualizing instruction in which the student and a teacher create an individualized program of learning. Contracts are verbal or written agreements made between a student (or a small group of students) and a classroom teacher and/or library media specialist for the completion of mutually developed learning activities. They can range from being totally unstructured—in which the student derives all learning alternatives, to being totally structured—in which the classroom teacher or library media specialist determines all learning activities.

Student-teacher contracts are closely related to LAP packs except that in a LAP pack the student independently works through a predetermined set of alternative activities during the completion of the package. In a student-teacher contract, the student has the opportunity to generate his or her own learning activities as the unit of study is in progress.

The use of varied textbook, reference, and audiovisual resources, and the incorporation of other instructional strategies such as learning centers, LAP packs, and individual and/or group study projects makes the use of student-teacher contracts a truly eclectic instructional method. Differences in learning styles, interests, and learning rates among students can be accommodated when deriving student-teacher contracts. They may also include provisions for an expected completion date, specifications of times for student-teacher conferences, signatures of persons or groups involved, and statements of mutually agreed criteria for evaluation or grading.

If a library media specialist or classroom teacher chooses the making of contracts with students on an individual or group basis as an instructional method to be used in a unit of study, careful structuring is necessary to ensure that all students are exposed to and meet the instructional objectives of the unit. Student-teacher contracts are most effectively used after a unit of study has been introduced and students have a background of introductory instructional experiences from which to make judgments concerning learning activity alternatives.

EXAMPLE

A fourth-grade class has begun a science unit on "Nutrition." One of the objectives to be developed within the instructional unit is: "Students will recognize and give examples of foods representing the 'Four Food Groups.'" The classroom teacher and the library media specialist have constructed a student-teacher contract as an instructional option for a small group of students designated as highly able learners. The library media specialist will supervise and coordinate the implementation of the student-teacher contract in the library media center with those students involved, while the classroom teacher will provide similar developmental instructional activities for the remaining students in the classroom. Figure 3.42 is a blank form for a student-teacher contract. Figure 3.43 (see p. 130) is a completed student-teacher contract developed by the classroom teacher and the library media specialist to fulfill the instructional objective concerning the "Four Food Groups."

(Text continues on page 131.)

Student-Teacher Contract

Content subject: _____   Content unit: _____

Classroom teacher : _____   Estimated time: _____

Instructional objective: _____

_____

Student Directions: _____

_____

_____

_____

_____ Activity 1: _____

_____

_____

_____ Activity 2: _____

_____

_____

_____ Activity 3: _____

_____

_____

_____ Activity 4: _____

_____

_____

_____ Activity 5: _____

_____

_____

Student: _____   Teacher:_____

Date started: _____   Date completed: _____

Fig. 3.42. Blank form.

Student-Teacher Contract

Content subject: __Science__   Content unit: __"Nutrition"__

Classroom teacher : __Ms. Bradley__   Estimated time: __two weeks__

Instructional objective: __The student will recognize and give__

__examples of foods representing the "Four Food Groups."__

Student Directions: __Select at least two alternative activities in__

__addition to Activity 4 to fulfill this contract. You may derive one__

__activity of your own and list it in the space provided under__

__Activity 5, but it must be approved.__

____ Activity 1: __View the filmstrip "Learning about Food" (Encyclo-__

__paedia Britannica Educational Corp., 1969). Write answers to__

__questions listed at the end of the filmstrip.__

____ Activity 2: __Construct a "Four Food Groups" chart on a large piece__

__of tagboard. Label the groups. Draw or cut out pictures from magazines__

__that represent examples of foods from each group.__

____ Activity 3: __Compose a poem, story, song, or television__

__commercial about the importance of eating a balanced diet of foods__

__from the four food groups.__

_X_ Activity 4: __Write a mini-report describing the four food groups.__
__Use at least three different sources in the library media center to__

__gather information. Include a listing of sources.__

____ Activity 5: _____

_____

_____

Student: __Derek M.__   Teacher: __Mr. Matthews (LMS)__

Date started: __12/05/84__   Date completed: _____

Fig. 3.43. Sample completed form.

Study Strategies

Study strategies are instructional methods through which students are taught to read independently and study assigned material in a procedural manner to increase comprehension and retention of information presented. Although study strategies may be applied in all content areas, they are especially helpful in social studies and science, as textbooks, reference books, and other print sources related to these content areas are often written in a complex expository style.

The oldest and perhaps most commonly taught study strategy is the "SQ3R study model" developed by Francis Robinson.[8] The procedural steps in the SQ3R study model (Survey, Question, Read, Recite, and Review) are similar to those of Stauffer's "directed reading-thinking activity."[9] (For a discussion of directed reading activity steps see the section of this chapter entitled "Directed Reading Activity.") There are differences however. The skills and processes used by students in a DRA are closely monitored by a classroom teacher as new material is presented to students; the skills and processes involved in the SQ3R model are applied by students as they independently review and study the information presented in a content unit in preparation for a test or other activity in which the recall of specific information is required.

It must be understood that most students do not learn and apply the SQ3R study model or other study strategies easily. A great number of experiences in following the procedural steps is necessary over a long period of time in varied content area units before students can be expected to internalize and apply these strategies independently. It is the author's view that through frequent exposure to the methods, skills, and processes involved in study strategies such as the SQ3R model in the upper elementary grades, students will be better prepared for the independent study skills expected of secondary school students. In the example that follows, the procedural steps inherent in the use of the SQ3R model as an instruction-strategy are explained in greater detail.

EXAMPLE

A fifth-grade classroom teacher is about to begin an instructional unit in science on Chemical and Physical Changes in Matter. Because of the difficulty of the complex concepts, terms, and investigations introduced in the textbook chapter entitled "Matter Changes Forms," the classroom teacher chooses to use the SQ3R study strategy as an instructional method to guide the students through the material presented. She will also have the students apply the SQ3R study strategy for reviewing the material for an end-of-chapter test. Since the textbook chapter is divided into five major sections, the classroom teacher demonstrates the application of the SQ3R study strategy for each of the five sections. Before the test, students are given a copy of the "SQ3R Study Strategy" steps (see fig. 3.44, p. 132), which they are expected to apply as they review and study for the test.

```
┌─────────────────────────────────────────────────────────────┐
│                     SQ3R Study Strategy                       │
├─────────────────────────────────────────────────────────────┤
│                          Survey                               │
│                                                               │
│  Look over the entire chapter, article, or section to get the │
│  main idea -- what it is about. Note its title, headings, and │
│  introductory or summary paragraphs. Look at any maps, tables,│
│  and charts listed. If there are questions at the end, look   │
│  them over to get a general idea of the information in the    │
│  chapter, article, or section that you should remember.       │
├─────────────────────────────────────────────────────────────┤
│                         Question                              │
│                                                               │
│  Turn the headings and subheadings into questions to give     │
│  yourself a purpose for reading each section.                 │
├─────────────────────────────────────────────────────────────┤
│                           Read                                │
│                                                               │
│  Find the answers to your questions by reading each section.  │
│  Think about what you are reading. Write notes or phrases on  │
│  the material by using the headings for an outline.           │
├─────────────────────────────────────────────────────────────┤
│                          Recite                               │
│                                                               │
│  Without looking at the book or your notes, try to answer the │
│  questions you asked before. If you cannot answer a particular│
│  question without looking at your book or notes, reread the   │
│  section.                                                     │
├─────────────────────────────────────────────────────────────┤
│                          Review                               │
│                                                               │
│  Try to remember the main ideas of each section without       │
│  looking at your book or notes. Reread any sections you are   │
│  not sure about.                                              │
└─────────────────────────────────────────────────────────────┘
```

Fig. 3.44. SQ3R study strategy steps.

DESIGNATION OF TEACHING RESPONSIBILITIES

When planning for an integrated program of content and library media skills instruction, classroom teachers and library media specialists must determine instructional roles prior to the actual implementation of instruction. If classroom teachers and library media specialists follow the procedure outlined in the beginning of this chapter, the teaching responsibilities are shared rather than increased by joint planning and joint teaching strategies.

As specified earlier, the classroom teacher first identifies content objectives for a unit of instruction, and then the library media specialist identifies library media research and study skills objectives that may be integrated into the content unit. Next, the library media specialist and the classroom teacher meet to develop integrated objectives and activities for the unit of study. It is at this point that designation of teaching responsibilities really begins. Once integrated content and library media research and study skills objectives are developed, teaching roles evolve naturally as the library media specialist and the classroom teacher plan instructional activities to meet their jointly developed instructional objectives. Decisions as to assessment procedures, preparation of materials, teaching strategies, sequence of instructional activities, designation of time, space, and student groupings for instruction, and teaching responsibilities will depend on the amount of integrated instruction each staff member is willing and able to do. The classroom teacher still has the same responsibility for teaching the content unit concepts, skills, and processes, just as the library media specialist has the same responsibility for teaching library media skills and processes. The difference, however, is that classroom teachers and library media specialists have an opportunity to share instructional responsibilities, materials, and ideas to provide more meaningful learning activities for students by integrating content and library media instruction.

EXAMPLE

One sixth-grade teacher and the library media specialist at his school began an integrated approach to teaching content and library media skills as the result of a conversation one day at lunch. The classroom teacher was frustrated, because he had asked his students to conduct research and write a short report on various representative bird species, and he had received reports seemingly copied from encyclopedias and other reference sources. The library media specialist offered to help the students learn how to take notes and paraphrase information rather than copying passages word for word. The library media specialist planned an activity in which students would take notes and paraphrase information. Each student was given a mammal information card (see fig. 3.45, p. 134) containing a paragraph about a particular mammal, and a mammal data card (see fig. 3.46, p. 135) on which to record pertinent information about the mammal. After the reading and recording exercise, the mammal information cards were collected, and the students were directed to write a paragraph about the mammal using the information recorded on their mammal data cards. The library media specialist shared the students' paragraphs with the classroom teacher, and both were pleased with the results. The classroom teacher liked the idea of taking notes on data cards, so he decided to expand the note-taking and paraphrasing activity. He prepared mammal data sheets (see figs. 3.47-3.49, pp. 136-38) for students to record information and bibliographic data. The library media specialist and the classroom teacher scheduled several research periods in which students would go to the library media center for data gathering experiences. Completed mammal data sheets were taken back to the classroom. Under the direction of their classroom teacher, students worked on organizing their notes into paragraph form, working on one section at a time. The library media specialist decided it was an opportune time to have the students create a filmstrip and an accompanying cassette recording about their respective mammals. She provided a storyboard worksheet (fig. 3.50, p. 139) for students to plan the visual and audio portions of their productions.

(Text continues on page 140.)

Mammals Information Cards

Armadillo	Bush Baby
Armadillos live in the grasslands and forests of South America. Armadillos are omnivorous animals, eating roots, leaves, and small animals. They are covered by jointed armor. When attacked, they roll into a ball and are protected by their armor.	The bush baby, or galago, is a primate, related to man, that lives in Africa. It is a small animal with large eyes, long ears, a long tail, long fingers on its hands, and long toes on its feet. It feeds on small birds, grasshoppers, eggs, fruit, and flowers.
Hyena	Mongoose
The hyena is a carnivore that lives in Africa and Asia. It is a scavenging animal, eating the meat left by lions and tigers after they have killed. The hyena's teeth are adapted for crushing bones. Hyenas sometimes hunt in packs.	The mongoose is a small carnivore that lives in Africa and Asia. It looks rather like a weasel, but the two are not related. Mongooses eat insects, small mammals, and reptiles. Some hunt alone, while others hunt in small packs.
Okapi	Pangolin
The okapi is a rare animal that was not discovered until 1900. It lives in Africa, in the Congo. It is related to the giraffe. It is a herbivore and has short legs, a short neck, and little horns on its head, like the giraffe.	Pangolins, or scaly anteaters, live in Africa and Asia. They can be as long as five feet. They have long noses, and long sticky tongues. Their bodies are covered with horny scales. They roll themselves into a ball when they are frightened.
Tapir	Wolverine
The tapir is a herbivore related to the horse and the rhinoceros. It lives in the forests of South America, Malaya, and the East Indies. It has a long nose, almost like a trunk. It is not very active, and spends most of its time grazing.	The wolverine, or glutton, is a carnivore. It lives in northern Canada and Alaska and from Siberia to Norway. A wolverine is a ferocious animal that can attack and kill an animal as large as a moose. It hunts alone, at night, leaping on its prey suddenly.
Wombat	Yak .
Wombats are small, bearlike animals. They are marsupials, living in and near Australia. They are herbivorous, eating grass, bark, and roots. They live in burrows, which they can dig quickly with their wide, shovel-like front paws.	Yaks are herbivores that live in the steppes of Central Asia. They are related to goats, cattle, and antelopes. They have long hair to protect them from the cold. Yaks are mountain animals.

Fig. 3.45. Mammals information cards.

Mammals Data Cards

Mammal: _____	Mammal: _____
Habitat: _____	Habitat: _____
Range: _____	Range: _____
Type of eater: _____	Type of eater: _____
Foods: _____	Foods: _____
Protection: _____	Protection: _____
Mammal: _____	Mammal: _____
Habitat: _____	Habitat: _____
Range: _____	Range: _____
Type of eater: _____	Type of eater: _____
Foods: _____	Foods: _____
Protection: _____	Protection: _____
Mammal: _____	Mammal: _____
Habitat: _____	Habitat: _____
Range: _____	Range: _____
Type of eater: _____	Type of eater: _____
Foods: _____	Foods: _____
Protection: _____	Protection: _____

Fig. 3.46. Mammals data cards.

Mammal Data Sheet 1

Mammal: _____

Researcher: _____

A. Classification information

Class: _____ Order: _____

Genus: _____ Species: _____

Common name(s): _____

Similar species: _____

B. Physical description

Average height: _____ Average length: _____

Average weight: _____ Life span: _____

Description of males: _____

_____

Description of females: _____

_____

Other notes: _____

_____

_____

Drawing of mammal: _____

Fig. 3.47. Worksheet.

Mammal Data Sheet 2

C. Environmental description

Habitat: _____

Home or shelter: _____

Range: _____

```
┌──────────────────────────────┬──────────────────────┐
│                              │                      │
│      Shade in the Range      │     [world map]      │
│                              │                      │
│      of this Mammal          │   THE WORLD          │
│                              │                      │
└──────────────────────────────┴──────────────────────┘
```

D. Description of behavior

Type of eater: _____

Foods: _____

_____

Protection: _____

_____

Enemies: _____

_____

Social system: _____

_____

Migration: _____

_____

Hibernation: _____

_____

Other notes: _____

_____

Fig. 3.48. Worksheet.

Mammal Data Sheet 3

E. Continuance of species

Gestation period: _____   Number of young: _____

Description of young: _____

_____

Care and training of young: _____

_____

F. Other important or interesting facts:

_____

_____

G. Bibliographic information

Encyclopedia
  Title: _____ Volume: _____

  Article title: _____

  Publisher: _____

  Copyright date: _____   Pages: _____

Book 1
  Author/Editor: _____

  Title: _____

  Publisher: _____

  Copyright date: _____   Pages: _____

Book 2
  Author/Editor: _____

  Title: _____

  Publisher: _____

  Copyright date: _____   Pages: _____

Fig. 3.49. Worksheet.

Storyboard

Visual   Audio

Fig. 3.50. Worksheet.

DETERMINATION OF STUDENT GROUPINGS FOR INSTRUCTION

The determination of alternative instructional groupings is an important component of any instructional plan. Grouping strategies are especially helpful in situations in which classroom teachers and library media specialists provide integrated content and library media skills instruction through jointly planned and implemented learning activities for students. Varied strategies for organizing students for instruction facilitate the ongoing instructional activities involving the interaction of students, resources, and teaching staff members. Library media specialists and classroom teachers should consider alternative student groupings that allow the optimal development of student knowledge, skills, abilities, and interests. Although management difficulties of scheduling may limit the frequency of variable student groupings, whenever possible adjustments can be made to consider alternative instructional groupings based upon students' needs.

Decisions concerning the grouping of students for instruction are best made after instructional objectives have been identified, teaching strategies have been selected, and preliminary planning for instructional activities has been accomplished. Alternative groupings of students for instruction include the following:

1. Total class instruction

2. Individualized instruction

3. Small group instruction
   a. Ability grouping
   b. Skills grouping
   c. Interest grouping

Total Class Instruction

Total class instruction is the most frequently used method of organizing students for instruction in the upper elementary grades. Although students are usually grouped by ability or skill proficiency in the content areas of reading/language arts and mathematics, total class instruction is the norm for curriculum areas related to art, library media, music, physical education, science, and social studies. Total class instruction involves no grouping of students in addition to their designated classroom assignments. If used as the only method of grouping for instruction, total class instruction does not meet the needs of individual students with varying abilities, interests, and learning rates or styles. It is most effective, however, if used in conjunction with other means of grouping students and with certain instructional methods and activities. Total class instruction is most effectively used as a means of: (1) introducing an instructional unit, skill, or process; (2) setting the purpose of an activity or a series of activities; (3) delivering content information through audiovisual presentations; (4) discussing content learnings with students in order to observe students' progress; and (5) reviewing an instructional unit, skill, or process in preparation for culminating activities.

EXAMPLE

A teaching team consisting of three fourth-grade teachers and the library media specialist of one school have combined literature and research in a series of activities to take place in the library media center and the classroom. The library media specialist meets with each fourth-grade class to introduce them to the author research activities. She demonstrates how students will choose an author, conduct biographic research on the author, use the "Author Research" worksheet (fig. 3.51) to record information, and select one book by the author to be read for a book report in the classroom.

Author Research

Directions: Use <u>The Junior Book of Authors</u>, "Author" cards in the card
catalog, and information listed on book jackets to find
information about an author.

Author: _____

Date of birth: _____ Place of birth: _____

Early life: _____

_____

_____

_____

Education: _____

_____

Adult life: _____

_____

_____

_____

Other facts of interest: _____

_____

_____

Books written by author: _____

_____

_____

_____

Book chosen to be read for book report:_____

(Bring book and this form to your classroom teacher.)

Fig. 3.51. Worksheet.

Individualized Instruction

Individualized instruction is most often used to differentiate instruction in order to meet the needs of individual students within a class or grade level. Students with varying learning rates, interest levels, skills proficiencies, learning styles, and ability levels are provided with assignments on which they work independently to accomplish instructional objectives. Diagnostic information concerning individual students is essential to library media specialist and classroom teachers using individualized instruction. On the basis of formal and/or informal assessment measures, classroom teachers and library media specialists prescribe learning alternatives for students. Individualized instruction is implemented through such teaching methods as learning centers, individual study projects, and student-teacher contracts. As a strategy for grouping students, individualized instruction is most effective when combined with other grouping techniques. Management difficulties may occur when a classroom teacher or library media specialist attempts to provide a totally individualized program that spans content areas.

EXAMPLE

In the previous example, the library media specialist used total class instruction to introduce the fourth-grade students to the series of activities relating literature and research. In that lesson, she gave the whole class an overview of the procedures for completing the author research activities. At this time, she uses individualized instruction to help students select an author, conduct biographic research, and select a book to be read for follow-up activities in the classroom. Students come to the library media center at prearranged times set up by the library media specialist and their classroom teachers. The library media specialist has set up a display with at least one popular book by each of the authors in the "Suggested Authors" list below. Based on interest and reading level, each student is matched with an author, and selects a book by that author for classroom use. Students return to the library media center individually during the next week to conduct the research necessary to complete the "Author Research" worksheet. Students work independently to gather the necessary data. The library media specialist or an aide is always present to help students if they are having difficulties. (The list of authors that follows may be helpful for generating student interest.)

Suggested authors:

Ludwig Bemelmans	Theodor Seuss Geisel	Mary Norton
Judy Blume	Carolyn Haywood	Scott O'Dell
Clyde Robert Bulla	Marguerite Henry	Beatrix Potter
Matt Christopher	Holling C. Holling	H. A. Rey
Beverly Cleary	Ezra Jack Keats	Thomas Rockwell
Elizabeth Coatsworth	Elaine Konigsburg	Maurice Sendak
Marguerite De Angeli	Robert Kraus	Shel Silverstein
Meindert De Jong	Evelyn Sibley Lampman	Peter Spier
Eleanor Estes	Robert Lawson	Eve Titus
Marie Hall Ets	Lois Lenski	E. B. White
John D. Fitzgerald	Astrid Lindgren	Laura Ingalls Wilder
Louise Fitzhugh	Leo Lionni	Elizabeth Yates
Doris Gates	Robert McCloskey	

Small Group Instruction

Small group instruction based on students' abilities, skills, or interests provides the flexibility of individualized instruction with the efficiency of total class instruction. Although used most often for teaching reading/language arts and mathematics, it is applicable to other content areas as well. Students may be provided with reinforcement of extension activities based on small group needs. As with total class and individualized instruction, small group instruction is most effective when used in conjunction with other methods of grouping students. The three most common forms of small group instruction are: ability grouping, skills grouping, and interest grouping.

Ability grouping is the most prevalent form of small group instruction. Students are grouped according to general achievement levels, and instructional activities are adjusted accordingly. The most commonly used form of ability grouping in the upper elementary grades is the traditional reading group in which students share in learning experiences with students at the same reading level. Although ability grouping is an effective means for some instructional activities, it should not be the only method of grouping students. Periodic reassessment of students is necessary to ensure that students are properly placed in ability groups. If students are grouped only on the basis of ability or achievement levels, a rigid tracking system may result.

Skills grouping is another form of small group instruction in which students are placed in specific groups on the basis of need for instruction in a particular skill or process. Students of varying ability levels may be placed in a skills group, since proficiency in a particular skill or process is the criterion for grouping. Diagnostic measures are also important to the formation of skills groups, however, their form differs from those used to place students in ability groups. Pretests and posttests for a particular skill are used to evaluate students for skills grouping, while general achievement tests are used to assess students for ability grouping. Skills groups are more flexible than ability groups. Skills groups change frequently as students meet mastery criterion for a particular skill or process.

Interest grouping is another form of small group instruction in which students are grouped together to explore a mutual interest. It is a highly motivational grouping strategy, since students select their group on the basis of interests. Students of differing ability levels work together effectively in interest groups. As with any alternative strategy for grouping students for instruction, interest grouping should be used in conjunction with other grouping methods in order to ensure a well-balanced instructional program.

EXAMPLE

In the previous example, the library media specialist used individualized instruction when students selected an author and a book by that author and later when students researched their authors independently. While students were involved in activities in the library media center, the classroom teacher used small group instruction to prepare students for follow-up activities in the classroom. The classroom teacher provided several developmental lessons with reading groups (ability grouping based on general reading achievement levels). Students participated in activities using narrative selections from their basal readers. Reading group discussions focused on the problem solving patterns represented by the characters in each narrative selection. Students identified (1) a problem experienced by a main character in the selection, (2) the action(s) taken by the character in attempting to solve the problem, and (3) the results of the character's action(s) in relation to the problem.

When all students had finished reading their book and had conducted research on its author, the classroom teacher prepared a "Book Report Form" (fig. 3.52, p. 144) that incorporated the biographical information gathered in the library media center and the problem-solving patterns studied in the classroom.

Book Report Form

Title: _____

Author: _____

Publisher: _____

Copyright date: _____   Number of pages: _____

A. Use the information listed on your "Author Research" worksheet to write a paragraph about the author's life.

_____

_____

_____

_____

_____

_____

_____

B. Think about a problem that one of the main characters had in the book that you read. Identify the problem, the action(s) taken by the character, and the result of the character's action(s).

Problem: _____

_____

_____

Action(s): _____

_____

_____

Result: _____

_____

_____

C. Draw an illustration depicting the character's problem on the back of this paper.

Fig. 3.52. Worksheet.

DESIGNATION OF TIME FOR INSTRUCTION

As library media specialists and classroom teachers plan for integrated content and library media research and study skills instruction, time is an important factor to be considered. They must consider a general time frame for the implementation of an instructional unit and specific scheduled times for instructional activities with students.

When identifying content objectives for a unit of study, the classroom teacher indicates the projected amount of time in terms of days, weeks, or months that an instructional unit will take. The library media specialist uses this general time frame when identifying library media research and study skills objectives to be integrated into the content unit.

When developing integrated objectives and planning for specific learning activities for students, the library media specialist and the classroom teacher must decide when students will participate in these activities. The library media specialist has many more limitations in terms of scheduling time for instruction than does the classroom teacher. The library media specialist must service an entire school, while the classroom teacher is concerned with only one class, grade, or team of students. In addition to teaching responsibilities, the library media specialist must provide assistance to individual students using the library media center, select appropriate library media resources, perform clerical duties related to library media center circulation, and provide resources to students and teachers as they are needed. Library media specialists usually designate instructional time for students in terms of either a *fixed* or a *flexible* schedule. With a fixed schedule, the library media specialist meets with each class in the school in the library media center for a specified period of time on a particular day on a weekly basis. When a flexible schedule is used, class time is determined by the library media specialist or an individual classroom teacher by what is to be taught, how it will be taught, and the rates at which the students progress. Regardless of the type of scheduling adhered to in a particular school, classroom teachers and library media specialists must consider time limitations when planning for instructional experiences with students. They must plan meaningful instructional activities for students within a workable time frame for all concerned.

EXAMPLE

An elementary school library media specialist had always operated under a fixed schedule. Each class in the school would come to the library media center for a thirty-minute library skills period per week. She had often experienced difficulty fitting in lessons within the allotted thirty-minute time frame, especially those with the upper grade classes. She instituted a new schedule with the principal in which classes would have their fixed library skills period every other week. On the alternate weeks, she had a flexible schedule in which classes came to the library media center as deemed appropriate by the classroom teacher or herself on the basis of student needs. The library media specialist found that the new scheduling procedure provided more flexibility in planning instructional activities with classroom teachers and in determining appropriate time periods for lessons.

DESIGNATION OF SPACE FOR INSTRUCTION

When library media specialists and classroom teachers plan for integrated content and library media research and study skills instruction, they must determine the location of instructional activities for students. Generally, the library media specialist teaches in the library media center where library media resources are readily available, and the classroom teacher instructs in the classroom that is his or her designated instructional space. If a particular activity requires a large space to accommodate large groups of students or movements, the all-purpose room, the gymnasium, or the playground may be the most appropriate location. For certain activities, an art or music room, or a reading, math, or science laboratory may be best suited to provide student access to special materials and/or resource persons. If learning centers are used, decisions must be made as to space available in the classroom or the library media center to provide maximum student access. In addition, library media specialists and classroom teachers must determine locations for the storage of media and materials used in integrated instructional activities.

EXAMPLE

A library media specialist works on a regular basis with a group of twelve highly able third graders on advanced library media research and study skills. At the present time, these students are involved in a science unit on "Animal Classifications" in the classroom. The library media specialist creates an activity in which these students must locate subject cards in the card catalog and record information on books about five different classes of vertebrates on the "Vertebrates" worksheet (fig. 3.53). This activity takes place in the library media center, since the students must have access to the card catalog and the library collection in order to complete the worksheet that the library media specialist has developed. After the students complete this activity, the library media specialist will make arrangements with the art teacher for a follow-up activity in which these students will go to the art room to make a water color painting of the animal that they selected from one of the books they had listed on the worksheet.

Vertebrates

Part A

Directions: Use Subject cards from the card catalog to complete the chart below. One example has been done for you.

Subject	Call Number	Author	Title
Amphibians	598.1 A	Allen, Gertrude E.	Everyday Turtles, Toads, and Their Kin.
Birds			
Fish			
Mammals			
Reptiles			

Part B

Directions: Locate one of the books that you listed above. Select an animal pictured in the book and draw a picture of it on the back of this paper.

Fig. 3.53. Worksheet.

IMPLEMENTATION OF INSTRUCTION

Once a library media specialist and a classroom teacher have developed instructional objectives and activities to integrate content and library media research and study skills instruction, the actual teaching of a unit of study commences. A series of structured learning experiences is provided to enable students to interact with the content and library media concepts, skills, processes, media, and materials included in the unit of study. The implementation of a unit of study entails the creating and assigning of appropriate learning activities to students. Instructional activities are presented in a sequential manner in the form of introductory, developmental, and culminating activities.

The examples for the section that follows will relate back to the fourth-grade unit of study in "Sound Energy" that was discussed in the first three sections of this chapter. For each of the three sections that follow, an example of an introductory, a developmental, and a culminating activity implemented by the classroom teacher or library media specialist will be provided.

INTRODUCTORY ACTIVITIES

As students begin a unit of study, their first learning experiences provide an introduction to the objectives, concepts, terms, processes, and skills involved in the instructional unit. Introductory activities may include learning situations to stimulate student interest through such means as audio-visual presentations, discussions, games, or brainstorming activities. These initiating experiences may incorporate activities to communicate the content and objectives of a unit of study to students through the use of such strategies as structured overviews, DRAs, or applications of the initial stages of the SQ3R study method. Often preassessment measures are administered to determine student placement if differentiated instructional practices are to be implemented. Preassessments may range from formal diagnostic tests or skills pretests to informal observations of student demonstration of skills performance.

Introductory activities are an essential part of a unit plan through which library media specialists and classroom teachers can determine what students already know in relation to the objectives of a unit of study. Student performance in initiating activities may in part determine the direction of developmental activities that follow. For instance, if preassessment measures indicate that students lack prerequisite skills needed for successful completion of an area of study, the classroom teacher or library media specialist must provide instruction in those requisite skills before proceeding to developmental activities that assume mastery of them.

EXAMPLE

The classroom teacher initiates instruction by preparing a structured overview of the instructional unit on "Sound Energy" (fig. 3.54). The structured overview is duplicated, and a copy is provided for each student. A discussion follows the presentation of the structured overview in which students demonstrate their current knowledge of the terms and concepts involved in the "Sound Energy" unit. A follow-up introductory lesson will include a survey of the textbook chapter to be used by students in developmental lessons of the unit in *Science 4* (Addison-Wesley, 1980).

Sound Energy

Terms to be learned:

1. Sounds

2. Vibrations

3. Volume (intensity)

4. Pitch (frequency)

5. Sound sources

6. Sound waves ("push" waves)

7. Conductors (solids, liquids, gases, vacuums)

8. Music

9. Noise

Terms to be explored:

1. Acoustics

2. Animal ears and sound production

3. Audiometers

4. Decibels

5. Echoes

6. Musical instruments (string, wind, percussion)

7. Noise pollution

8. Oscilloscopes

9. Radar

10. Sonar

11. Sound barrier

12. Thunder

13. Ultrasonic sounds

14. Vocal chords

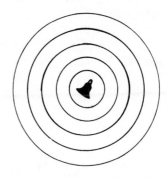

SOUND WAVES

PUSH WAVES

THE EAR

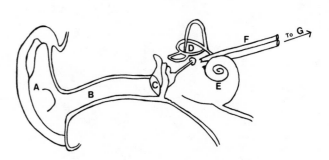

Parts of the ear: a, outer ear; b, ear canal; c, eardrum; d, middle ear; e, inner ear; f, nerves; g, brain.

Fig. 3.54. Structured overview of sound energy unit.

EXAMPLE

The library media specialist has selected "locating books in the library media center by the use of the Dewey decimal system" as a general objective for all fourth graders. She now integrates this objective into the science unit on "Sound Energy." She creates and administers a pretest/posttest (fig. 3.55) to determine student use and knowledge of call numbers to identify and locate print sources in the library media center, using books related to the "Sound Energy" unit. Based on pretest performance, students are grouped for instruction into skills groups for developmental activities to follow.

Call Numbers Pretest/Posttest

Part A

Directions: Indicate whether you would look for an Author, Subject, or Title
card in the card catalog to locate each of the following.

1. A book by Margaret Cosgrove _____

2. The book <u>Musical Insects</u> _____

3. A book about sound _____

4. The book <u>The Story of Your Ear</u> _____

5. A book by Illa Podendorf _____

Part B

Directions: Match each book with its call number. Choose from the call
numbers listed below:

591.59   595.72   612.85   621.389   534.07   612   534   598.2   534
  C   D   S   M   A   E   B   G   F

6. <u>Sound Science</u> by Melvin M. Alexenberg _____

7. <u>Sound and Ultrasonics</u> by Ira M. Freeman _____

8. <u>The Story of Your Ear</u> by Alvin and Virginia Silverstein _____

9. <u>High Sounds, Low Sounds</u> by Franklyn M. Branley _____

10. <u>Messages and Voices: The Communication of Animals</u> by Margaret Cosgrove

    _____

11. <u>Bird Talk</u> by Roma Gans _____

12. <u>The World of Sound Recording</u> by Don Murray _____

13. <u>Musical Insects</u> by Bette J. Davis _____

14. <u>Human Body: The Ear</u> by Kathleen Elgin _____

Part C

Directions: List the call numbers from Part B in the order in which the books
would be arranged on the shelves in the library media center.

15. _____   20. _____
16. _____   21. _____
17. _____   22. _____
18. _____   23. _____
19. _____

Fig. 3.55 Pretest/Posttest.

DEVELOPMENTAL ACTIVITIES

After students, classroom teachers, and library media specialists have engaged in introductory activities, the classroom teacher and the library media specialist provide students with developmental activities in which students are exposed to the specific content and library media research and study skills, concepts, and processes that have been identified as instructional objectives for the unit of study. Often developmental activities entail the use of directed reading and drill/practice instructional strategies to reinforce student learnings. At this time, some small group or independent activities may be implemented in which students practice and extend instructional concepts, skills, and processes through the use of learning centers, student-teacher contracts, computer-assisted instruction, problem-solving activities, programmed instruction materials, simulations, or LAP packs. Assessment measures used for developmental activities are usually informal observations by the classroom teacher and/or library media specialist, although many written developmental activities may be assessed for grading purposes. Developmental activities provide structured learning opportunities through which students meet the instructional objectives of the integrated unit of study.

EXAMPLE

The classroom teacher, while presenting developmental lessons using the student textbook *Science 4* (Addison-Wesley, 1980), creates and posts a "Sound" learning center (see fig. 3.56) at which small groups of students work independently to reinforce and extend instructional learnings. The learning center contains four activities with accompanying worksheets (figs. 3.57-60, pp. 154-57).

(Text continues on page 158.)

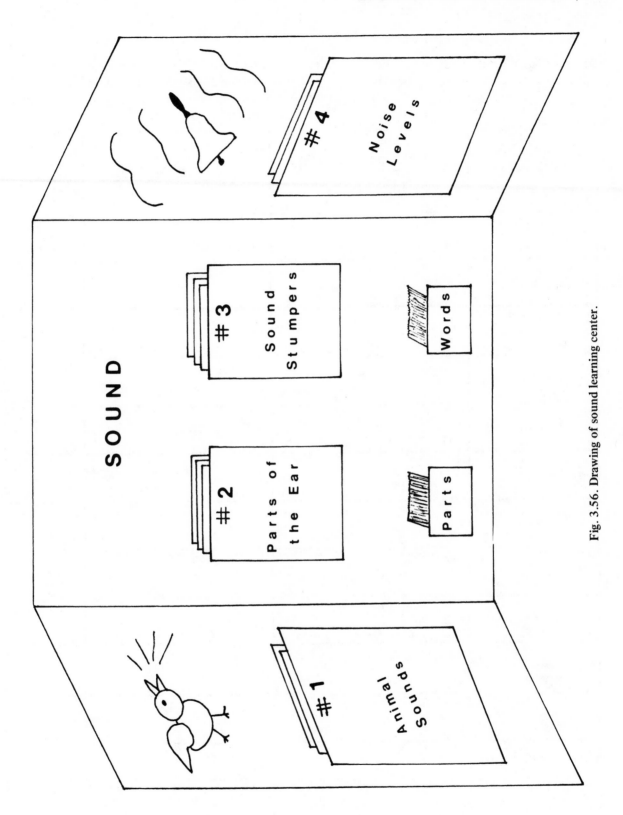

Fig. 3.56. Drawing of sound learning center.

Activity 1 -- Animal Sounds

Directions: Use the three books at the "Sound" center to find out if the entries listed below are found in each of the indexes. Put an <u>X</u> in the box if the entry appears in the index of that particular book. The first entry has been done for you.

Index Entry	Messages and Voices: The Communication of Animals	Musical Insects	Sounds in the Sea
1. barnacles	X		X
2. cicada			
3. crickets			
4. grasshopper			
5. hydrophone			
6. katydid			
7. porpoise			
8. shark			
9. sonar			
10. spectro-graph			
11. swim bladder			
12. toadfish			
13. trigger fish			

Fig. 3.57. Worksheet.

Activity 2 -- Parts of the Ear

Directions: Take the "Parts" cards out of the pocket and arrange them to fit
in the outline below. List the Parts as title, main topics, and
subentries on the outline form. Use the dictionary if you are
not sure of all of the meanings.

_____

I. _____

    A. _____

    B. _____

II. _____

    A. _____

    B. _____

    C. _____

III. _____

    A. _____

    B. _____

    C. _____

Fig. 3.58. Worksheet.

Activity 3 -- Sound Stumpers

Directions: Take the "Words" cards out of the pocket and arrange them in
             alphabetical order. List them in order on the lines below. Then
             look up each word in the dictionary and write its meaning.

1. _____ - _____

   _____

2. _____ - _____

   _____

3. _____ - _____

   _____

4. _____ - _____

   _____

5. _____ - _____

   _____

6. _____ - _____

   _____

7. _____ - _____

   _____

8. _____ - _____

   _____

9. _____ - _____

   _____

10. _____ - _____

    _____

11. _____ - _____

    _____

12. _____ - _____

    _____

Fig. 3.59. Worksheet.

Activity 4 -- Noise Levels

Part A

Directions: Number the "sound levels" in order from the softest (1) to the
             loudest (11).

____ Rock music   ____ A whisper; leaves rustling

____ A noisy office   ____ Normal conversation

____ A rocket launch   ____ A typewriter; loud conversation

____ A jet takeoff   ____ Busy traffic; thunder

____ Normal traffic   ____ Quiet conversation

____ Light traffic

Part B

Directions: Underline the noise from each pair that would annoy you the
             most. Then explain why on the line provided.

1. a. Dropping a book in class   b. Dropping a loaded tray in the
                                            cafeteria

    _____

2. a. Band practice indoors   b. Band practice outdoors

    _____

3. a. Cheering at a football game   b. Cheering at a basketball game

    _____

4. a. Group discussions in class   b. Talking in an empty school hallway

    _____

5. a. A jet takeoff   b. A jackhammer digging in a city
                                            street

    _____

6. a. Students exercising in the   b. Students exercising on a football
        gymnasium   field

    _____

Fig. 3.60. Worksheet.

For Activity 1—Animal Sounds, the students must use the index of three books to locate entries, and indicate on the worksheet whether such entries appear in each of the books. The three books selected for this activity are:

Cosgrove, Margaret. *Messages and Voices: The Communication of Animals.* New York: Dodd, Mead, 1974.

Davis, Bette J. *Musical Insects.* New York: Lothrup, Lee, and Shepard, 1971.

Jacobs, Francine. *Sounds in the Sea.* New York: Morrow, 1977.

For Activity 2—Parts of the Ear, students must complete an outline by arranging the title, main topics, and subentries contained in the "Parts" pocket in proper outline order, on the worksheet provided. The "Parts" pocket items include: Parts of the Ear, Outer Ear, Pinna, Auditory Canal, Middle Ear, Hammer, Anvil, Stirrup, Inner Ear, Semi-circular Canals, Cochlea, and Auditory Nerve.

For Activity 3—Sound Stumpers, students practice alphabetizing words and locating and interpreting dictionary entries by arranging the terms in the "Words" pocket in alphabetical order, looking up the dictionary entries, and writing the words and dictionary meanings on the worksheet provided at the center. The "Words" pocket items include: pandemonium, cacophony, reverberation, dissonance, stridulation, amplification, discordance, ululation, acoustics, resonance, sonar, and radar.

For Activity 4—Noise Levels, students must order a list of sounds from loudest to softest, choose among annoying noises, and write explanations as to their choices on the worksheet provided.

EXAMPLE

The library media specialist places students in skills groups according to their performance on the "Call Numbers Pretest/Posttest" given as an introductory activity. The library media specialist schedules instructional time with the skills groups and provides three activities.

The library media specialist works with students displaying difficulty in determining whether to look for author, subject, or title cards in the card catalog when given specific information about a book. Students are given an "Author, Subject, and Title Cards" worksheet (fig. 3.61) for practice. After completing the worksheet, individual students are asked to locate specific catalog cards for selected items from the worksheet. When a student locates a specified catalog card, he or she must identify and explain the call number for that particular book.

Author, Subject, and Title Cards

Directions: Indicate whether you would use an <u>author</u>, <u>subject</u>, or <u>title</u>
            card to locate each of the following items listed in the card
            catalog.

1. A book called <u>Sound Science</u> _____

2. A book about sound _____

3. A book by Franklyn M. Branley _____

4. A book about animal sounds _____

5. A book called <u>Musical Insects</u> _____

6. A book by Kathleen Elgin _____

7. A book called <u>Wonders of Sound</u> _____

8. A book about ultrasonics _____

9. **A book by Judith Fryer** _____

10. A book called <u>Bird Talk</u> _____

11. A book called <u>Sound and Hearing</u> _____

12. A book by Francine Jacobs _____

13. A book about acoustics _____

14. A book called <u>Make Your Own Musical Instruments</u> _____

15. A book by George F. Mason _____

16. A book called <u>Sound and Its Reproduction</u> _____

17. A book about sound recording _____

18. A book called **Sounds All About** _____

19. A book by Paul Showers _____

20. A book called <u>The Story of Your Ear</u> _____

21. A book called <u>Science Experiments with Sound</u> _____

22. A book by Eric Windle _____

Fig. 3.61. Worksheet.

Students that experienced difficulty matching books with call numbers on the "Call Numbers Pretest/Posttest" are placed in a skills group and presented with this activity. First, the library media specialist has individual students from the group locate author and title cards in the card catalog. Each student must locate and explain the call number on the catalog card he or she finds. Examples may be used from the worksheet (fig. 3.61). Then, each student is given a copy of the "Call Number Matching" worksheet (fig. 3.62) to practice matching call numbers and books. When students have completed the worksheet, they check their own work, verifying their answers by locating author or title cards in the card catalog.

The library media specialist provides an activity in which call numbers must be put in sequential order as the books would be shelved in the library media center. This activity is for those students that are in the skills group (based on their performance on the "Call Numbers Pretest/Posttest) requiring more instruction and practice in this process skill. Each student is provided with a "Call Number Order" worksheet (fig. 3.63, see p. 162) to practice ordering call numbers. After the students complete the worksheet examples, the library media specialist has individuals check their answers by locating the books in each set on the shelves.

Call Number Matching

Directions: Match each book with its call number. Write the call number
on the line next to the title and author.

Call
Numbers

612
S

621.385
B

621.389
O

789
W

598.2
G

534
P

534
F

621.389
M

534
A

591.59
J

793.8
V

595.72
D

612
K

612
E

591.59
C

1. Sounds in the Sea by Francine Jacobs _____

2. How You Talk by Paul Showers _____

3. Messages and Voices: The Communication of Animals by

    Margaret Cosgrove _____

4. The World of Sound Recording by Don Murray _____

5. Junior Science Book of Sound by Dorothy S. Anderson

    _____

6. Things That Go Bang by Lisl Weil _____

7. Human Body: The Ear by Kathleen Elgin _____

8. Sound All Around: How Hi-Fi and Stereo Work by Ross. R.

    Olney _____

9. Bird Talk by Roma Gans _____

10. Sounds All About by Illa Podendorf _____

11. The Telephone by Henry Brinton _____

12. Fun with Ventriloquism by Alexander Van Renselaer

    _____

13. Musical Insects by Bette J. Davis _____

14. Song, Speech, and Ventriloquism by Larry Kettelkamp

    _____

15. Sound and Ultrasonics by Ira M. Freeman

Fig. 3.62. Worksheet.

Call Number Order

Directions: List the call numbers from each set in the order in which the
books would be arranged on the shelves in the library media
center.

Set A:	612	612	612.85	612	612
	K	E	S	S	F

1. _____   2. _____   3. _____   4. _____   5. _____

Set B:	591.59	595.72	591.5	598.2	591.59
	J	D	M	G	C

1. _____   2. _____   3. _____   4. _____   5. _____

Set C:	621.389	621.385	621.385	621.389	621.385
	O	K	S	M	B

1. _____   2. _____   3. _____   4. _____   5. _____

Set D:	789	781.9	788	789	787	793.8
	K	M	K	W	K	M

1. _____   2. _____   3. _____   4. _____   5. _____

6. _____

Set E:	534	534	534	534.07	534	534	534.07	534
	G	S	B	S	A	P	A	M
	534	534.07	534	534
	W	F	K	F

1. _____   2. _____   3. _____   4. _____   5. _____

6. _____   7. _____   8. _____   9. _____   10. _____

11. _____   12. _____

Fig. 3.63. Worksheet.

CULMINATING ACTIVITIES

Following developmental activities in which students engage in structured learning situations involving the concepts, skills, and processes identified as instructional objectives for a unit of study, classroom teachers and library media specialists must provide culminating activities to determine the students' achievement of the designated instructional objectives. When teaching units that integrate content and library media research and study skills, library media specialists and classroom teachers may require students to display attainment of instructional objectives through postassessment activities. Such activities can be either the creation of a product or the taking of a formal posttest. The intent of such culminating activities is to focus on student performance in relation to the instructional objectives of the unit of study and to make decisions about subsequent instructional planning.

Often students are asked to create a product as a culminating activity. Products include such creations as individual or group projects; written reports; demonstrations; experiments; dramatizations, or oral reports presented to the class or group; or construction activities in which a model, filmstrip, diorama, mural, display, bulletin board, or some other artistic representation is made. Through the creation of products, students demonstrate the application of the concepts, skills, and processes gained through participation in the developmental activities of the instructional unit.

Classroom teachers and library media specialists may use either formal or informal assessment measures to determine student attainment of unit objectives. Informal assessments may involve the observation of student behavior as students create and present products for culminating activities. Formal assessment may entail the administration of a posttest made by the classroom teacher or library media specialist. Often classroom teachers ask students to apply "study strategies" as they review content learnings for a unit test. Library media specialists may use formal posttests or informal observation to determine student achievement of library media research and study skills and processes. Whatever the means, classroom teachers and library media specialists use culminating activities to assess student attainment of unit objectives.

EXAMPLE

In addition to a unit test on "Sound Energy," the classroom teacher assigns a project as a culminating activity. Each student must create and demonstrate some principle or concept about sound energy. The classroom teacher gives students a list of questions (fig. 3.64, p. 164) to stimulate the planning for their investigations. Students must research their chosen investigation in the library media center, and the library media specialist has agreed to aid students in their search for information upon which to base their investigations. The classroom teacher distributes a "Science Project Worksheet" (fig. 3.39), which will help students in planning their projects. Students determine a hypothesis, create an investigation, choose and list materials and/or equipment, conduct the investigation, record their results, and support or refute their original hypothesis. Students must report their findings to the class or group in the form of a demonstration of the investigation itself or through the production of a visual display.

Sound Energy Questions

1. How do people differ in their ability to hear a sound of very high pitch?

2. How are sound waves like water waves?

3. How can you make a stethoscope?

4. How can you transmit speech through a string telephone?

5. How does a megaphone increase the volume of a sound?

6. How does sound travel through solids?

7. How does sound travel through liquids?

8. How does sound travel through gases?

9. How are echoes made?

10. How do human vocal **cords work?**

11. How does a cricket chirp?

12. How does a frog croak?

13. How do propoises **communicate** with each other and with man?

14. How do our outer ears help us to hear?

15. How do most reptiles hear?

16. How can we hear sounds through our teeth?

17. What is the advantage of having two ears rather than just one ear?

18. How does sound travel through a tube?

19. Why do we see lightning before we hear thunder?

20. Do sea shells have the sound of the sea in them?

21. How does a phonograph record produce a sound?

22. How does soundproofing a room work?

23. How does sonar work to help ships at sea detect other ships and underwater obstacles?

24. How are bats able to fly in total darkness without striking objects?

25. How does the amount of furniture in a room affect sound?

26. How can you demonstrate how sound waves travel?

27. How does a tuning fork work?

28. How does a trumpet produce sound?

29. How does a piano produce sound?

30. How does a violin produce sound?

31. How does a drum produce sound?

32. How does a tape recorder work?

33. How does a telephone transmit your voice?

34. How does ventriloquism work?

35. What are ultrasonic sounds?

36. How does noise pollution affect different people?

Fig. 3.64. List of questions.

EXAMPLE

Individual students are sent to the library media center by the classroom teacher to gather information pertinent to their science project for the unit on "Sound Energy." The library media specialist aids students in locating appropriate print and nonprint sources to support their chosen topic of study or investigation.

The library media specialist meets with the whole class for a culminating activity in which students review skills related to developmental instructional activities in a game situation. Students will be assessed as the library media specialist observes their skills proficiency as they play the game. Students are divided into relay teams of no more than six members each, and each team is seated at a separate table. The game consists of three rounds in which one student at a time attempts to score a point for the team. The skills assessed in the game are (1) identifying author, subject, and title cards; (2) locating call numbers of specific books listed on catalog cards; and (3) arranging call numbers in sequential order. The team with the highest number of points at the end of round 3 is declared the winner. Examples for questions can be taken from the developmental activities worksheets ("Author, Subject, and Title Cards"; "Call Number Matching"; and, "Call Number Order"). What follows are sample questions that are appropriate for the three rounds. For Round 1, questions could include which type of catalog card would you use to find (1) a book by Illa Podendorf? (2) a book about acoustics? and (3) a book called *Sounds in the Sea*? For Round 2, students could be asked to locate the call number on the title card for the book *High Sounds, Low Sounds* by Franklyn M. Branley or locate the call number on the author card for the book by Eric Windle called *Sounds You Cannot Hear.* For Round 3, questions could include which call number would come first in Dewey decimal order?

(1)   612   or 612?
     S   R

(2)   621.385   or   621.385?
     B   K

(3)   591.59   or 591.5?
     C   M

EVALUATION OF STUDENT LEARNINGS

Once classroom teachers and library media specialists have implemented instruction through introductory, developmental, and culminating activities, it is necessary to evaluate student learnings in relation to attainment of instructional objectives. In most cases, culminating activities and/or postassessment measures are evaluated to determine how students performed. At this time, it must be determined if reteaching is necessary for groups or individuals who did not perform well in culminating activities or on posttest measures. The classroom teacher or library media specialist may need to select additional learning activities to help students achieve objectives not yet attained.

EXAMPLE

After observing student performance in the culminating game activity, the library media specialist determined that several students required additional instruction in the skill of ordering call numbers. Rather than reteaching this skill in relation to the science unit on "Sound Energy," she decides to incorporate ordering call numbers as an instructional objective in the next integrated unit to be taught in conjunction with a classroom social studies unit on "The Civil War."

REVISION OF INSTRUCTIONAL UNIT AND ACTIVITIES

After classroom teachers and library media specialists have evaluated student learnings gained from an instructional unit, they must focus on the unit plan and its instructional activities to determine if any revision of the unit is necessary before using it again with another group of students. Any revision decisions would be made in relation to student performance in culminating activities and/or postassessment measures. Revision decisions would focus on such areas as (1) concurrence between the instructional plan and actual instructional activities; (2) appropriateness of instructional materials and activities for students; and (3) congruence of instructional objectives and instructional activities.

EXAMPLE

The classroom teacher determined that students had performed at a satisfactory level on the unit test on "Sound Energy." Nevertheless, she found that several students had had difficulty in formulating and evaluating a hypothesis on which to base their investigations when working on the project assigned as a culminating activity. She, therefore, added another content objective for the unit of study on Sound Energy. The objective stated: "The student will formulate, test, and evaluate a hypothesis when conducting investigative experiments." At this time, she makes the decision that if the unit on Sound Energy is to be implemented again with another group of students, she would plan several total class activities in which students would experience those processes before being asked to do them independently.

SUMMARY

The proposed Integrated Model of Library Media Research and Study Skills Instruction involves a set of procedural steps by which library media specialists and classroom teachers plan, implement, and evaluate instructional activities for students in the form of instructional units. An instructional unit may include one activity or a series of activities, depending upon the complexity of the subject matter and the library media research and study skills and processes to be taught. The preparation and implementation of units of study in which content subject concepts, skills, and processes are integrated with library media research and study skills processes involves the development of joint planning techniques and joint teaching strategies and practices by library media specialists and classroom teachers. The steps involved in the integrated model are as follows.

1. The classroom teacher identifies content skills objectives for the specified unit of study.

2. The library media specialist identifies appropriate library media research and study skills objectives that may be integrated into the content unit.

3. The classroom teacher and the library media specialist develop integrated instructional objectives for those skills and processes that may be taught jointly.

4. The library media specialist and the classroom teacher develop instructional activities through which students will be exposed to the content and skills involved in the integrated instructional unit. Decisions about instructional variables must be made as classroom teachers and library media specialists develop learning activities for students. These instructional variables include: the sequencing of instructional activities, the selection of appropriate instructional resources, the selection of instructional strategies to be employed, the designation of teaching responsibilities, the grouping of students for instruction, and the designation of time and space for instruction.

5. The library media specialist and the classroom teacher implement the unit of instruction through structured learning experiences for students in the form of introductory, developmental, and culminating activities.

6. The classroom teacher and the library media specialist evaluate student learnings on the basis of student performance in culminating activities and/or on postassessment measures.

7. The library media specialist and the classroom teacher revise the instructional unit, including its instructional objectives and activities, for future use with other student groupings.

(Answer keys for Chapter 3 are on pages 168-172.)

ANSWER KEYS FOR CHAPTER 3

Figure Number	Title and Answers
3.8	**Opaque Projector Operation** Part A: 4; 7; 2; 5; 1; 6; 3. Part B: 1. c; 2. b; 3. b; 4. b; 5. c.
3.13	**Energy Sources** (Answers will vary.)
3.14	**Fiction or Nonfiction** 1. N; 2. F; 3. N; 4. N; 5. F; 6. N; 7. F; 8. N; 9. F; 10. F; 11. N; 12. N; 13. F; 14. N; 15. F; 16. F; 17. F; 18. N; 19. F; 20. N. (Note: Fiction = F Nonfiction = N)
3.17	**Table Tackle Pretest** 1. Asia; 2. Australia; 3. 9,366,000; 4. 4,017,000; 5. 27.9; 6. 12.0; 7. Asia; 8. Antarctica; 9. The World Almanac, 1983; 10. 21,016,000 sq. mi.; 11. 2,485,000 sq. mi.; 12. Africa; 13. Australia.
3.18	**Activity 1 -- Wind Chill Factor** 1. b; 2. c; 3. a; 4. b; 5. c; 6. a; 7. c; 8. b; 9. c.
3.19	**Activity 2 -- Metric Measurements** 1. kg, metric ton; 2. km, hectare; 3. km/hr., $^{\circ}$C, cm; 4. mm, kilowatt; 5. gram, kg; 6. gram, ml; 7. liter, sq. m; 8. cm; 9. mm, cubic m; 10. km; 11. cm, m; 12. $^{\circ}$C, sq. m; 13. m, kg, kilowatt; 14. km, sq. m, $^{\circ}$C; 15. cm, sq cm; 16. hectare, km; 17. liter.

Figure Number	Title and Answers
3.20	**Activity 3 -- Calendar Caper** Month: May 	S	M	T	W	T	F	S
---	---	---	---	---	---	---
						1
2	3	4	5	6	7	8
9	10	11	12	13	14	15
16	17	18	19	20	21	22
23/30	24/31	25	26	27	28	29	 1. Saturday; 2. 21st; 3. Monday; 4. Monday; 5. 13th; 6. Wednesday; 7. 31; 8. Jan., Feb., Mar., Apr., May, June, July, Aug., Sept., Oct., Nov., Dec.; 9. 365; 10. Sun., Mon., Tues., Wed., Thurs., Fri., Sat.; 11. 52; 12. 4, February.
3.21	**Activity 4 -- Science TV Guide** (Answers will vary.)
3.22	**Activity 5 -- Astro Airlines** 1. Gate 22; 2. 9:30; 3. St. Louis; 4. 8:00; 5. Gate 30; 6. Gate 35; 7. leaves (departs); 8. arrives; 9. Gate 35; 10. Gates 22, 26, 30; 11. Flight 136; 12. 146; 13. destination; 14. two flights; 15. origin; 16. leaving (departing); 17. Miami; 18. Gate 22.
3.23	**Activity 6 -- Store Directory** 1. 2; 2. 6; 3. 3; 4. 4; 5. 5; 6. 5; 7. 1; 8. 6; 9. 3; 10. 4; 11. 2; 12. 2; 13. 1; 14. 5; 15. 4; 16. 3; 17. 3; 18. 6; 19. 1; 20. 2; 21. 4; 22. 4; 23. 2; 24. 6; 25. 3; 26. 3; 27. 1; 28. 5; 29. 4; 30. 4; 31. 5; 32. 2; 33. 2; 34. 5.
3.24	**Activity 7 -- Precipitation Table** Table: Boston -- 1.0; Chicago -- 2.2; Los Angeles -- 1.95; New York -- 1.0; Reno -- 0.9. 1. Atlanta; 2. Jan.; 3. Atlanta; 4. Reno; 5. Jan.; 6. Reno; 7. Atlanta; 8. July; 9. Boston, New York; 10. Atlanta or Baltimore; 11. July; 12. .05; 13. Reno; 14. July; 15. 4.9; 16. 3.3.

Figure Number	Title and Answers
3.25	Table Tackle Posttest Weight Table: 1. basketball; 2. tennis ball; 3. 200; 4. 90; 5. 1,250. Area Table: 1. Pacific; 2. Arctic; 3. 28,350,500; 4. 22.9; 5. <u>The World Almanac</u>, 1983; 6. Atlantic; 7. Arctic; 8. 30,766,300; 9. 61,770,500.
3.27	Emergency! 1. 555-4422; 2. 555-0178; 3. 411; 4. 555-9634; 5. seven; 6. 301; 7. 555-1234; 8. 555-0178; 9. 555-4422; 10. 555-9634.
3.30	Source Search (Many answers will vary due to publication date of reference source cited in answers.)
3.33	TV Commercials Monitoring Form (Answers will vary according to program viewed.)
3.34	Planetary Facts (Answers are in fig. 3.35.)
3.36	Card Catalog Guide Letters 1. P-Q; 2. Sm-Sz; 3. M; 4. D-E; 5. A; 6. B; 7. K-L; 8. P-Q; 9. P-Q; 10. Sm-Sz; 11. B; 12. A; 13. B; 14. Sh-Sl; 15. Sh-Sl; 16. G-H; 17. K-L; 18. C-Ch; 19. F; 20. Sm-Sz; 21. S-Se; 22. I-J; 23. W; 24. C-Ch; 25. Ci-Cz; 26. S-Se; 27. Sm-Sz; 28. Sm-Sz; 29. C-Ch; 30. S-Se.
3.37	Fabulous Fairy Tales Part A: 1. b; 2. g; 3. f; 4. a; 5. e; 6. d; 7. c. Part B: 1. e, E, C; 2. d, C, E; 3. g, E, C; 4. a, C, E; 5. c, E, C; 6. b, E, C; 7. f, C, E.

Figure Number	Title and Answers

3.55	**Call Numbers Pretest/Posttest**
	
	Part A: 1. Author; 2. Title; 3. Subject; 4. Title; 5. Author.
	Part B: 6. 534.07; 7. 534; 8. 612.85; 9. 534; 10. 591.59;
	            A F S B C
	    11. 598.2; 12. 621.389; 13. 595.72; 14. 612.
	          G M D E
	Part C: 15. 534; 16. 534; 17. 534.07; 18. 591.59;
	          B F A C
	    19. 595.72; 20. 598.2; 21. 612; 22. 612.85; 23. 621.389.
	        D G E S M

3.57	**Activity 1 -- Animal Sounds** 1. X-X; 2. XX-; 3. XX-; 4. XX-; 5. X-X; 6. XX-; 7. X-X; 8. X-X; 9. X-X; 10. X-X; 11. X-X; 12. X-X.

3.58	**Activity 2 -- Parts of the Ear**
	
	Title: Parts of the Ear
	    I. Outer Ear
	        A. Pinna
	        B. Auditory canal
	   II. Middle Ear
	        A. Hammer
	        B. Anvil
	        C. Stirrup
	 III. Inner Ear
	        A. Semi-circular canals
	        B. Cochlea
	        C. Auditory nerve

3.59	**Activity 3 -- Sound Stumpers** 1. acoustics; 2. amplification; 3. cacophony; 4. discordance; 5. dissonance; 6. pandemonium; 7. radar; 8. resonance; 9. reverberation; 10. sonar; 11. stridulation; 12. ululation.

Figure Number	Title and Answers
3.60	Activity 4 -- Noise Levels Part A: (Accept reasonable answers.) 1. A rocket launch; 2. A jet takeoff; 3. Busy traffic, thunder; 4. Rock music; 5. Normal traffic; 6. A noisy office; 7. A typewriter; loud conversation; 8. Light traffic; 9. Normal conversation; 10. Quiet conversation; 11. A whisper, leaves rustling. Part B: (Accept answers on the basis of explanations.) 1. b; 2. a; 3. b; 4. a or b; 5. a or b; 6. a.
3.61	Author, Subject, and Title Cards 1. Title; 2. Subject; 3. Author; 4. Subject; 5. Title; 6. Author; 7. Title; 8. Subject; 9. Author; 10. Title; 11. Title; 12. Author; 13. Subject; 14. Title; 15. Author; 16. Title; 17. Subject; 18. Title; 19. Author; 20. Title; 21. Title; 22. Author.

3.62	Call Number Matching
	
	1. 591.59; 2. 612; 3. 591.59; 4. 621.389; 5. 534; 6. 789;
	   J S C M A W
	7. 612; 8. 621.389; 9. 598.2; 10. 534; 11. 621.385;
	   E M G P B
	12. 793.8; 13. 595.72; 14. 612; 15. 534.
	   V D K F

3.63	Call Number Order
	
	Set A: 1. 612; 2. 612; 3. 612; 4. 612; 5. 612.85.
	      E F K S S
	Set B: 1. 591.5; 2. 591.59; 3. 591.59; 4. 595.72; 5. 598.2.
	      M C J D G
	Set C: 1. 621.385; 2. 621.385; 3. 621.385; 4. 621.389;
	      B K S M
	5. 621.389.
	   O
	Set D: 1. 781.9; 2. 787; 3. 788; 4. 789; 5. 789; 6. 793.8.
	      M K K K W V
	Set E: 1. 534; 2. 534; 3. 534; 4. 534; 5. 534; 6. 534;
	      A B F G K M
	7. 534; 8. 534; 9. 534; 10. 534.07; 11. 534.07;
	   P S W A F
	12. 534.07.
	   S

NOTES

[1] Russell G. Stauffer, *Teaching Reading as a Thinking Process* (New York: Harper and Row Publishers, 1969), 14-15.

[2] Lou E. Burmeister, *Reading Strategies for Secondary School Teachers* (Reading, MA: Addison-Wesley Publishing Co., Inc., 1978), 94-100.

[3] Harold L. Herber, *Teaching Reading in Content Areas*, 2d ed. (Englewood Cliffs, NJ: Prentice-Hall, Inc., 1978), 226-27.

[4] Harry Singer and Dan Donlan, *Reading and Learning from Text* (Boston: Little, Brown and Co., 1980), 52-53.

[5] Earl H. Cheek, Jr. and Martha Collins Cheek, *Reading Instruction through Content Teaching* (Columbus, OH: Charles E. Merrill Publishing Co., 1983), 175-181.

[6] Ibid.

[7] David Ausubel, "The Use of Advanced Organizers in the Learning and Retention of Meaningful Verbal Material," *Journal of Educational Psychology* 51 (1960): 267-72.

[8] H. Alan Robinson, *Teaching Reading and Study Strategies*, 2d ed. (Boston: Allyn and Bacon, Inc., 1978), 40-50.

[9] Stauffer, *Teaching Reading*, 14-15.

4 Selected Activities to Integrate Library Media Research and Study Skills with Content Instruction

The activities selected for inclusion in this chapter represent sample learning experiences that integrate library media research and study skills and processes with content area concepts, skills, and processes. Included are learning activities that promote the application of location and reference skills, interpretation skills, and organizational skills. Sample learning activities are listed by content area subjects and include: art, careers, computer literacy, dance/drama, mathematics, music, physical education, reading/language arts, science, and social studies. Although an instructional level is designated for each activity, many suggested activities can be adapted for differentiated instruction for grades three through six. Each selected activity includes the notation of objectives, instructional strategies, resources, teaching responsibilities, instructional groupings, and assessment criteria.

ART

LESSON 1

Title: Book Illustrators and Their Art

Library Media Research and Study Skills Objectives:

Introduce book illustrations as an art form.

Analyze, compare, and contrast the styles of various book illustrators and record observations.

Level: 5-6

Instructional Strategy: Demonstration/Practice/Discussion

Performance Objective: Given two books representing the work of two different book illustrators, the students will analyze, compare, and contrast the work of two illustrators; record their observations on a worksheet; and present their findings orally to the total class.

Resources: Sets of books representing the work of two book illustrators (see "Suggested List of Illustrators," fig. 4.1, p. 176), and copies of the "Illustrations Analysis" worksheet (fig. 4.2, p. 177).

Instructional Responsibility: Library media specialist

Instructional Grouping: Total class divided into work pairs of two students.

Activity: Following a demonstration of a comparison of the works of two book illustrators by the library media specialist, each pair of students is given a set of two books representing two different book illustrators, and a copy of the "Illustrations Analysis" worksheet. Each student pair designates one student to be the recorder, to record their observations on the worksheet, and one student to be the presenter, to present orally their findings to the class. Student pairs spend one class period analyzing the illustrations and recording their findings on the worksheet. Because of time limitations, a follow-up class period may need to be scheduled for oral presentations.

Assessment Criteria: Students will be assessed on the basis of their application of critical thinking skills as evidenced by their observations recorded on the "Illustrations Analysis" worksheet and their oral presentations.

(Text continues on page 178.)

Joan Anglund	Ezra Jack Keats
Edward Ardizzone	Elaine L. Konigsburg
Ludwig Bemelmans	Robert Lawson
Virginia Lee Burton	Lois Lenski
Randolph Caldecott	Leo Lionni
James Daugherty	Robert McCloskey
Marguerite L. de Angeli	Edna Miller
Roger Duvoisin	Leo Politi
Ed Emberley	Beatrix Potter
Marie Hall Ets	Arthur Rackham
Katherine Evans	Norman Rockwell
Gyo Fujikawa	Maurice Sendak
Paul Galdone	E. H. Shepard
Theodor Seuss Geisel	Tasha Tudor
Janusz Grabianski	Edwin Tunis
Hardie Gramatky	Lynd Ward
Carolyn Haywood	Brian Wildsmith
Holling C. Holling	Newell C. Wyeth

Fig. 4.1. Suggested list of illustrators.

Illustrations Analysis

Example 1

    Illustrator: _____

    Title: _____

    Author: _____

    Art medium: _____

    Use of color: _____

    Use of lines, shapes, and forms: _____

    _____

    Mood conveyed: _____

Example 2

    Illustrator: _____

    Title: _____

    Author: _____

    Art medium: _____

    Use of color: _____

    Use of lines, shapes, and forms: _____

    _____

    Mood Conveyed: _____

* * * * * *

Compare the illustrations for likenesses: _____

_____

_____

Contrast the illustrations for differences: _____

_____

_____

Fig. 4.2. Worksheet.

LESSON 2

Title: Careers in Art—Activity 1

Library Media Research and Study Skills Objective:

Locate and record bibliographic information for a given set of sources.

Level: 4-6

Instructional Strategy: Group practice

Performance Objective: Given a set of materials on Careers in Art, consisting of four nonfiction books, a filmstrip, and a reference source, the student will locate and record bibliographic information on a data sheet.

Resources: Sets of source materials for four groups (fig. 4.3, pp. 179-80) and copies of "Bibliographic Data Sheet" worksheets (fig. 4.4, p. 181).

Instructional Responsibility: Library media specialist

Instructional Grouping: Four groups of six to eight students

Activity: This lesson would follow introductory lesson(s) on bibliographic skills by either the classroom teacher and/or the library media specialist. Students are divided into groups of about equal size. Each group is given a set of sources for information on Careers in Art. Each student is provided with a copy of the "Bibliographic Data Sheet." Students in each group fill out the appropriate information on their data sheet. The library media specialist circulates to aid students who need help.

Assessment Criteria: Given a set of materials on "Careers in Art," consisting of four nonfiction books, a filmstrip, and a reference source, the student will locate and record bibliographic information with 80 percent accuracy.

(Text continues on page 182.)

Careers in Art

Group 1

Designing Cloth for Clothes. (Filmstrip in the series "Cotton Clothing from
   Field to You.") Los Angeles: Churchill Films, 1968.

Baker, Eugene H. I Want to Be an Architect. Chicago: Childrens Press, 1969.

Bendick, Jeanne. Filming Works like This. New York: McGraw-Hill, 1970.

Downer, Marion. Discovering Design. New York: Lothrop, Lee, & Shepard, 1947.

Munro, Eleanor C. The Encyclopedia of Art. New York: Golden Press, 1961.

Schwartz, Alvin. Museum: The Story of America's Treasure Houses. New York:
   E. P. Dutton & Co., Inc., 1967.

Group 2

Silk Screen Printing. (Filmstrip in the series "Cotton Clothing from Field
   to You.") Los Angeles: Churchill Films, 1968.

De Borhegyi, Suzanne. A Book to Begin on Museums. New York: Holt, Rinehart,
   & Winston, 1962.

Goldreich, Gloria. What Can She Be? An Architect. New York: Lothrop, Lee,
   & Shepard, 1974.

Nault, W. H., ed. World Book Encyclopedia -- Volume 1. Chicago: Field
   Enterprises, 1972.

Reid, Giorgina. The Delights of Photography: A Working Manual. Cranbury, NJ:
   A. S. Barnes & Co., Inc., 1963.

Siegel, Margot. Looking Forward to a Career: Fashion. Minneapolis: Dillon
   Press, Inc., 1970.

Fig. 4.3. Source materials.

(Figure continues on page 180.)

Group 3

Commercial Artist. (Filmstrip in the series "Career Mothers.") Audio-Visual
    Instructional Devices and Systems, 1974.

Adkins, Jan. How a House Happens. New York: Walker & Co., 1972.

Belgrano, Giovanni. Let's Make a Movie. New York: Scroll Press, Inc., 1972.

Berger, Melvin. Jobs in Fine Arts and Humanities. New York: Lothrop, Lee
    & Shepard, 1974.

Cayne, Bernard S. Merit Students Encyclopedia -- Volume 1. Riverside, NJ:
    Macmillan, 1975.

Sagara, Peter. Written on Film. Chicago: Childrens Press, 1970.

Group 4

Furniture Designer. (Filmstrip in the series "So Many Jobs to Think
    About." -- Set 1.) Fairfax, VA: Learning Resources Corp., 1974.

Childcraft: The How and Why Library. Vol. 8, What People Do. Chicago:
    Field Enterprises, 1973.

Helfman, Harry. Making Your Own Movies. New York: William Morrow & Co.,
    Inc., 1970.

Janson, H. W. The Story of Painting for Young People: From Cave Painting
    to Modern Times. New York: Harry N. Abrams, Inc., n. d.

Johnson, Lillian. Sculpture: The Basic Methods and Materials. New York:
    David McKay Co., Inc., 1960.

Webster, David. Photo Fun: An Idea Book for Shutterbugs. New York:
    Franklin Watts, Inc., 1973.

Fig. 4.3.–*continued*

Bibliographic Data Sheet

Book 1	Book 2
Author/Editor: _____	Author/Editor: _____
Title: _____	Title: _____
Publisher: _____	Publisher: _____
Place: _____	Place: _____
Copyright date: _____	Copyright date: _____
Pages used: _____	Pages used: _____
Book 3	**Book 4**
Author/Editor: _____	Author/Editor: _____
Title: _____	Title: _____
Publisher: _____	Publisher: _____
Place: _____	Place: _____
Copyright date: _____	Copyright date: _____
Pages used: _____	Pages used: _____
Filmstrip	**Encyclopedia**
Editor/Author: _____	Editor/Author: _____
Title: _____	Encyclopedia: _____
Series title: _____	Article: _____
Publisher: _____	Publisher: _____
Place: _____	Place: _____
Copyright date: _____	Copyright date: _____
	Volume: _____ Pages: _____

Fig. 4.4. Worksheet.

LESSON 3

Title: Careers in Art—Activity 2

Library Media Research and Study Skills Objective:

Write a bibliography using correct form for books, filmstrips, and reference sources.

Level: 4-6

Instructional Strategy: Practice

Performance Objective: Given data gathered on a "Bibliographic Data Sheet" worksheet listing four nonfiction books, a filmstrip, and a reference source, the student will use the data to write a bibliography in correct form.

Resources: Completed "Bibliographic Data Sheet" worksheet (fig. 4.4), paper.

Instructional Responsibility: Classroom teacher

Instructional Grouping: Total class or instructional group

Activity: This lesson follows the activity in which the library media specialist had the students gather bibliographic data on a set of materials related to "Careers in Art." The classroom teacher reviews the data on the "Bibliographic Data Sheet" and the correct procedure for preparing a bibliography. The students then write a bibliography, using correct form for the books, filmstrips, and reference sources listed on their "Bibliographic Data Sheet" worksheets. Follow-up activities in which the students gather information and report findings may follow this activity if the classroom teacher and/or library media specialist desire to have the students conduct formalized research on careers in art.

Assessment Criteria: Given data gathered on a "Bibliographic Data Sheet" worksheet listing four nonfiction books, a filmstrip, and a reference source, the student will write a bibliography from this data in correct form with 80 percent accuracy.

LESSON 4

Title: Dewey Decimal Collage

Library Media Research and Study Skills Objective:

> Increase student awareness of the subjects associated with Dewey Decimal Classification numbers.

Level: 5-6

Instructional Strategy: Demonstration/Group project

Performance Objective: Given a particular Dewey Decimal Classification number, students will familiarize themselves with subjects associated with the number, select or draw pictures associated with the subjects, and create a collage representative of a particular Dewey Decimal Classification.

Resources: Old magazines and catalogs for cutting, scissors, drawing paper, poster board (15" x 20"), and rubber cement.

Instructional Responsibility: Library media specialist and classroom teacher

Instructional Grouping: Small groups of two to four students

Activity: This activity would follow developmental lessons in the classroom and the library media center concerning the Dewey decimal system of classifying nonfiction books. Students meet in the library media center with the library media specialist. They are divided into groups of two to four students each. Each group is assigned a Dewey Decimal Classification number. (Suggested numbers might be: 394, 520, 550, 580, 590, 745, 788, 789, 794, 796, 970, 974, 975, 976, 977, 978, and 979.) Student groups are given about twenty minutes to examine the shelves bearing books with their classification number and to make a list of the subjects represented by their particular number. Students return to the classroom with their listings. The classroom teacher explains that they are going to make a collage to represent their subject listings or Dewey Decimal Classification numbers. Students may cut out pictures from old magazines or catalogs or they may draw pictures themselves. A few days later, students meet in their small groups in the classroom to arrange and glue their pictures to form a collage on a piece of tagboard. Each group's Dewey Decimal Classification number must be prominently placed somewhere on the collage. When all collages are complete, the small groups meet in the library media center to share their collages with the library media specialist and the class. The library media specialist displays the collages in the nonfiction section of the library media center.

Assessment Criteria: Students are evaluated on the basis of how well their collage displays the subjects associated with its particular Dewey Decimal Classification number.

CAREERS

LESSON 5

Title: Calling All Careers

Library Media Research and Study Skills Objectives:

Locate entry words in a dictionary.

Increase word knowledge through the interpretation of dictionary entries.

Increase awareness of the variety of career options.

Level: 3-4

Instructional Strategy: Learning center

Performance Objective: The student will locate and interpret dictionary entries to match occupational terms, associations, places, and tools.

Resources: "Calling All Careers" learning center (see fig. 4.5), including task cards for matching "Jobs," "Tools," "Clues," and "Places"; several dictionaries; paper and pencils.

Instructional Responsibility: Classroom teacher and library media specialist

Instructional Grouping: Individuals or small groups of students

Fig. 4.5. Drawing of calling all careers learning center.

Activities: The classroom teacher presents several introductory lessons on using dictionaries to locate entry words and interpret dictionary entries. The library media specialist follows up classroom instruction with a learning center in which students use the dictionary to increase their awareness of the variety of career options open to them. The learning center includes three matching activities in which students must interpret dictionary entries. Student directions and suggested task cards for each activity are listed below.

Activity 1 Directions: Use the dictionary to help you match the "Jobs" cards with the "Tools" cards representing tools or instruments used by persons employed in particular occupations. List at least fifteen matches on your paper. *Suggested "Jobs" and "Tools" cards:* 1. surgeon—scalpel; 2. astronomer—telescope; 3. photographer—telephoto lens; 4. welder—blowtorch; 5. carpenter—plane; 6. meteorologist—barometer; 7. airplane pilot—altimeter; 8. electrician—voltmeter; 9. surveyor—transit; 10. sculptor—chisel; 11. car mechanic—ratchet; 12. pugilist—boxing gloves; 13. artist (painter)—palette; 14. optometrist—optical lenses; 15. radio annoucer—microphone; 16. pathologist—microscope; 17. lumberjack—axe; 18. glazier—glass cutter; 19. architect—blueprints; 20. butcher—cleaver.

Activity 2 Directions: Use the dictionary to help you match the "Jobs" cards with the "Clues" cards to identify what a person in each occupation would be required to know about or work with in that particular job. List at least twenty matches on your paper. *Suggested "Jobs" and "Clues" cards:* 1. orthopedist—skeletal system; 2. librarian—alphabetical order; 3. florist—flower arrangement; 4. paleontologist—fossils; 5. statistician—numerical data; 6. psychologist—human behavior; 7. surgeon—sutures; 8. toxicologist—poisonous substances; 9. stenographer—shorthand; 10. herpetologist—snakes; 11. numismatist—coins and medals; 12. aeronaut—hot air balloons; 13. philatelist—postage stamps; 14. airplane pilot—wind currents; 15. taxidermist—mounting animal skins; 16. surveyor—measuring perimeter and area; 17. cryptographer—decoding secret codes; 18. chef—condiments; 19. anthropologist—cultures; 20. cartographer—mapmaking; 21. radiologist—taking X rays; 22. bookkeeper—keeping ledgers; 23. dermatologist—skin disorders; 24. news commentator—correct diction; 25. cosmetologist—applying hair dye.

Activity 3 Directions: Use the dictionary to help you match the "Jobs" cards with the "Places" cards to identify where people in various occupations might work. List at least twenty matches on your paper. *Suggested "Jobs" and "Places" cards:* 1. veterinarian—animal hospital; 2. photographer—studio; 3. teller—bank; 4. pharmacist—drugstore; 5. attorney—courtroom; 6. chemist—laboratory; 7. choreographer—theater; 8. astronomer—observatory; 9. clerk—department store; 10. professor—college classroom; 11. ornithologist—bird sanctuary; 12. meteorologist—weather station; 13. zoologist—zoological garden; 14. surgeon—hospital operating room; 15. porter—railroad station; 16. stevedore—docks or piers; 17. paleontologist—ruins of an ancient civilization; 18. nutritionist—cafeteria; 19. editor—publishing office; 20. curator—museum; 21. cobbler—shoe repair shop; 22. diplomat—embassy or chancellery; 23. aquanaut—beneath the ocean; 24. beekeeper—apiary; 25. astronaut—beyond the atmosphere of the earth.

Assessment Criteria: Students will locate and interpret dictionary entries and match occupational terms, associations, places, and tools with 80 percent accuracy.

LESSON 6

Title: Career Clues

Library Media Research and Study Skills Objectives:

Locate entry words in a dictionary.

Increase word knowledge through interpreting dictionary entries.

Increase student awareness of varied career options.

Level: 3-4

Instructional Strategy: Game/Practice

Performance Objective: Given occupations to find in a dictionary, the students will locate the occupations and match the meanings clues in order to play a game.

Resources: Four to six dictionaries and a chalkboard or chart.

Instructional Responsibility: Classroom teacher or library media specialist

Instructional Grouping: Four to six small groups within a class

Activity: This game is a culminating activity for students after participating in developmental activities in locating and interpreting dictionary entries. It may be implemented by either the library media specialist or the classroom teacher. The instructor will list the clue words on the blackboard or a chart before the game begins. (Suggested occupations and clue words are listed below.) The students are divided into four to six groups or teams. An explanation is given that students are to match occupations with what the person would study (clue words). The game is played as a relay with one person from each team competing at the same time. Each player must locate the occupation in the dictionary to verify his or her matching with the proper clue word. To begin the game, the first player from each team is given a dictionary. The instructor pronounces an occupation and writes it in large letters on the blackboard or chart. The first players look up the occupation in the dictionary. When a player feels that he or she can correctly match the occupation with the appropriate clue word, he or she raises his or her hand. The instructor notes the order in which hands are raised and calls on the first player. In order to score a point for his or her team, the player must give the matching clue word, and read the supporting definition from the dictionary entry. The game continues in this manner until all players have had at least two turns. At the end of the game, the team or group with the highest total score is declared the winning team, and an appropriate award is presented to all winning team members.

Suggested occupations and clue words: 1. geologist–rocks; 2. ichthyologist–fish; 3. chemist–elements; 4. meteorologist–weather; 5. anthropologist–cultures; 6. optometrist–eyes; 7. economist–money; 8. entomologist–insects; 9. zoologist–animals; 10. pharmacist–medicines; 11. botanist–plants; 12. podiatrist–feet; 13. audiologist–ears; 14. orthodontist–teeth; 15. sociologist–human groups; 16. physicist–matter and energy; 17. osteologist–bones; 18. ornithologist–birds; 19. pathologist–diseases; 20. cardiologist–hearts; 21. dermatologist–skin; 22. paleontologist–fossils; 23. mycologist–fungi; 24. herpetologist–snakes; 25. toxicologist–poisons; 26. numismatist–coins and medals; 27. mineralogist–ores; 28. hematologist–blood; 29. philatelist–postage stamps; 30. psychologist–human behavior; 31. pugilist–boxing; 32. apiarist–bees; 33. lawyer–statutes; 34. astronomer–planets; 35. surgeon–sutures;

36. cryptographer—secret codes; 37. cartographer—maps; 38. choreographer—dancing; 39. nutritionist—vitamins; 40. broadcaster—diction.

Assessment Criteria: Students will participate in the game and use the dictionary to locate entries and match occupations with clue words.

LESSON 7

Title: Informative Interviews

Library Media Research and Study Skills Objectives:

Conduct an interview.

Practice note-taking skills.

Recreate an interview in a role-playing situation.

Operate a cassette tape recorder without assistance.

Level: 4-5

Instructional Strategy: Project/Role-playing

Performance Objective: Given a school worker, the students will conduct and take notes in an interview and role-play and record an interview using a cassette tape recorder.

Resources: Copies of the "Informative Interviews" worksheet (fig. 4.6, p. 190), several cassette tape recorders, and blank cassette tapes.

Instructional Responsibility: Classroom teacher and library media specialist

Instructional Grouping: Total class and student pairs

Activity: The classroom teacher demonstrates the interviewing process to the total class as an alternative way of gaining information. Proper courtesy, clear speaking, and brief note-taking skills are emphasized. The activity that follows has two distinct parts in which students will participate.

Part 1: Students are divided into pairs who are assigned to conduct an interview with someone who works in the school. (Suggested school workers to be interviewed are physical education teacher, reading teacher, student council sponsor, library media specialist, library media aide, crossing guard, school secretary, cafeteria manager, cafeteria workers, P. T. A. officers, school bus driver, music teacher, resource teacher, school nurse, classroom teachers, principal, custodians, parent volunteer workers, playground aides, safety patrol sponsor, and art teacher.) Each student pair is provided with an "Informative Interviews" worksheet to record notes during the interview. The classroom teacher and the students will arrange and schedule appointments with school personnel prior to the actual interviews. As each student pair interviews a school worker, the questioning and note-taking roles will be alternated.

Part 2: After student pairs have interviewed school personnel, they will participate in the second part of the project. The classroom teacher arranges for the library media specialist to review the operation of a cassette tape recorder with the total class before students engage in Part 2. Student pairs then role-play the interviewing process, using the data from the "Informative Interviews" worksheet. Prior to recording the role-played interview on a blank cassette tape, the student pairs designate which role each will play. When all student pairs have completed Parts 1 and 2, a "School Careers Day" is held. Interview tapes are presented to the class, and school workers who have agreed to speak to the class are invited.

Assessment Criteria: Student pairs will be evaluated on the basis of their interview tapes as they are presented to the total class.

Informative Interviews

Interviewers: _____

Interviewee: _____

Date: _____ Place: _____

1. What is your job title? _____

2. Describe what you do in your job. _____

   _____

3. What made you decide to do this kind of work? _____

   _____

4. What special skills or training did you need to prepare for this job? ___

   _____

   a. Where did you get the training? _____

   b. How long did the training take? _____

5. How much experience do you have at this job? _____

6. Does your job require working before or after school hours? _____

   If so, how much? _____

7. What, in your opinion, are some advantages of your job? _____

   _____

8. What, in your opinion, are some disadvantages of your job? _____

   _____

9. Do you encourage young people to go into this kind of work? _____

   Why? _____

10. Do you have any advice for students about their career choices? _____

    _____

11. Would you be willing to speak to our class about your work? _____

Fig. 4.6. Worksheet.

COMPUTER LITERACY

LESSON 8

Title: Computer Language

Library Media Research and Study Skills Objectives:

Use an index to locate specific information within a sourcebook.

Use a glossary to interpret word meanings within a sourcebook.

Familiarize students with the vocabulary necessary for understanding computer parts and processes.

Familiarize students with computer-related careers.

Level: 5-6

Instructional Strategy: Learning center project

Performance Objective: Given information sources, the students will use the indexes and/or glossaries to complete a "mini-dictionary" of computer terms, processes, and related careers; and the students will create a puzzle to reinforce the vocabulary gained.

Resources: A "Computer Language" learning center (see fig. 4.7, p. 192); several information sourcebooks; pencils, paper (writing and construction), crayons and/or marking pens.

Instructional Responsibility: Library media specialist

Instructional Grouping: Individuals or small groups

Fig. 4.7. Drawing of computer language learning center.

Activities: The library media specialist prepares a learning center that includes two activities.

Activity 1: Within the pocket labeled "Make a Mini-Dictionary," the library media specialist provides directions for compiling the mini-dictionary and a list of terms to be included. Suggested terms may vary according to the available sourcebooks and types of computer hardware and software available. Some suggested terms are BASIC, boot, bug, byte, cassette, chip, circuit, CPU (central processing unit), computer, computer programmer, computer search, cursor, data entry operator, debug, disk, END, ENTER, GOTO, hardware, input, keyboard (input unit), key punch operator, LET, LIST, LOAD, log, memory, microcomputer, monitor (output unit), output, PRINT, printer, program, programming, RAM (random access memory), ROM (read only memory), RUN, software, ?SYNTAX ERROR, systems analyst, and word processing unit.

Some suggested sourcebooks:

Ball, Marion, and Sylvia Charp. *Be a Computer Literate.* Morristown, NJ: Creative Computing, 1977.

Bitter, Gary. *Exploring with Computers.* New York: Julian Messner, 1981.

D'Ignazio, Fred. *The Creative Kid's Guide to Home Computers.* New York: Doubleday & Co., Inc., 1981.

Jacobsen, Karen. *A New True Book, Computers.* Chicago: Childrens Press, 1982.

Rice, Jean. *My Friend the Computer.* rev. ed. Minneapolis: T. S. Denison and Co., Inc., 1976.

Rice, Jean, and Marien Haley. *My Computer Dictionary.* Minneapolis: T. S. Denison and Co., Inc., 1981.

Rice, Jean, and Sandy O'Connor. *Computers Are Fun.* Minneapolis: T. S. Denison and Co., Inc., 1981.

Spencer, Donald D. *What Computers Can Do.* Ormond Beach, FL: Camelot Publishing Company, 1982.

Activity 2: Within the pocket labeled "Make a Puzzle," the library media specialist provides directions for creating a puzzle to reinforce the vocabulary learned through completing Activity 1. A list specifying the terms to be included in the puzzle may also be included. Students may be given the option to complete this activity by choosing alternative puzzle forms, such as crossword or word search puzzles, or by creating a manipulative game for this activity.

Assessment Criteria: Students will be assessed on the basis of the quality of their completed "Mini-Dictionaries" and "Puzzles."

LESSON 9

Title: Computer Scavenger Hunt

Library Media Research and Study Skills Objectives:

Participate in a discussion following the presentation of information from a sourcebook.

Interpret and apply information presented in a sourcebook.

Describe computer uses in the home, school, and community.

Describe the various processes computers can perform at home, at school, and in the community.

Level: 3

Instructional Strategy: Demonstration/Discussion/Project

Performance Objective: Given a demonstration of computer uses in the home, school, and community, students will participate in discussions, collect pictures and/or items related to computer use and processes, and create a mural depicting the varied computer-related items.

Resources: A copy of the book *Computers Are Fun* by Jean Rice and Sandy O'Connor (Minneapolis: T. S. Denison and Co., Inc., 1981) and a large sheet of paper for a mural.

Instructional Responsibility: Library media specialist and classroom teacher

Instructional Grouping: Total class and small group

Activities:

Introductory Activity: The library media specialist meets with the total class in the library media center and reads pp. 9-17 from *Computers Are Fun* by Jean Rice and Sandy O'Connor. Following the presentation, students participate in a discussion on computer uses in the home, at school, and in the community. The discussion is based on the information presented in the book and student experiences with computers and computer-related usage.

Developmental Activities: The classroom teacher assigns a "Computer Scavenger Hunt" project in which students will apply the information gained in their lesson and discussion in the library media center. Students are given one week to gather evidence of computer use in the home, at school, and in the community. Evidence can be in the form of pictures (cut from magazines or drawn) or actual items (grocery sales slips, library or fare cards, universal product codes, computer-generated reports and graphics, etc.). Each day students share the pictures or items collected and discuss where the computer was, who used the computer, what information must have been fed to the computer, and how the information was used.

Culminating Activity: After students have collected evidence of computer use and its applications for a week, the classroom teacher directs students in making a mural to display the evidence gathered. The mural is divided into three parts representing computer-related usage "At Home," "At School," and "In the Community." Students work in small groups to organize, select, and mount items for the mural. The completed mural is displayed in the library media center, after the library media specialist leads a discussion in which students explain the evidences of computer-related usage as presented in the mural.

Assessment Criteria: Students will be evaluated informally as they participate in the discussions and activities related to the "Computer Scavenger Hunt."

LESSON 10

Title: Computer Survey

Library Media Research and Study Skills Objectives:

Conduct a survey.

Organize gathered survey data into graphic representations in the form of bar graphs.

Level: 3-4

Instructional Strategy: Project/Discussion

Performance Objective: Given a tally sheet and a form for making bar graphs, the student will conduct a survey, record and tally the data, and organize the data on bar graphs.

Resources: Copies of the "Computer Survey Tally Sheet" (fig. 4.8, p. 196) and the "Computer Survey Bar Graphs Sheet" (fig. 4.9, p. 197).

Instructional Responsibility: Classroom teacher

Instructional Grouping: Total class

Activity: The activity will follow introductory and developmental lessons on making surveys and interpreting and constructing bar graphs. Each student is assigned to conduct a survey and record the results on a copy of the "Computer Survey Tally Sheet." After students have conducted their surveys, a class discussion is held to compare their results. The "Reasons for Response" columns for surveys A and B are shared in reference to adult and student attitudes toward computer games. Next, the students are given a copy of the "Computer Survey Bar Graphs Sheet." They are directed to transfer the data from their "Computer Survey Tally Sheet" to the three bar graphs represented on the bar graphs worksheet.

Assessment Criteria: Students will be evaluated on the basis of the data recorded on their tally sheets, the accuracy of the representative bar graphs on their bar graphs worksheets, and their participation in related classroom discussions.

(Text continues on page 198.)

Computer Survey Tally Sheet

A. Ask ten adults the question: "Are computer games good or bad for children and why?" Tally and list the responses below.

	Good	Bad	Both	Reason for Response
1				
2				
3				
4				
5				
6				
7				
8				
9				
10				

B. Ask ten students the question:"Are computer games good or bad for children and why?" Tally and list the responses below.

	Good	Bad	Both	Reason for Response
1				
2				
3				
4				
5				
6				
7				
8				
9				
10				

C. Ask ten students the question: "What computer games have you played?" List and tally the computer games mentioned on the listing below.

Tally Column	Computer Games Listing

Fig. 4.8. Worksheet.

Computer Survey Bar Graphs Sheet

Directions: Organize your data from your "Computer Survey Tally Sheet" to complete the bar graphs below.

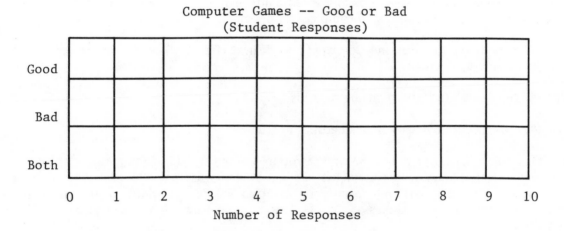

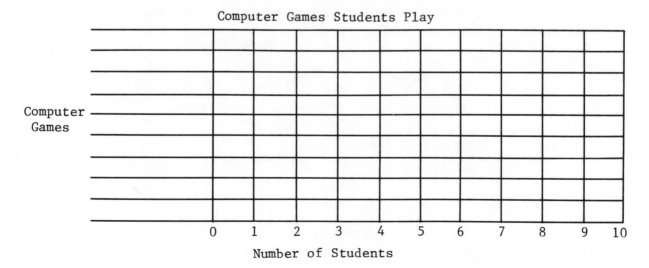

Fig. 4.9. Worksheet.

DANCE/DRAMA

LESSON 11

Title: Dances and Countries

Library Media Research and Study Skills Objectives:

>Alphabetize a group of words.

>Use an encyclopedia index to locate volumes that contain specific information.

>Locate specific information within encyclopedia articles.

>Interpret information presented in encyclopedia articles.

Level: 4-5

Instructional Strategy: Practice

Performance Objective: Given a list of dances, the student will alphabetize the dances, write them in alphabetical order, use an encyclopedia index to locate articles containing specific information about the dances, locate the articles and specific information within the articles, and interpret the encyclopedia articles in order to complete a worksheet.

Resources: Copies of the "Dances and Countries" worksheet (fig. 4.10), several encyclopedias that include indexes, and pencils.

Instructional Responsibility: Library media specialist

Instructional Grouping: Individuals or small groups of students

Activity: This practice activity follows several introductory and developmental lessons on encyclopedia skills. The library media specialist has had students use encyclopedia indexes, locate encyclopedia articles, and find specific information within encyclopedia articles in prior lessons. Students are given copies of the "Dances and Countries" worksheet to practice these encyclopedia skills.

Assessment Criteria: Students will be evaluated on the accuracy of the completed worksheets, thus indicating the application of alphabetizing skills, the use of encyclopedia indexes, and the location and interpretation of specific information within encyclopedia articles.

Dances and Countries

Directions: Alphabetize the list of dances below and write them in alphabetical order in the Dance column of the chart below. Use an
encyclopedia index to help you locate the specific information
you need in order to complete the Country of Origin and Brief
Description columns of the chart.

pavane gavotte passepied waltz hora reel tarantella
mazurka jig minuet

Dance	Country of Origin	Brief Description

Fig. 4.10. Worksheet.

LESSON 12

Title: Novel Dramatization

Library Media Research and Study Skills Objectives:

> Read and interpret literature in the form of realistic fiction novels.
>
> Report on a realistic fiction novel in dramatic form.
>
> Write scripts based on passages from a realistic fiction novel.

Level: 4-6

Instructional Strategy: Directed reading/Dramatization

Performance Objective: After reading a realistic fiction novel under the direction of the classroom teacher, students will select a passage, write a script, and present a dramatization of the passage.

Resources: Sets of realistic fiction novels to be read by students in their reading groups (third- through fourth-grade level novels)

Instructional Responsibility: Classroom teacher

Instructional Grouping: Small groups (reading groups)

Activity: Students are reading realistic fiction novels in their reading groups. The library media specialist provides multiple copies of three novels to be used by the classroom teacher for instruction. (Examples for a fourth-grade class with varying reading levels might be: *Ramona and Her Father* by Beverly Cleary, *The Bully of Barkham Street* by Mary Stolz, and *The Winged Watchman* by Hilda Van Stockum.) Upon completion of the novels, the students in each reading group select a passage to dramatize for their classmates and other members of their grade level. The classroom teacher suggests that they select a passage with several characters and a lot of dialogue. Students in each group write a script for the passage that they have selected to dramatize. The script will include a description of the setting and a list of characters represented in the dramatization. The dialogue for the characters in the script will include stage directions. Once a group has completed its script, the students will practice their dramatization, make decisions about costuming and props, and prepare scenery.

Assessment Criteria: Students will be assessed on the basis of their participation in: the selection of the passage to be dramatized, the writing of the script, the planning of the presentation, and the actual dramatization itself.

LESSON 13

Title: Theater Terms

Library Media Research and Study Skills Objectives:

Arrange a group of words in alphabetical order.

Increase word meaning through the interpretation of dictionary entries.

Interpret and label a graphic aid in the form of a diagram.

Level: 4-6

Instructional Strategy: Learning center

Performance Objective: Students will alphabetize words, interpret dictionary entries, and interpret a diagrammatic representation to complete learning center activities.

Resources: "Theater Terms" learning center (see fig. 4.11, p. 202), several dictionaries, pencils and paper.

Instructional Responsibility: Library media specialist or classroom teacher

Instructional Grouping: Individuals or small groups of students

Activities: Students will have experienced several developmental lessons in alphabetizing words and locating and interpreting dictionary entries before this center is assigned. The first activity provides practice in alphabetizing words and locating and interpreting dictionary entries. The second activity provides practice in interpreting and labeling a diagrammatic representation. Either the classroom teacher or the library media specialist will prepare the activity items.

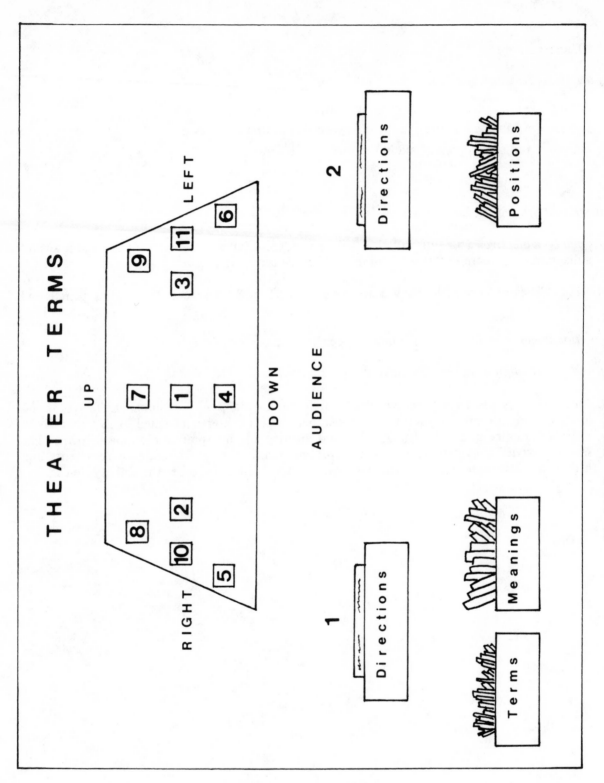

Fig. 4.11. Drawing of theater terms learning center.

Activity 1 Directions: Take out the cards from the "Terms" pocket and arrange them in alphabetical order. Next, take out the cards from the "Meanings" pocket and match them with the "Terms" cards. (Use the dictionary to help you with any meanings that you have difficulty matching with terms.) Make a "Mini-dictionary of Theater Terms" on the paper provided at the center. (Be sure your mini-dictionary lists the terms in alphabetical order.) *Suggested "Terms" and "Meanings" cards:* 1. actor—a male cast member representing a character in the play; 2. actress—a female cast member representing a character in the play; 3. cast—all of the actors and actresses in the play; 4. character—a person portrayed in the play; 5. costumes—what actors and actresses wear when playing their roles in the play; 6. crew—all of the stage-hands who work backstage during the play's preparation and performance; 7. cue—a signal for a specific speech or movement in a play; 8. director—the person who tells the cast members how to talk and move onstage; 9. double cast—to give each part or role in the play two cast members so that the play can be performed by two different casts; 10. gesture—any movement that a cast member uses to emphasize what is being said or felt; 11. in character—continuing to maintain the voice, body position, and facial expressions that are appropriate to the role being played; 12. leading role—a main character's role or part; 13. lines—the actual words spoken by an actor or actress while "in character"; 14. projection—the cast member's exaggeration of gestures and lines onstage so that the audience will understand their importance; 15. props—objects that appear onstage to make the stage setting more realistic; 16. script—a written representation of the play that includes a description of the setting and characters in the play, lines to be said by cast members, and stage directions for cast and crew members; 17. sets—stage scenery to be used as a background for the presentation of the play; 18. setting—the time and place where the play is occurring; 19. stage directions—the positions of the cast members as they face the audience onstage; 20. stagehands—crew members who assist the stage manager backstage during the play's preparation and performance; 21. stage manager—the person who supervises the crew backstage during the play's preparation and performance.

Activity 2 Directions: Study the stage diagram pictured on the center. Take the "Positions" cards out of the pocket and arrange them in order as in the diagram. Number your paper from 1 to 11. Match the numbers in the diagram with the "Positions" cards. Remember: Stage directions describe the positions of the actors and actresses as they *face* the audience. *Diagram numbers and "Positions" cards:* (The numbers correspond to the numbers in the diagram. Do not write the numbers on the "Positions" cards.) 1=C, or center stage; 2=R, or stage right; 3=L, or stage left; 4=DC, or down center; 5=DR, or down right; 6=DL, or down left; 7=UC, or up center; 8=UR, or up right; 9= UL, or up left; 10=RC, or right center; 11=LC, or left center.

Assessment Criteria: Students will be evaluated on the basis of their completed papers for activities 1 and 2.

MATHEMATICS

LESSON 14

Title: Catalog Computation

Library Media Research and Study Skills Objective:

Use a mail-order catalog to simulate ordering procedures.

Level: 5-6

Instructional Strategy: Demonstration/Practice

Performance Objective: The student will use a mail-order catalog to: select five items to order; fill out a form with shipping and ordering information; and compute the total amount including merchandise, shipping, and tax costs.

Resources: Copies of the "Catalog Computation" worksheet (fig. 4.12), transparency of the worksheet, several mail-order catalogs (8-10), pencils

Instructional Responsibility: Classroom teacher or library media specialist

Instructional Grouping: Small groups of eight to ten students

Activity: The classroom teacher or library media specialist produces a transparency of the "Catalog Computation" worksheet. The instructor projects the transparency on a screen and demonstrates the procedure for ordering and computing costs for a five-item mail order. Students are given a worksheet and access to several mail-order catalogs to complete the assignment.

Assessment Criteria: Students will be assessed on the accuracy of their completed "Computer Computation" worksheets.

Catalog Computation

Directions: Select a mail-order catalog and specify on this sheet the one
you are using. Choose any five items from the catalog that you
would like to buy. Fill out the order blank below. Be sure to
include all information needed. Print your name and address
clearly on the form to enable the company to send your order. Add
a sales tax of 5% and a shipping cost of 50¢ per pound to the cost
of your merchandise when you total your order.

Catalog: _____

Ship to:
Name: _____

Address: _____

City: _____ State: _____ Zip: _____

Page	Item	Catalog Number	Quantity	Size	Color	Weight	Price Each	Total

Merchandise Total	
Sales Tax	
Shipping Cost	
Total	

Fig. 4.12. Worksheet.

LESSON 15

Title: Dewey Decimal Derby

Library Media Research and Study Skills Objective:

Put a series of Dewey decimal numbers in order.

Level: 5-6

Instructional Strategy: Game/Practice

Performance Objective: Given a set of index cards with a Dewey decimal number printed on each, students will arrange the cards in Dewey decimal order.

Resources: At least six sets of index cards with a Dewey decimal number printed on each card. Each set should contain five or six cards representing numbers from the same Dewey decimal division. Example:

629.202	629.22	629.22	629.45	629.45
F	A	S	B	W

A stopwatch or a watch with a second hand.

Instructional Responsibility: Library media specialist

Instructional Grouping: Total class divided into teams of five to six members

Activity: This game will follow introductory lessons in ordering Dewey decimal numbers. The library media specialist prepares at least six sets of index cards for the game prior to the actual activity. Students are divided into teams of five to six members. To start play, the team members of one team stand and are presented with one index card each (face down). At the signal, "Go," the library media specialist begins timing the team. The team members turn over their cards and silently arrange themselves in the Dewey decimal order of their cards. The library media specialist records the number of seconds taken by the team to order the numbers. The team is awarded two points for each card in proper Dewey decimal order. Play continues in this manner until all teams have had a turn. Then, the library media specialist reviews the recorded times, and awards the team with the least time a bonus of five points. The other teams are awarded four, three, two, and one bonus points, respectively, in accordance with their recorded times. The team with the highest number of points is declared the winning team, and appropriate rewards are presented to winning team members.

Assessment Criteria: Students will be evaluated informally as they participate in the game situation.

LESSON 16

Title: Newspaper Math

Library Media Research and Study Skills Objectives:

Use a newspaper index to locate information.

Identify sections of a newspaper.

Locate specific information within newspaper sections and articles.

Level: 5-6

Instructional Strategy: Game/Practice

Performance Objective: Given a newspaper, students will use the index, identify sections, and locate specific information in a game situation.

Resources: Copies of the "Newspaper Math" worksheets (fig. 4.13), several newspapers (preferably five or six copies of the same newspaper), pencils.

Instructional Responsibility: Library media specialist or classroom teacher

Instructional Grouping: Total class divided into five or six groups

Activity: This game/practice activity would follow introductory lessons in using a newspaper index, identifying the sections of a newspaper, and locating specific information within newspaper sections and articles. To prepare students for the activity, the library media specialist divides the class into five or six teams. Each team is given a newspaper and a copy of the "Newspaper Math" worksheet. Students are told that they must find as many of the mathematical terms, symbols, and measures listed on the worksheet as possible within a twenty-five minute period. Notation of example, section, page, and column number must be listed for each item found. At the end of the given time period, the team that has found the most items is declared the winning team, and appropriate rewards are given to each member.

Assessment Criteria: Students will be assessed informally as they use the newspaper index, identify newspaper sections, and locate specific information within newspaper sections and articles in the game situation.

Things to Find	Example	Section	Page	Column
Amount of money over $10.00				
Amount of money under $10.00				
Bar graph				
Celsius or centrigrade temperature				
Circle graph				
Date (month, day, and year)				
Decimal fraction				
English unit of measurement				
Fahrenheit temperature				
Line graph				
Measure of area				
Measure of capacity				
Measure of length				
Measure of volume				
Metric unit of measurement				
Mixed number				
Number between 500 and 1,000				
Number greater than 10,000				
Number written in words				
Percent				
Prime number (digits and words)				
Telephone number whose digits total thirty-five				
Telephone number whose digits total thirty-nine				
Time measurement unit (hour, minute, or second)				

Fig. 4.13. Worksheet: Newspaper Math.

LESSON 17

Title: Occupational Measurement

Library Media Research and Study Skills Objective:

    Locate information from a variety of reference sources.

Level: 5-6

Instructional Strategy: Practice

Performance Objective: Given a list of occupations, the student will use a variety of reference sources to locate and record current measurements and metric measurements for these occupations.

Resources: Copies of the "Occupational Measurements" worksheet (fig. 4.14, p. 210), pencils, a variety of reference sources.

Instructional Responsibility: Library media specialist and/or classroom teacher

Instructional Grouping: Individuals, small groups, or total class

Activity: This practice activity involves the use of a variety of information-seeking skills and reference sources. Students should have received instruction in locating information through the use of the card catalog and encyclopedia and book indexes before attempting to complete the "Occupational Measurements" worksheet independently.

Assessment Criteria: Students should complete the "Occupational Measurements" worksheet with at least 80 percent accuracy.

Occupational Measurements

Directions: Fill in the missing Current Measurements and Metric Measurements
columns for the occupations listed in the chart below. Find the
information you need in an encyclopedia or in another reference
source. You may need to use the card catalog and book indexes to
complete the chart.

Occupation	Current Measurements	Metric Measurements
Carpenter		
Clothing salesperson		
Cook		
Electrician		
Engineer		
Forester		
Gasoline station attendant		
Meat cutter		
Meteorologist		
Optometrist		
Painter (house)		
Photographer		
Plumber		
Shipping clerk		
Shoemaker		
Taxi driver		

Fig. 4.14. Worksheet.

MUSIC

LESSON 18

Title: Composers

Library Media Research and Study Skill Objective:

Locate specific information in a biographical dictionary.

Level: 5-6

Instructional Strategy: Practice

Performance Objective: Given a list of composers, the student will locate specific information about the composers in a biographical dictionary.

Resources: Copies of the "Composers" worksheet (fig. 4.15, p. 212), several copies of *Webster's New Biographical Dictionary*, pencils.

Instructional Responsibility: Library media specialist

Instructional Grouping: Small groups of students (Size of groups will depend on the number of biographical dictionaries available.)

Activity: This practice activity would follow an introductory lesson in which the library media specialist demonstrates the use and contents of a biographical dictionary. Students would work as individuals or in small groups to complete the activity worksheet. Students must locate specific information within entries in a biographical dictionary to complete the "Composers" worksheet.

Assessment Criteria: Students will be evaluated on the basis of the completed "Composers" worksheet.

Composers

Directions: Use a biographical dictionary to complete the chart below.
The first example has been done for you.

Composer	Dates	Country
Johann Sebastian Bach	1685-1750	Germany
Béla Bartók		
Ludwig van Beethoven		
Aleksandr Borodin		
Johannes Brahms		
Frédéric Chopin		
Claude Achille Debussy		
Antonín Dvořák		
Edvard Grieg		
George Friderick Handel		
Joseph Haydn		
Franz Liszt		
Felix Mendelssohn		
Wolfgang Amadeus Mozart		
Sergey Prokofiev		
Giacomo Puccini		
Sergey Rachmaninoff		
Maurice Ravel		
Jean Sibelius		
Igor Stravinsky		
Pyotr Tchaikovsky		
Giuseppe Verdi		
Richard Wagner		

Fig. 4.15. Worksheet.

LESSON 19

Title: Listen and Write

Library Media Research and Study Skills Objectives:

Operate a record player.

Operate a listening station.

Interpret the mood of a musical composition and translate it into a creative writing composition.

Level: 3-6

Instructional Strategy: Learning center

Performance Objective: Given a musical recording, a record player, and a listening station, the student will operate the record player and listening station, listen to a recording of a musical composition, interpret the mood of the music, and translate it into a creative writing composition.

Instructional Responsibility: Library media specialist or classroom teacher

Instructional Grouping: Individuals or small groups of students

Activity: Students will listen to a musical composition to motivate creative writing. Prior to setting up the learning center, the library media specialist or classroom teacher should review the operation of a record player and a listening station. After they complete the activity, students may share their creative writing compositions stimulated by the music. Suggested musical compositions to be used at this learning center are:

Bach—"Little Fugue in G Minor"

Copland—"Appalachian Spring"

Debussy— "Clair de Lune," "La Mer"

Grieg— "Peer Gynt Suite"

Grofe—"Grand Canyon Suite"

Haydn—"The Toy Symphony," "The Surprise Symphony"

Herbert—"March of the Toys"

Mendelssohn—"Midsummer Night's Dream," "Fingel's Cave"

Mozart—"Eine kleine Nachtmusik"

Pierne—"March of the Little Lead Soldiers"

Poldini—"The Waltzing Doll"

Prokofiev—"Peter and the Wolf"

Ravel—"Mother Goose Suite"

Rimsky-Korsakov—"Scheherazade"

Rossini—"William Tell Overture"

Saint-Saëns—"Animal's Carnival," "Dance Macabre"

Schumann—"Papillon," "The Wild Horsemen"

Strauss—"Pizzicato"

Stravinsky—"Firebird Suite"

Tchaikovsky—"1812 Overture," "Nutcracker Suite"

Assessment Criteria: Given a musical recording, students will operate the necessary equipment, and create a written composition that reflects the mood of the musical piece.

LESSON 20

Title: Musical Mini-Report

Library Media Research and Study Skills Objectives:

>   Use a variety of information sources to research a topic.

>   Take notes to research a topic.

>   Organize research notes to write a short, factual report.

Level: 5-6

Instructional Strategy: Individual project

Performance Objective: Given a musical instrument as a research topic, the student will use a variety of sources to locate information, take notes, and organize the notes to write a short, factual report.

Resources: A variety of information sources, copies of the "Musical Instruments Data Sheet" (fig. 4.16, p. 216), pencils and paper.

Instructional Responsibility: Classroom teacher and library media specialist

Instructional Grouping: Small group or individuals

Activity: The classroom teacher assigns a research report to coordinate language arts skills in locating information, taking notes, and writing short, factual reports with a science unit in Sound Energy and a music unit in Musical Instruments. The library media specialist supervises and aids students while they collect data and take abbreviated notes on the "Musical Instruments Data Sheet" in the library media center. When students have completed their research, the classroom teacher helps students as they organize their notes into paragraph form in order to write a short, factual report on their instruments. As part of the project, students must do one of these three activities: (1) draw a poster to illustrate the instruments, (2) make or play a recording that features the instruments, or (3) demonstrate the actual instruments themselves. Suggested instruments for research are accordion, banjo, bass clarinet, bass drum, bassoon, bells, bongo drums, castanets, cello, chimes, clarinet, cymbals, double bass, English horn, flute, French horn, glockenspiel, gong, guitar, harp, harpsichord, oboe, organ, piano, pianoforte, piccolo, saxophone, snare drum, string bass, tambourine, timpani (kettle drum), triangle, trombone, trumpet, tuba, ukelele, viola, violin, and xylophone.

Assessment Criteria: The library media specialist will assess students on their performance as they locate information and take notes, and the classroom teacher will evaluate students based on their completed projects.

Musical Instruments Data Sheet

Musical instrument: _____

Description: _____

_____

_____

_____

History and development: _____

_____

_____

_____

Materials and manufacture: _____

_____

_____

_____

Method of playing: _____

_____

_____

Range and tone: _____

_____

_____

Well-known players: _____

_____

_____

Other interesting facts: _____

_____

_____

Fig. 4.16. Worksheet.

PHYSICAL EDUCATION

LESSON 21

Title: Graphathon

Library Media Research and Study Skills Objectives:

Collect and record data in table form.

Interpret data in table form in order to make a line graph to represent the data.

Level: 4-6

Instructional Strategy: Game/Practice

Performance Objective: Given a set of physical activities to perform, the student will perform the physical activities, record data in table form, and interpret data in table form in order to make a line graph to represent the data.

Resources: Basketball and basket, tennis racket and tennis ball, jump rope, measuring tape, masking tape, copies of the "Graphathon" worksheet (fig. 4.17, p. 218).

Instructional Responsibility: Classroom teacher and physical education teacher

Instructional Grouping: Five groups of students

Activity: Students are engaged in instructional lessons on making and interpreting graphs in the classroom. The classroom teacher makes prior arrangements with the physical education teacher to schedule an instructional period in which students can participate in five different athletic events. A copy of the "Graphathon" worksheet is provided for each student, and the classroom teacher demonstrates how to record scores for each of the five events for themselves and their team members. Student groups or teams are selected and names are recorded on the "Graphathon" worksheet. Meanwhile, the physical education teacher sets up five stations in the all-purpose room or gymnasium for the student teams to do their "Graphathon" events. Each student is allowed three trials for each event; the highest score is recorded on the worksheet for each student. The events or stations are (1) ball bouncing (bounce a tennis ball to the floor using a tennis racket); (2) basketball throw (throw a basketball into a bushel basket from a specified distance); (3) broad jump (jump and measure the distance); (4) hopping (hop on one foot for as long as possible); and (5) rope jumping (jump as many times as possible). After participating in the "Graphathon" events, the students return to the classroom where they rank each student on their team and fill in the line graph. Follow-up activities may include representing data by events or by the total class in the form of bar graphs, pictographs, or line graphs.

Assessment Criteria: Students will participate in the "Graphathon" events, record data in table form, and make a line graph to represent the data.

Students	Ball Bouncing		Basketball Throw		Broad Jump		Hopping		Rope Jumping	
	Score	Rank	Score	Rank	Score	Rank	Score	Rank	Score	Rank
1.										
2.										
3.										
4.										
5.										
6.										
7.										
8.										

_____'s Rank in the Graphathon

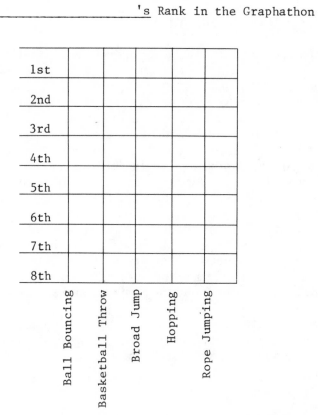

Fig. 4.17. Worksheet: Graphathon

LESSON 22

Title: Guinness Records

Library Media Research and Study Skills Objectives:

Use an index to locate specific information within a reference source.

Use headings, subheadings, and captions to locate specific information in tables within a reference source.

Use the *Guinness Book of World Records* as an information source.

Level: 4-6

Instructional Strategy: Practice

Performance Objective: Given a copy of the current edition of *Guinness Book of World Records*, the student will use the index, headings, subheadings, and captions to locate specific information.

Resources: Copies of the current edition of *Guinness Book of World Records*, copies of the "Guinness Records" worksheet (fig. 4.18, p. 220), pencils.

Instructional Responsibility: Library media specialist or classroom teacher

Instructional Grouping: Individuals or small groups of students

Activity: This practice activity would follow several developmental activities in which students would use indexes, and locate and interpret information as presented in tabular form. Prerequisite instruction may be provided by either the library media specialist or the classroom teacher. Students work as individuals or in small groups (in order to have access to copies of the *Guinness Book of World Records*) to complete the "Guinness Records" practice worksheet.

Assessment Criteria: Students will use the index, headings, subheadings, and captions in the *Guinness Book of World Records* to complete the "Guinness Records" worksheet.

Guinness Records

Directions: Use the current year <u>Guinness Book of World Records</u> to find out the facts about sports below. Use the index, headings, subheadings, and captions to help you locate the specific information you need.

1. Who is the holder of the greatest number of Olympic medals in archery?

   _____

2. Who is the only heavyweight boxing champion to have been undefeated in his entire professional career? _____

3. What was the longest recorded nonstop rope-jumping marathon in hours and minutes? _____

4. When did the first Indianapolis 500-mile race take place?

   _____

5. Who was the holder of the shortest pentathlon world record?

   _____

6. Who holds the record for the most fumbles in a football game?

   _____

7. What sport did William J. Cobb, the heaviest sportsman of all time, play? _____

8. When did the earliest recorded bicycle race take place? _____

9. What is the only country to have won the Olympic football title three times? _____

10. What is the name of the youngest major league baseball player of all time? _____

11. How long was the longest recorded fight between a fisherman and a fish?

    _____

12. Which sport has the highest ratio of officials to participants?

    _____

Fig. 4.18. Worksheet.

LESSON 23

Title: Sports Classification

Library Media Research and Study Skills Objectives:

>Classify information into categories.
>
>Distinguish between main topic and subtopic entries in an outline.
>
>Write an outline using correct form for main topics and subtopics.

Level: 3-4

Instructional Strategy: Practice

Performance Objective: Given a list of sports, students will classify the sports into three categories, and then write the categories in proper outline form for main topics and subtopics.

Resources: Copies of the "Sports Classification" worksheet (fig. 4.19, p. 222), pencils and paper.

Instructional Responsibility: Classroom teacher

Instructional Grouping: Total class

Activity: The classroom teacher provides this practice activity after introductory lessons in categorizing and simple outlining skills.

Assessment Criteria: Given a list of sports, students will complete a worksheet in which they classify the sports into three categories and write the categories in proper outline form.

Sports Classification

Part A
Directions: Decide in which category each sport in the list belongs. Write
each sport under the proper headings of the chart.

baseball   lacrosse   swimming
bobsledding   sailing   tobogganing
fishing   snow skiing   volleyball
football   snowmobiling   water skiing
hockey   soccer   yachting
ice skating   surfing

Team Sports	Water Sports	Winter Sports

Part B
Directions: Make an outline from the completed chart above. The title of
the outline should be Sports Categories. Use Roman numerals
and capital letters properly.

Title: _____

__· _____   __· _____
__· _____   __· _____
__· _____   __· _____
__· _____   __· _____
__· _____   __· _____
__· _____   __· _____
__· _____   __· _____
__· _____   __· _____
__· _____   __· _____
__· _____
__· _____

Fig. 4.19. Worksheet.

READING/LANGUAGE ARTS

LESSON 24

Title: Abbreviations

Library Media Research and Study Skills Objective:

Identify abbreviations frequently used on a catalog card.

Level: 5-6

Instructional Strategy: Drill/Practice/Game

Performance Objective: Given flash cards representing card catalog abbreviations and their meanings, students will match the flash cards in a drill/game situation.

Resources: Set of flash cards with card catalog abbreviations and a set of flash cards with their meanings.

Instructional Responsibility: Library media specialist

Instructional Grouping: Small groups of students

Activity: The library media specialist prepares a set of flash cards with abbreviations frequently used in the card catalog and another set with their meanings. Students in small groups are introduced to the abbreviations through a drill/game consisting of two rounds. In the first round, the library media specialist displays a flash card with an abbreviation, and students are given opportunities to guess the abbreviation meaning. If a student correctly identifies the abbreviation, he or she keeps the flash card. When all the cards have been identified, the students record the number of cards that they are holding and the cards are collected. In the second round, the same procedure is followed using the flash cards with the meanings. When the library media specialist displays a meaning, students are given opportunities to guess the abbreviations. When all the cards have been identified, totals are recorded, cards are collected, a winner is designated, and an appropriate reward is given to the winner. If time permits, a third round may be played in which students match the abbreviations cards with the meanings cards. *Suggested matching abbreviations and meanings:* 1. b & w = black and white; 2. CH = charts; 3. cm =centimeter(s); 4. col = color; 5. CT = cassette tape; 6. DM = ditto master; 7. fr = frame(s); 8. FS = filmstrip, 9. FSS = filmstrip (sound); 10. GA = game(s); 11. ill, illus = illustrated, illustrations; 12. in = inches; 13. min = minutes; 14. MP = film(s); 15. nd = no date; 16. p = page(s); 17. photo = photographs; 18. PIC - pictures (posters, study prints, art prints); 19. RD = record; 20. RT = tape recording; 21. SD, SL = slides; 22. ser = series; 23. tg = teacher's guide; 24. TRA = transparencies; 25. unp = unpaged; 26. v, vol = volume.

Assessment Criteria: Students will identify catalog card abbreviations as they participate in a drill/game situation.

LESSON 25

Title: Dictionary Derivation

Library Media Research and Study Skills Objectives:

Use a dictionary to determine word origins (derivation, etymology).

Classify words as by language of origin (derivation, etymology).

Locate dictionary entries and interpret dictionary meanings.

Level: 4-6

Instructional Strategy: Learning center

Performance Objective: Given a dictionary and a list of words, the student will identify the language of origin and match the dictionary meaning to the words.

Resources: "Dictionary Derivation" learning center (see fig. 4.20), several different dictionaries, pencils and paper.

Instructional Responsibility: Classroom teacher or library media specialist

Instructional Grouping: Individuals or small groups

Activity: This series of developmental activities would follow introductory lessons in the location and interpretation of dictionary entries, including word derivations, by the classroom teacher or library media specialist. Students would complete the learning center stations independently or in small groups.

Directions: There are four stations at the "Dictionary Derivation" learning center. Do the following six steps for each station:

1. Make a chart. Label three columns: Word, Language of Origin, and Dictionary Meaning.

2. Take the cards out of the "Words" and "Meanings" pockets.

3. Use the dictionary to help you determine the language of origin and the dictionary meaning of each word. Write this information on your chart.

4. As you complete the chart for each word, hang the word card on a hook under the appropriate language at that station.

5. When you have completed the chart, return the "Words" and "Meanings" cards to the proper pockets.

6. When you have completed all four stations of the "Dictionary Derivation" center, turn in your papers to the library media specialist or classroom teacher.

Suggested "Words" and "Meanings" cards for Station 1: Greek–1. telescope–a device used to observe distant objects; 2. eureka–an expression of triumphant discovery; 3. nautilus–a tropical marine mollusk with a partitioned shell; 4. dialect–a regional speech pattern or language; 5. phobia–a strong fear of a specific thing or situation. Latin–1. wine–the fermented juice of grapes or sometimes other fruits or plants; 2. veil–a piece of transparent cloth worn over the face; 3. vein–a vessel that transports blood toward the heart; 4. ointment–a viscous substance used on the skin for cosmetic or medical purposes; 5. campus–the grounds of a school, college or university.

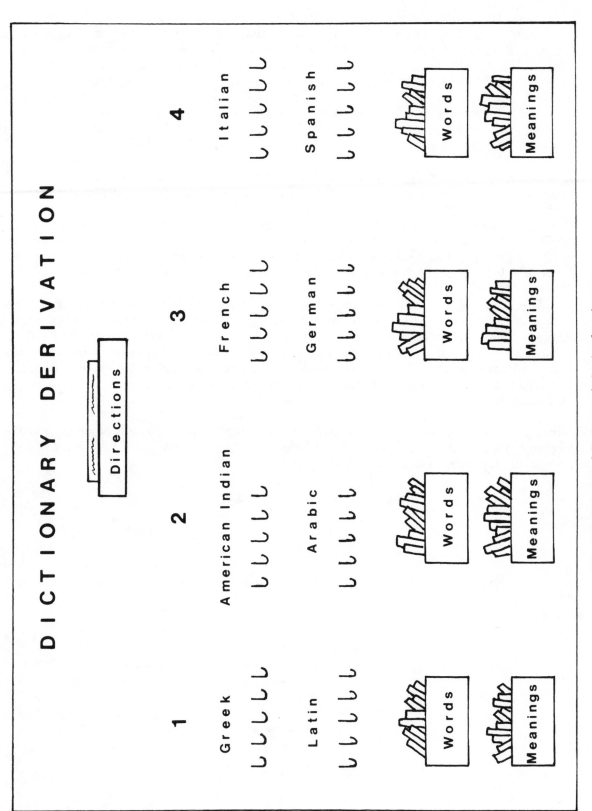

Fig. 4.20. Drawing of dictionary derivation learning center.

Suggested "Words" and "Meanings" cards for Station 2: American Indian—1. caucus—a political meeting to determine policy or to select candidates; 2. chipmunk—a small squirrellike rodent with a striped back; 3. skunk—a black and white furry mammal that can eject a malodorous secretion; 4. raccoon—a mammal with a bushy, black-ringed tail; 5. toboggan—a long, runnerless sled. Arabic—1. algebra—the science of arithmetic involving symbols representing numbers and operations; 2. magazine—a storage place for ammunition, firearms, literature, film, etc.; 3. mattress—a pad filled with soft material used as a bed; 4. sherbert—a sweet-flavored ice to which milk, egg whites, or gelatin has been added; 5. sofa—a long, upholstered couch with a back and arms.

Suggested "Words" and "Meanings" cards for Station 3: French—1. purchase—to buy something or something that is bought; 2. fuselage—the central body of an airplane; 3. garage—a place to keep or fix vehicles; 4. levee—an embankment raised to keep a river from overflowing; 5. sabotage—to deliberately damage someone's property. German—1. noodle—a thin strip of food made from flour and eggs; 2. delicatessen—a shop that sells freshly prepared foods ready for serving; 3. hamburger—a cooked patty of chopped or ground meat; 4. kindergarten—a school class for young children; 5. pumpernickel—a dark, coarse, rye bread.

Suggested "Words" and "Meanings" cards for Station 4: Italian—1. trombone—a brass musical instrument related to the trumpet; 2. regatta—an organized boat race or series of boat races; 3. pilot—one who operates a ship or an aircraft; 4. fiasco—a complete failure; 5. balcony—a platform projecting out from the wall of a building. Spanish—1. bonanza—any source of great wealth, 2. bronco—a wild or semiwild horse; 3. burro—a small donkey; 4. canyon—a narrow valley with steep walls eroded by running water; 5. rodeo—a public exhibition of cowboy skills.

Assessment Criteria: Students will use a dictionary to identify the language of origin and the meanings for a list of words. Students will be evaluated on the basis of the accuracy of their completed "Dictionary Derivation" Center papers.

LESSON 26

Title: Dictionary Picture Clues

Library Media Research and Study Skills Objectives:

Locate dictionary entries.

Use dictionary pictures and/or diagrams to help interpret dictionary meanings.

Level: 3-4

Instructional Strategy: Drill/Practice

Performance Objective: The students will locate dictionary entries and use dictionary pictures and/ or diagrams to help interpret word meanings in order to complete a worksheet.

Resources: Copies of the "Dictionary Picture Clues" worksheet (fig. 4.21, p. 228), dictionaries (one per student), pencils.

Instructional Responsibility: Classroom teacher

Instructional Grouping: Total class or small group (depending on number of dictionaries available)

Activity: This developmental activity should follow introductory lessons involving the location of dictionary entries. Each student is given a copy of the "Dictionary Picture Clues" worksheet and a dictionary.

Assessment Criteria: Students will use the dictionary to complete the "Dictionary Picture Clues" worksheet, and will be assessed on the accuracy of the completed paper.

Dictionary Picture Clues

Part A
Directions: Find the words listed below in the dictionary. If the dictionary
         entry includes a picture or diagram to illustrate the word, put
         an x on the blank next to the word.

1. ___ abacus	11. ___ isosceles	21. ___ perambulator	31. ___ tracery
2. ___ aigrette	12. ___ larynx	22. ___ peruke	32. ___ umbel
3. ___ beret	13. ___ lugger	23. ___ prawn	33. ___ umiak
4. ___ caduceus	14. ___ metronome	24. ___ quatrefoil	34. ___ wainscot
5. ___ chalice	15. ___ minaret	25. ___ rebec	35. ___ warp
6. ___ chaps	16. ___ monocle	26. ___ sabot	36. ___ whelk
7. ___ conger	17. ___ obelisk	27. ___ scimitar	37. ___ whirligig
8. ___ dingo	18. ___ octagon	28. ___ tankard	38. ___ willet
9. ___ fife	19. ___ oval	29. ___ terrapin	39. ___ wimple
10. ___ Ionic	20. ___ parquetry	30. ___ toggle	40. ___ zeppelin

Part B
Directions: Choose any six words with an x from the list above. For each word,
         draw a picture or diagram in the box. Then, write the entry word
         and a definition on the lines below the box.

Fig. 4.21. Worksheet.

LESSON 27

Title: Figures of Speech

Library Media Research and Study Skills Objectives:

Interpret figurative language in the form of similes, metaphors, idioms, and personifications.

Distinguish among figures of speech in order to identify similes, metaphors, idioms, and personifications.

Level: 5-6

Instructional Strategy: Game/Practice

Performance Objective: Given examples of figures of speech, the students will: identify their forms as similes, metaphors, idioms, or personifications; and interpret their meanings in a game situation.

Resources: List of sentences containing similes, metaphors, idioms, and personifications.

Instructional Responsibility: Classroom teacher

Instructional Grouping: Total class divided into four or five teams

Activity: This game/practice activity would follow developmental lessons on figures of speech in the form of similes, metaphors, idioms, and personifications. Students are divided into four or five teams, and the game is played as a relay. Only one player is involved at a time. Each player listens to a sentence containing a figure of speech and must either identify its form or interpret its meaning. Players earn a point for their respective teams if they answer correctly. When all students have had at least one turn at identification and at least one turn at interpretation, team scores are tallied, a winning team is declared, and appropriate rewards are given to winning team members. A follow-up activity might be to have the students illustrate selected examples from the game. This list which follows illustrates selected sentences for the game.

Similes: 1. He acted like an angry bull. 2. The ice cream was as hard as a brick. 3. A still pond is like a mirror. 4. The box is as light as a feather. 5. Harold's car is like a dream. 6. John is as happy as a lark. 7. Her hair is like silk. 8. My head is spinning like a top. 9. Alice is as sharp as a tack. 10. She is as sour as a pickle.

Metaphors: 1. My dog is a pain in the neck. 2. That child is a silly goose. 3. Your room is a pigpen! 4. She's a tiger when she's angry! 5. The moon is a big balloon. 6. That driver is a road hog! 7. That job is a piece of cake. 8. He's a chip off the old block. 9. That job is a real dog. 10. That lady is a busy bee.

Idioms: 1. He had to foot the bill for lunch. 2. Jane had to face the music. 3. Their team won by a hair. 4. Dad gave him a tongue-lashing. 5. The boy spilled the beans when he told the teacher. 6. Jack was killing time before the game. 7. It's raining cats and dogs! 8. I was racking my brain trying to remember her name. 9. Tom decided to turn over a new leaf. 10. Once in a blue moon, she finishes her work.

Personifications: 1. The wind is whispering secrets to me. 2. The stream is running over the rocks. 3. Flowers were nodding their heads. 4. The tree tapped its fingers on my window. 5. The chair groaned when he sat on it. 6. The blanket hugged me during the night. 7. The kite was jumping wildly. 8. The candy bar was begging to be eaten. 9. The bike has a mind of its own. 10. The sun kissed their happy faces.

Assessment Criteria: Students will be evaluated informally as they identify figures of speech and interpret their meanings in a game situation.

LESSON 28

Title: Listen and Draw

Library Media Research and Study Skills Objectives:

Operate a cassette recorder.

Follow oral directions in sequential order to make a map.

Determine directionality on a specific map.

Level: 3-6

Instructional Strategy: Learning center

Performance Objective: Given an outline map of a city, the student will operate a cassette recorder, listen to and follow oral directions, determine directionality, and draw a map accurately.

Resources: "Listen and Draw" learning center (see fig. 4.22, p. 232), copies of the blank city outline map (fig. 4.23, p. 233), cassette tape recorder and cassette tape with directions, listening station, pencils.

Instructional Responsibility: Library media specialist or classroom teacher

Instructional Grouping: Individuals or small groups of students

(Text continues on page 234.)

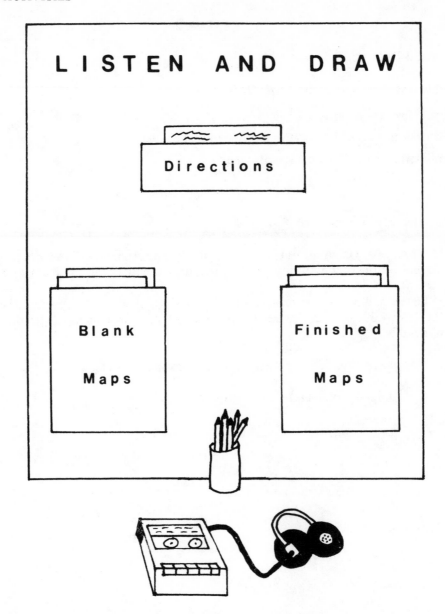

Fig. 4.22. Drawing of listen and draw learning center.

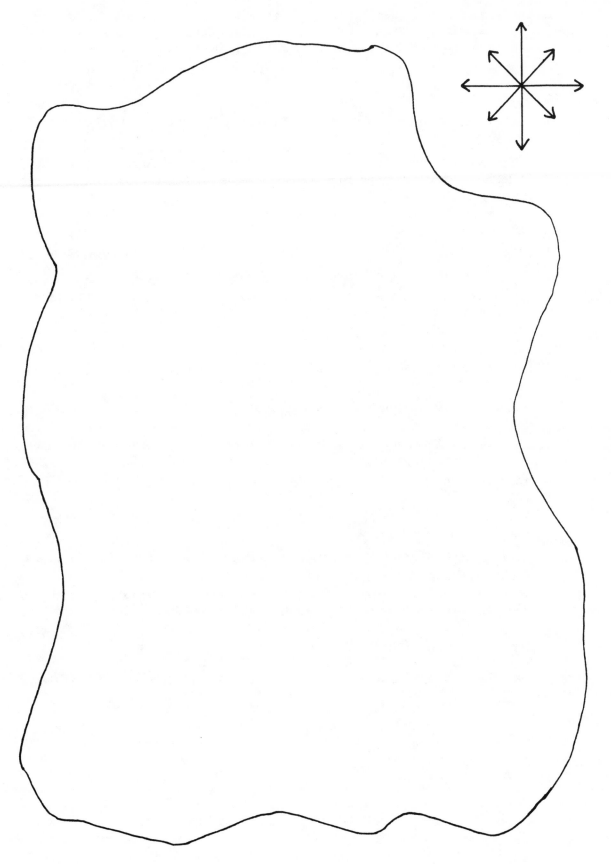

Fig. 4.23. Outline map of city.

Activity: Students should be introduced to this learning center by the classroom teacher or the library media specialist. The operation of the cassette recorder and the use of the listening station should be reviewed prior to assigning this activity to students. The following directions should be posted on the "Listen and Draw" learning center.

Directions:

1. Take a city outline map out of the "Blank Maps" pocket and a pencil from the pencil can.
2. Turn on the tape recorder and listen to the directions carefully.
3. After each set of directions, turn the tape recorder off while you draw that part of the map.

Script for the Tape Recording:

1. Hold your paper so that the compass rose is in the lower right-hand corner. Stop.
2. Label the compass rose directions: N, E, S, W, NE, SE, SW, and NW. Stop.
3. Draw and label Main Street. It passes through the center of the city and runs north and south. Stop.
4. Draw and label Maple Avenue. It runs east and west near the southern edge of the city. Stop.
5. Draw and label Frank Street. It runs parallel to Main Street through the eastern side of the city. Stop.
6. Draw and label Jackson Road. It runs east and west through the northern edge of the city. Stop.
7. Draw and label Western Avenue. It runs parallel to Main Street through the western part of the city. Stop.
8. Draw and label Central Highway. It runs east and west through the center of the city. Stop.
9. Draw and label Jones Lane. It runs from Western Avenue to Frank Street. It is to the south of Central Highway. Stop.
10. Draw a small lake near the northeast corner of Jackson Road and Frank Street. Stop.
11. Draw a railroad entering the southwest corner of the city. It crosses Maple Avenue and Central Highway. It exits the city just to the south of Jackson Road. Stop.
12. Your map is now complete. Put your map in the "Finished Maps" pocket. Rewind the tape and turn off the tape recorder.

Assessment Criteria: Students will be assessed on the basis of their completed maps.

SCIENCE

LESSON 29

Title: Animal Longevity

Library Media Research and Study Skills Objectives:

Use an almanac index to locate specific information.

Use headings and subheadings to locate information arranged in tabular form.

Interpret data listed in tabular form in order to transfer it to a bar graph.

Level: 4-6

Instructional Strategy: Practice

Performance Objective: Given an almanac, the students will: use the index, headings, and sub-headings to locate a table containing specific information concerning animal longevity; interpret the information listed in the table; and fill in a bar graph representing the data.

Resources: Copies of *The World Almanac*, copies of the "Animal Longevity" worksheet (fig. 4.24, p. 236), pencils.

Instructional Responsibility: Library media specialist or classroom teacher

Instructional Grouping: Small groups of students

Activity: This practice activity would follow review lessons on using an index, interpreting tables, and representing data graphically in the form of bar graphs. Students work in small groups because of the limited quantity of almanacs available. Each student is given an almanac and a copy of the "Animal Longevity" worksheet.

Assessment Criteria: Students will be observed informally as they locate the necessary information in the almanac and complete the bar graph on the worksheet.

Animal Longevity

Directions: Use the index of <u>The World Almanac</u> to locate a table that lists
information on animal longevity. Find the average longevity or
life span for each animal listed below. Then, fill in the bar
graph to represent the average longevity for each animal listed.

Average Longevity of Animals

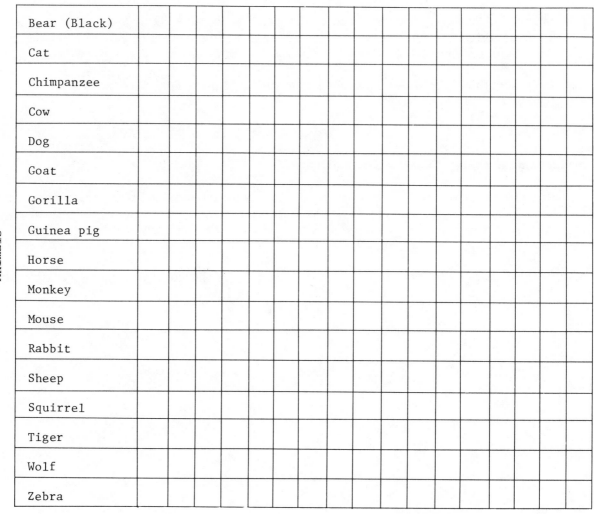

Fig. 4.24. Worksheet.

LESSON 30

Title: Colorful Synonyms

Library Media Research and Study Skills Objectives:

Distinguish between the content of a general and a special dictionary (thesaurus).

Use an index to locate the appropriate page for a given entry word in a thesaurus.

Use guide words/letters to locate the appropriate page for a given entry word in a thesaurus.

Interpret thesaurus entries to distinguish between synonyms.

Level: 5-6

Instructional Strategy: Practice/Learning center

Performance Objective: Given a thesaurus and a list of color words, the student will use an index or guide words/letters to locate thesaurus entries, and interpret thesaurus entries in order to complete a worksheet in which specific color words are associated with general colors.

Resources: Several different examples of thesauri, copies of the "Colorful Synonyms" worksheet (fig. 4.25, p. 238), pencils.

Instructional Responsibility: Library media specialist or classroom teacher

Instructional Grouping: Individuals or small groups of students

Activity: This activity may be assigned as a practice activity or may be used with a learning center. This activity should follow instruction in the content and use of a thesaurus. Students should have previously participated in learning activities in which indexes and guide words/letters are used to locate specific dictionary entries. Each student is given a copy of the "Colorful Synonyms" worksheet and should have access to several types of thesauri in order to complete the worksheet.

Assessment Criteria: Students will be evaluated on the basis of the accuracy of the completed "Colorful Synonyms" worksheet. It should be completed with 80 percent accuracy.

Colorful Synonyms

Directions: Use a thesaurus to identify the color associated with each word
listed below. (Remember to determine whether the thesaurus you
are using contains an index or lists words in alphabetical order
as in a general dictionary.) Use the code below to identify the
colors. If a word has a __/__ before it, list two colors.

R = Red   O = Orange   Y = Yellow   G = Green   B = Blue   P = Purple
Br = Brown   Bl = Black   W = White

1. ___ amber	19. ___ indigo	37. ___ scarlet
2. ___ amethyst	20. ___ ivory	38. ___ snowy
3. ___ apricot	21. ___ jade	39. ___ tan
4. ___ azure	22. ___ kelly	40. ___ tawny
5. ___ beige	23. ___ lavender	41. ___ topaz
6. _/_ brunette	24. ___ lemon	42. ___ umber
7. ___ cherry	25. ___ lilac	43. ___ verdant
8. ___ chocolate	26. ___ mahogany	44. ___ vermillion
9. ___ cinnamon	27. ___ milky	45. ___ violet
10. ___ claret	28. ___ navy	46. ___ viridescent
11. ___ crimson	29. _/_ ocher	
12. ___ cyanic	30. ___ olive	
13. ___ ebony	31. ___ peach	
14. ___ emerald	32. ___ pearl	
15. ___ flaxen	33. _/_ plum	
16. ___ frosty	34. ___ raven	
17. ___ garnet	35. ___ saffron	
18. _/_ henna	36. ___ sapphire	

Fig. 4.25. Worksheet.

LESSON 31

Title: Food Groups

Library Media Research and Study Skills Objectives:

Classify information into headings and subheadings.

Distinguish between main topics and subtopics in an outline.

Complete an outline using proper form.

Level: 4-5

Instructional Strategy: Practice

Performance Objective: Given a listing of food categories and food examples, the student will identify and list food category headings on a chart, identify and list food subheadings on a chart, and use the chart to complete an outline.

Resources: Copies of the "Food Groups" worksheet (fig. 4.26, p. 240), pencils.

Instructional Responsibility: Classroom teacher or library media specialist

Instructional Grouping: Total class

Activity: This practice activity would be best used if integrated into a science or health unit on Nutrition. If students are not engaged in such a unit, then resource books that contain information about food groups should be provided. Students should have received instruction in categorizing and outlining skills prior to the assignment of this activity. Students are presented with a copy of the "Food Groups" worksheet and access to resource books in order to complete this practice activity.

Assessment Criteria: Students will be evaluated on the quality of the completed "Food Groups" worksheet. It should be completed with at least 90 percent accuracy.

Food Groups

Part A

Directions: Read the list of items below. Choose the five food group headings and list them at the top of the chart. Then classify and write the remaining foods under the proper food headings in the chart.

Apples	Bananas	Beef	Beets	Bread	Butter	Carbo-
Carrots	Cheese	Cherries	Celery	Cereal	Dairy Products	hydrates
Fruits	Grapes	Ice Cream	Lettuce	Meats	Milk	Oranges
Pork	Potatoes	Radishes	Rice	Veal	Vegetables	

_____ _____ _____ _____ _____ _____
_____ _____ _____ _____ _____ _____

_____

Part B

Directions: Use the completed chart above to determine where each food group and food listing would fit in the outline below. List all the items from the chart in the outline. Be sure to capitalize all outline entries.

Food Groups

I. _____   IV. _____
   A. _____   A. _____
   B. _____   B. _____
   C. _____   C. _____

II. _____   V. _____
   A. _____   A. _____
   B. _____   B. _____
   C. _____   C. _____
   D. _____   D. _____
                                         E. _____
III. _____   F. _____
   A. _____
   B. _____
   C. _____
   D. _____
   E. _____

Fig. 4.26. Worksheet.

LESSON 32

Title: Geologic Events

Library Media Research and Study Skills Objective:

Interpret information listed in the form of a time line.

Level: 4-6

Instructional Strategy: Practice

Performance Objective: Given a geologic time line, the student will read and interpret the time line and answer questions that pertain to it.

Resources: Copies of the "Geologic Events" worksheet (fig. 4.27, p. 242), pencils

Instructional Responsibility: Classroom teacher or library media specialist

Instructional Grouping: Total class, small groups, or individuals

Activity: This practice activity is best suited for introduction in conjunction with a science unit on Geology or Early Plants and Animals. Students should have experienced some lessons pertaining to the interpretation of time lines prior to the assignment of this practice exercise. Students are given copies of the "Geologic Events" worksheet, which they are to complete independently.

Assessment Criteria: Students will be evaluated on the completed "Geologic Events" worksheet. It should be completed with at least 80 percent accuracy.

Geologic Events

Part A Directions: Use the Geologic Time Line to answer the questions below.
Write your answers on the blank following each question.

Geologic Time Line

Pennsylvanian Period

325 million years ago.
Earth covered by huge
swamps. Giant ferns and
mosses thrive. First
reptiles appear. Insects
grow to enormous size.

Permian Period

280 million years ago.
Climate warm but dry.
Size, number, and kinds
of reptiles increase.
Appalachian Mountains have
high peaks.

Triassic Period

225 million years ago.
Earth is wet and warm.
First, primitive dino-
saurs appear. Conifer
trees thrive.

Jurassic Period

200 million years ago.
Dinosaurs dominate the
earth. The first birds
appear.

Cretaceous Period.

136 million years ago.
Seas and swamps recede.
Last dinosaurs appear and
become extinct. Mammals
arise and rule.

1. During which period did primitive dinosaurs
   first appear? _____

2. How long ago did the Permian period exist?
   _____

3. During which period did huge ferns live?
   _____

4. How long ago did the Jurassic period exist?
   _____

5. During which period did the first birds
   appear? _____

6. During which period did the first reptiles
   appear? _____

7. How long ago did dinosaurs become extinct?
   _____

8. During which period might you have seen many
   evergreen trees? _____

9. Which mountains had sharp peaks 280 million
   years ago? _____

10. How much time passed between the first and
    last dinosaurs? _____

Part B Directions: Read each statement to decide
whether it is true or false.
Then write True or False
on the line after the statement.

11. Primitive dinosaurs first appeared during
    the Permian period. _____

12. The Jurassic period came after the Permian period. _____

13. The earth's climate was wet and warm 225 million years ago. _____

14. There were 189 years between the Pennsylvanian period and the Cretaceous
    period. _____

15. Mammals ruled during the Permian period. _____

16. Reptiles became much larger during the Permian period. _____

Fig. 4.27. Worksheet.

SOCIAL STUDIES

LESSON 33

Title: Continents, Countries, Cities

Library Media Research and Study Skills Objectives:

Distinguish between general and special dictionaries.

Use alphabetical order and guide words/letters to locate entries in a geographical dictionary.

Interpret entries in a geographical dictionary.

Level: 5-6

Instructional Strategy: Practice/Learning center/Game

Performance Objective: Given a list of places, the student will locate and interpret entries in a geographical dictionary to identify whether the places are continents, countries, or cities.

Resources: Copies of the "Continents, Countries, Cities" worksheet (fig. 4.28, p. 244), copies of as many geographical dictionaries as possible, pencils.

Instructional Responsibility: Library media specialist

Instructional Grouping: Individuals or small groups

Activity: Depending upon the number of geographical dictionaries available, this practice activity can be easily adapted for use at a learning center or in a game situation. Students should be introduced to geographical dictionaries prior to taking part in this activity. The "Continents, Countries, Cities" worksheet can be used by students for a learning center, a game activity, or a practice exercise.

Assessment Criteria: If the "Continents, Countries, Cities" worksheet is used as a practice exercise or a learning center activity, students will complete the worksheet with 80 percent accuracy. If this activity is used in a game situation, students will be assessed informally as they use a geographical dictionary to locate specific information.

Continents, Countries, Cities

Directions: Use a geographical dictionary to determine whether each place
listed below is a continent, a country, or a city. Write the
code letter on the blank next to each place. The code letters are:

A = Continent
B = Country
C = City

1. ___ Aden	23. ___ Damascus	45. ___ Panama City	67. ___ Wellington
2. ___ Africa	24. ___ Denmark	46. ___ Peru	68. ___ Yugoslavia
3. ___ Albania	25. ___ Ecuador	47. ___ Rome	69. ___ Zaire
4. ___ Ammon	26. ___ Europe	48. ___ Rumania	70. ___ Zambia
5. ___ Antarctica	27. ___ Finland	49. ___ Senegal	
6. ___ Argentina	28. ___ Gangtok	50. ___ Sierra Leone	
7. ___ Asia	29. ___ Ghana	51. ___ Sikkim	
8. ___ Austria	30. ___ Islamabad	52. ___ Somalia	
9. ___ Australia	31. ___ Juneau	53. ___ South Africa	
10. ___ Bangkok	32. ___ Lebanon	54. ___ South America	
11. ___ Barbados	33. ___ Libya	55. ___ Spain	
12. ___ Bern	34. ___ Lhasa	56. ___ Stockholm	
13. ___ Brazil	35. ___ Lima	57. ___ St. Paul	
14. ___ Bucharest	36. ___ Mauritania	58. ___ Syria	
15. ___ Bulgaria	37. ___ Mozambique	59. ___ Tanzania	
16. ___ Canada	38. ___ Niger	60. ___ Tehran	
17. ___ Canberra	39. ___ Nigeria	61. ___ Thailand	
18. ___ Chicago	40. ___ North America	62. ___ Togo	
19. ___ Concord	41. ___ Norway	63. ___ Toronto	
20. ___ Costa Rica	42. ___ Oslo	64. ___ Tunis	
21. ___ Czechoslovakia	43. ___ Pakistan	65. ___ Venezuela	
22. ___ Dakar	44. ___ Panama	66. ___ Warsaw	

Fig. 4.28. Worksheet.

LESSON 34

Title: Holiday Research

Library Media Research and Study Skills Objectives:

> Use a variety of sources to locate specific information.
>
> Practice taking notes in an abbreviated form.
>
> Prepare an oral report from notes.

Level: 4-6

Instructional Strategy: Individual project

Resources: A variety of reference sources, copies of the "Holiday Research Information Sheet" (fig. 4.29, p. 246), pencils.

Instructional Responsibility: Library media specialist or classroom teacher

Instructional Grouping: Individuals

Activity: This research project may be assigned individually or be included as part of an ongoing interest center. Students are given a "Holiday Research Information Sheet" with which to take notes as they research a particular holiday. Students must cite at least three different information sources from which they gathered data about the particular holiday. After students have recorded information in abbreviated note form, they organize the notes in order to make an oral presentation to their classmates.

Assessment Criteria: Students will be evaluated on the basis of their oral presentation of information on the holiday they researched. The library media specialist or classroom teacher will collect the "Holiday Research Information Sheet" after the presentation.

Holiday Research Information Sheet

Holiday: _____

Country of origin: _____

When it started: _____

Original purpose or reason: _____
_____
_____
_____

Customs: _____
_____
_____
_____

Symbols: _____
_____
_____

Early celebrations: _____
_____
_____

Modern celebrations: _____
_____
_____

Other important information: _____
_____
_____
_____

Realia, pictures, etc., to be included in your oral report: _____
_____
_____
_____

Information sources:

1. _____
_____

2. _____
_____
_____

3. _____
_____
_____

Fig. 4.29. Worksheet.

LESSON 35

Title: State Research

Library Media Research and Study Skills Objectives:

Use a variety of information sources to locate specific information.

Practice taking notes in an abbreviated form.

Organize notes in order to write a factual report.

Level: 5-6

Instructional Strategy: Individual or group project

Performance Objective: Given a state as a research topic, the student will gather information from a variety of sources, take notes in abbreviated form, and organize the notes to write a factual report.

Resources: A variety of information sources, copies of the "State Data Sheets 1 and 2" (figs. 4.30, 4.31, pp. 248-9), pencils and paper.

Instructional Responsibility: Classroom teacher or library media specialist

Instructional Grouping: Individuals or small groups

Activity: This project would serve as a culminating activity for a social studies unit on Geographical Regions. Students could be assigned a state to research individually or in small groups. The "State Data Sheets 1 and 2" would serve to help students record and organize information in order to write a factual report. Students are directed to include at least one almanac, one encyclopedia, and one other reference source in their research. Statistical information should be found in the latest almanac edition.

Assessment Criteria: Students will be evaluated on the basis of their completed written reports on their respective states.

(Text continues on page 250.)

State Data Sheet 1

I. Important facts

    A. Official name: _____

    B. Location (in United States): _____

    C. Size

        1. Area: _____

        2. Rank: _____

    D. Bordering states, countries, bodies of water, etc.:

        1. N - _____

        2. E - _____

        3. S - _____

        4. W - _____

    E. Capital: _____

        1. Location: _____

        2. Population: _____

    F. Population

        1. Size: _____

        2. Rank: _____

    G. State symbols

        1. Bird: _____

        2. Flower: _____

        3. Tree: _____

        4. Nickname(s): _____

                _____

        5. State flag (description): _____

                _____

Fig. 4.30. Worksheet.

State Data Sheet 2

II. Physical features

    A. Geographical areas: _____

    _____

    B. Bodies of water: _____

    _____

    C. Highest elevation: _____

    D. Lowest elevation: _____

III. Climate

    A. Average temperatures

        1. January (winter): _____

        2. July (summer): _____

    B. Average rainfall (per year): _____

IV. Natural resources and industries

    A. Important natural resources: _____

    _____

    B. Major industries: _____

    _____

    C. Major products: _____

    _____

    D. Agriculture (important crops): _____

    _____

  V. Interesting places to visit: _____

    _____

VI. Information sources: (Include a listing on the back of this paper. You must have at least one almanac, one encyclopedia, and one other type of reference source.)

Fig. 4.31. Worksheet.

LESSON 36

Title: View the States

Library Media Research and Study Skills Objective:

Use an atlas to locate specific information.

Level: 3-4

Instructional Strategy: Practice

Performance Objective: Given an atlas and an unlabeled map of the United States, the student will use the atlas to identify and label the states and to identify and list the state capitals.

Resources: Multiple copies of an atlas, copies of the unlabeled map of the United States (fig. 4.32), pencils and paper.

Instructional Responsibility: Classroom teacher or library media specialist

Instructional Grouping: Total class or small group

Activity: Students are given a copy of the unlabeled United States map and are asked to label the states and identify the capital of each state. They must use the atlas to help them find the information needed. On the front of the map, students are to write the names of the states. They must list the capitals on another piece of paper.

Assessment Criteria: Students will label the states and list the capitals with 100 percent accuracy.

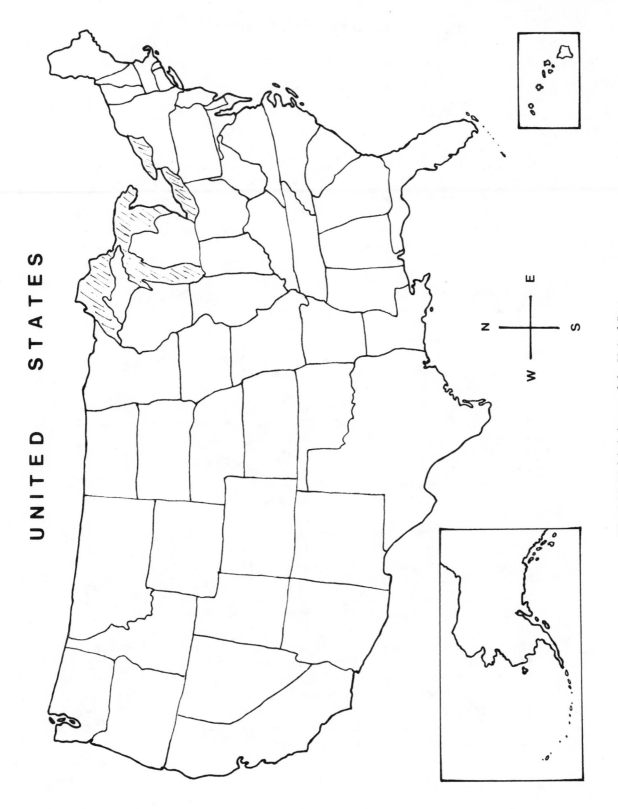

UNITED STATES

Fig. 4.32. Unlabeled map of the United States.

ANSWER KEYS FOR CHAPTER 4

Figure Number	Title and Answers
4.10	**Dances and Countries** 1. gavotte -- France; 2. hora -- Romania and Israel; 3. jig -- England, Scotland, and Ireland; 4. mazurka -- Poland; 5. minuet -- France and England; 6. passepied -- France; 7. pavane -- Italy (southern Europe); 8. reel -- Scotland; 9. tarantella -- Italy; 10. waltz -- Austria and Germany.
4.14	**Occupational Measurements** 1. Carpenter -- in., ft. -- cm, m; 2. Clothing salesperson -- whole sizes -- cm; 3. Cook -- teaspoon, cup -- g, mL; 4. Electrician -- in., horsepower,-- mm, kilowatt; 5. Engineer -- ft., lb., horsepower -- m, kg, kilowatt; 6. Forester -- mi., acre -- km, hectare; 7. Gasoline station attendant -- gal -- L; 8. Meat cutter -- ounce, lb. -- g, kg; 9. Meteorologist -- mi./hr., °F, in. -- km/hr., °C, cm; 10. Optometrist -- mm, cm -- mm, cm; 11. Painter (house) -- gal., sq. ft. -- L, sq. m; 12. Photographer -- mm -- mm; 13. Plumber -- in., gal. -- mm, cu m; 14. Shipping clerk -- lb., ton -- kg, ton; 15. Shoemaker -- in., sq. in. -- cm, sq. cm; 16. Taxi driver -- mi. -- km.
4.15	**Composers** 1. Bartók -- 1881-1945 -- Hungary; 2. Beethoven -- 1770-1827 -- Germany; 3. Borodin -- 1834-1887 -- Russia; 4. Brahms -- 1833-1897 -- Germany; 5. Chopin -- 1810-1849 -- Poland; 6. Debussy -- 1862-1918 -- France; 7. Dvořák -- 1841-1904 -- Czechoslovakia; 8. Grieg -- 1843-1907 -- Norway; 9. Handel -- 1685-1757 -- Germany; 10. Haydn -- 1732-1809 -- Austria; 11. Liszt -- 1811-1886 -- Hungary; 12. Mendelssohn -- 1809-1847 -- Germany; 13. Mozart -- 1756-1791 -- Austria; 14. Prokofiev -- 1891-1953 -- Russia; 15. Puccini -- 1858-1924 -- Italy; 16. Rachmaninoff -- 1873-1943 -- Russia; 17. Ravel -- 1875-1937 -- France; 18. Sibelius -- 1865-1957 -- Finland; 19. Stravinsky -- 1882-1971 -- U.S.-Russia; 20. Tchaikovsky -- 1840-1893 -- Russia; 21. Verdi -- 1813-1901 -- Italy; 22 22. Wagner -- 1813-1883 -- Germany.

Figure Number	Title and Answers
4.18	Guinness Records (Answers from Guinness Book of World Records, 1983 edition) 1. Hubert van Innis; 2. Rocky Marciano; 3. 12 hours, 8 min.; 4. May 30, 1911; 5. Olga Rukavishnikova; 6. Len Dawson; 7. wrestling; 8. May 31, 1868; 9. Hungary; 10. Joe Nuxhall; 11. 32 hrs., 5 min.; 12. tennis.
4.19	Sports Classification Part A: Team sports: baseball, football, hockey, lacrosse, soccer, volleyball. Water sports: fishing, sailing, surfing, swimming, water skiing, yachting. Winter sports: bobsledding, ice skating, snow skiing, snowmobiling, tobogganing. Part B: Outline should follow chart.
4.24	Animal Longevity (Answers from The World Almanac, 1983 edition) Bear -- 18; Cat -- 12; Chimpanzee -- 20; Cow -- 15; Dog -- 12; Goat -- 8; Gorilla -- 20; Guinea pig -- 4; Horse -- 20; Monkey -- 15; Mouse -- 3; Rabbit -- 5; Sheep -- 12; Squirrel -- 10; Tiger -- 16; Wolf -- 5; Zebra -- 15.
4.25	Colorful Synonyms 1. Y; 2. P; 3. O; 4. B; 5. Br; 6. Br/Bl; 7. R; 8. Br; 9. Br; 10. R; 11. R; 12. B; 13. Bl; 14. G; 15. Y; 16. W; 17. R; 18. O/R; 19. B; 20. W; 21. G; 22. G; 23. P; 24. Y; 25. P; 26. Br; 27. W; 28. B; 29. Br/O; 30. G; 31. O; 32. W; 33. R/P; 34. Bl; 35. Y; 36. B; 37. R; 38. W; 39. Br; 40. Br; 41. Y; 42. Br; 43. G; 44. R; 45. P; 46. G.
4.26	Food Groups I. Carbohydrates: Bread, Cereal, Rice; II. Dairy Products: Butter, Cheese, Ice Cream, Milk; III. Fruits: Apples, Bananas, Cherries, Grapes, Oranges; IV. Meats: Beef, Pork, Veal; V. Vegetables: Beets, Carrots, Celery, Lettuce, Potatoes, Radishes.

Figure Number	Title and Answers
4.27	Geologic Events Part A: 1. Triassic; 2. 280 million years ago; 3. Pennsylvanian; 4. 200 million years ago; 5. Jurassic; 6. Pennsylvanian; 7. 136 million years ago; 8. Triassic; 9. Appalachian; 10. 89 million years Part B: 11. false; 12. true; 13. true; 14. true; 15. false; 16. true.
4.28	Continents, Countries, Cities 1. C; 2. A; 3. B; 4. C; 5. A; 6. C; 7. A; 8. B; 9. A; 10. C; 11. B; 12. C; 13. B; 14. C; 15. B; 16. B; 17. C; 18. C; 19. C; 20. B; 21. B; 22. C; 23. C; 24. B; 25. B; 26. A; 27. B; 28. C; 29. B; 30. C; 31. C; 32. B; 33. B; 34. C; 35. C; 36. B; 37. B; 38. B; 39. B; 40. A; 41. B; 42. C; 43. B; 44. B; 45. C; 46. B; 47. C; 48. B; 49. B; 50. B; 51. B; 52. B; 53. B; 54. A; 55. B; 56. C; 57. C; 58. B; 59. B; 60. C; 61. B; 62. B; 63. C; 64. C; 65. B; 66. C; 67. C; 68. B; 69. B; 70. B.

Bibliography

Adams, Anne H., Anne Flowers, and Elsa E. Woods. *Reading for Survival in Today's Society, Volume 1.* Santa Monica, CA: Goodyear Publishing Co., Inc., 1978.
Grade level: 1-12
This source book for functional reading skills includes such topics as labels, printed directions, magazines, schedules, newspapers, weather reports, signs, maps, dictionary, and telephone directory.

Adams, Dennis M. *Simulation Games: An Approach to Learning.* Worthington, OH: Charles A. Jones Publishing Co., 1973.
Grade level: Professional
Extensive examples of simulation games and activities are provided for all levels of students.

Ahlers, Eleanor E. "Instruction in Library Skills." *School Libraries* 21 (Spring 1972): 23-25.
Grade level: Professional
The article focuses on problems in integrating library skills instruction into the classroom teaching process, specifically, lack of teacher training in instructional media, lack of preparation for media specialists in educational practices, and lack of information exchange and planning time for teachers and media specialists.

Arizona State Library Association. *SSRG (Study Skills for Reading).* Phoenix, AZ: Arizona State Library Association, 1975. ED 117652.
Grade level: Professional
Included in this curriculum guide are behavioral objectives for orientation in the use of the library media center, care of materials, materials selection, circulation procedures, library media technology, nonbook materials and equipment, parts of a book, library media center arrangement, the card catalog, reference materials, periodicals, information file, bibliographies, *Abridged Reader's Guide to Periodical Literature,* and advanced reference materials. Performance criteria are listed for each objective as are introductory and mastery levels. Skills tests are given for grades three through eight.

Ausubel, David. "The Use of Advanced Organizers in the Learning and Retention of Meaningful Verbal Material," *Journal of Educational Psychology* 51 (1960): 267-72.
Grade level: Professional
The author provides the rationale for advanced organizers and structured overviews.

Bartch, Marian R., and Jerry J. Mallett. *Reading Rousers: 114 Ways to Reading Fun.* Santa Monica, CA: Goodyear Publishing Co., Inc., 1980.
Grade level: 3-6
Reproducible activity worksheets are set up for book reporting in modern fantasy, historical fiction, informational books, realistic fiction, biography, and traditional literature.

Beck, Margaret V., and Vera M. Pace. *A Guidebook for Teaching Library Skills, Book One.* Minneapolis: T. S. Denison, Co., 1965.
Grade level: K-2
Activities are suggested for motivating students to use the library and the card catalog.

Beck, Margaret V., and Vera M. Pace. *A Guidebook for Teaching Library Skills, Book Two.* Minneapolis: T. S. Denison, Co., 1965.
Grade level: 3-6
Sequential practice exercises are identified on the Dewey Decimal System.

Beck, Margaret V., and Vera M. Pace. *A Guidebook for Teaching Library Skills, Book Three.* Minneapolis: T. S. Denison, Co., 1966.
Grade level: 3-6
Exercises for use with reference tools (encyclopedia, almanac, atlas, biographical dictionary, and *Reader's Guide to Periodical Literature*) model simple research techniques.

Berg, David W., George Daugherty, Ann Richards Taylor, Sheldon F. Katz, and Sophie Y. Stauroff. "Research and Reporting." *Instructor* 82 (November 1972): 86-92.
Grade level: Professional
This professional article offers tips for teaching research and report writing skills.

Blackburn, Jack E., and W. Conrad Powell. *One at a Time All at Once: The Creative Teacher's Guide to Individualized Instruction without Anarchy.* Santa Monica, CA: Goodyear Publishing Co., Inc., 1976.
Grade level: Professional
This book contains alternative procedures for individualizing learning, including learning centers, learning packages, student contracts, specific individualization strategies, educational games, and reproducible worksheets.

Bloom, Benjamin, et al. *Taxonomy of Educational Objectives: The Classification of Educational Goals. Handbook I: Cognitive Domain.* New York: Longmans, Green and Co., Inc., 1956.
Grade level: Professional
This document has become a classic in the development of cognitive objectives.

Bowers, Melvyn K. *Library Instruction in the Elementary School.* Metuchen, NJ: Scarecrow Press, Inc., 1971.
Grade level: Professional
Practical activities are designated for each grade level. Examples of programmed materials are included in the appendix.

Buckingham, Betty Jo. "Peer Six: Six Projects Selected by the Participants in Teaching Library Skills, A Workshop, June 27-July 1, 1977." Des Moines, IA: Iowa State Department of Public Instruction, 1978. ED 184544.
Grade level: Professional
Team teaching projects to integrate library media skills into subject areas of the curriculum include: (1) Dictionary skills game for fifth grade students on etymology of words, (2) Fairy tales from Ginn 360 reading program to improve self-image, (3) Library skills instruction integrated with classroom assignments in junior high, (4) Fifth-grade social studies biographies, (5) Fourth-grade make-your-own book, and (6) Card catalog skills.

Burmeister, Lou E. *Reading Strategies for Secondary School Teachers.* Reading, MA: Addison-Wesley Publishing Co., Inc., 1978.
Grade level: Professional
Among many useful strategies for reading are steps for directed reading activities (DRA).

Burns, Julie, and Dorothy Swan. *Reading without Books.* Belmont, CA: Fearon Pitman Publishers, Inc., 1979.
Grade level: Professional
A supplemental functional reading program with reproducible activity sheets and task cards, includes menus, TV guides, magazines, telephone books, newspaper ads, and recipes.

Cheek, Earl H., Jr., and Martha Collins Cheek. *Reading Instruction through Content Teaching.* Columbus, OH: Charles E. Merrill Publishing Co., 1983.
Grade level: Professional
This college text provides useful guidance for introducing and reinforcing good student study habits in the content areas.

Cleary, Florence D. *Blueprints for Better Reading.* New York: H. W. Wilson Co., 1972.
Grade level: Professional
This book emphasizes a whole-school approach to library program planning especially in the area of reading. Programs and activities to promote critical reading skills show the joint effort required in organization and scheduling for reading guidance and selection.

Cleary, Florence D. *Discovering Books and Libraries: A Handbook for Students in the Middle and Upper Grades.* 2d ed. New York: H. W. Wilson Co., 1977.
Grade level: Professional
Suggestions are given to library media specialists and teachers for introducing books and materials to students.

Colvin, Mary Paris, ed. *Instructor's Big Holiday Book.* Dansville, NY: Instructor Publications, Inc., 1979.
Grade level: K-6
Holiday-related activities for teaching skills from every area of curriculum provide ideas for joint planning by library media specialist and teacher.

Contra Costa County Department of Education. *Handbook for Elementary Library-Media Instruction.* rev. ed. Pleasant Hills, CA: Contra Costa County Department of Education, 1975.
Grade level: Professional
The handbook of K-8 units includes orientation and care of materials, parts of a book, the card catalog, classification, materials arrangement, research and reference, magazines, and nonprint materials. Detailed lessons and ample worksheets are noted for different grade levels.

Cory, Beverly. *Birdseye View of Language Arts*. Belmont, CA: Fearon Pitman Publishers, Inc., 1977.
Grade level: 3-6
Reproducible worksheets provide practice in dictionary skills, phonics, word structure, word meaning, and grammar.

Cotler, Harold I. *Encyclopedic Desk-book of Teaching Ideas and Classroom Activities*. West Nyack, NY: Parker Publishing Co., Inc., 1977.
Grade level: Professional
The author suggests an interrelated approach to ideas for classroom activities.

Danes, Margaret F., and Elizabeth W. Koenig. *Stepping Stones to the Library*. Bronx, NY: Fordham Equipment and Publishing Co., 1972.
Grade level: K-2
Teacher's guide and spirit masters teach beginning library media skills through puzzles and activities.

Davies, Ruth Ann. *The School Library Media Center: A Force for Educational Excellence*. New York: R. R. Bowker Co., 1974.
Grade level: Professional
This edition advocates total involvement of students, teachers, and library media specialists in the instruction of library media skills.

De Leeuw, William L. *Study Skills with Stacy Stegosaurus*. Greensboro, NC: The Education Center, 1978.
Grade level: 4
Using a dinosaur theme, the author provides reproducible activity sheets that focus on location and reference skills, interpretation skills, and organization skills.

Durkin, Delores. *Teaching Them to Read*. 3rd ed. Boston: Allyn and Bacon, Inc., 1978.
Grade level: Professional
This reading text also deals with study skills in the content and subject areas.

Farnette, Cherrie, Imogene Forte, and Barbara Loss. *Special Kid's Stuff*. Nashville: Incentive Publications, 1976.
Grade level: Professional
This book contains high-interest, low-vocabulary reading and language skills learning center ideas, reproducible worksheets, and a section on study skills.

Forgan, Harry W. *Read All About It!* Santa Monica, CA: Goodyear Publishing Co., Inc., 1979.
Grade level: 3-8
Children's interests and hobbies are used as motivation for teaching reading as a source of information and enjoyment.

Forgan, Harry W. *A Reading Skillbuilder; Lesson Plans, Ideas and Activities for Teaching Functional Reading Skills*. Glenville, IL: Scott, Foresman and Co., 1982.
Grade level: 3-6
Strategies, plans, ideas, and hands-on activities are useful for teaching reading symbols and abbreviations; map skills; reading graphs, tables, and diagrams; parts of a book; reference skills; study strategies; and recreational reading.

Forgan, Harry W., and Charles T. Mangrum II. *Teaching Content Area Reading Skills.* 2d ed. Columbus, OH: Charles E. Merrill Publishing Co., 1981.
Grade level: Professional
Guidance to teaching staff and actual activities are provided in this textual material.

Forte, Imogene. *Skillstuff, Volume I. Reading.* Nashville: Incentive Publications, Inc., 1979.
Grade level: 3-6
This basic skills activity encyclopedia provides reproducible materials for a diagnostic/prescriptive approach to reading study skills.

Forte, Imogene, and Mary Ann Pangle. *Comprehension Magic.* Nashville: Incentive Publications, Inc., 1977.
Grade level: 2-6
Game boards and student activity sheets are designed to teach or reinforce basic comprehension skills such as predicting outcomes, main ideas, characterization, fantasy/reality, skimming, drawing conclusions, making inferences, using maps, and locating information.

Forte, Imogene, and Mary Ann Pangle. *Vocabulary Magic.* Nashville: Incentive Publications, Inc., 1977.
Grade level: 2-6
Games, game boards, and individual and group activities provide motivation and extension of basic vocabulary skills (word structure, word meaning, and dictionary skills).

Freeman, Doris L, et al. *Action and Interaction: An Elementary Library Media Program.* King of Prussia, PA: Upper Merion Area School District, 1977.
Grade level: Professional
The curriculum guide provides a program of essential library skills where the library media specialist and classroom teacher design learning activities to locate, use, search, appreciate, and produce materials.

Freund, Roberta Bishop. *Open the Book.* Metuchen, NJ: Scarecrow Press, Inc., 1966.
Grade level: 3-8
Lessons teach the card catalog, encyclopedia, reference sources, bibliographies, and note taking.

Gagne, Robert M., and Leslie J. Briggs. *Principles of Instructional Design.* 2d ed. New York: Holt, Rinehart and Winston, Inc., 1979.
Grade level: Professional
Library media specialists lead teachers through the process of instructional design.

Gentile, Lance M. *Using Sport and Physical Education to Strengthen Reading Skills.* Newark, DE: International Reading Association, 1980.
Grade level: Professional
The brief document integrates physical education and reading instruction.

Gillespie, John T., and Diana L. Spirt. *Creating a School Media Program.* New York: R. R. Bowker Co., 1973.
Grade level: Professional
Elements that distinguish a media center from the conventional library are discussed in light of the classroom teaching process.

Gillespie, Mary, Marilynn Hazard, Anne Hyland, and Linda Williams. *Curriculum Guide for Teaching Library Media Skills, Kindergarten-Eighth Grade.* Toledo, OH: Toledo Public Schools, 1974. ED 102962.
  Grade level: Professional
  The curriculum guide offers strategies for the instruction of locating, using, appreciating, and understanding all kinds of print and nonprint materials.

Hart, Thomas L., ed. *Instruction in School Media Use.* Chicago: American Library Association, 1978.
  Grade level: Professional
  An overview of the status of library skills instruction is given by the editor.

Herber, Harold L. *Teaching Reading in Content Areas.* 2d ed. Englewood Cliffs, NJ: Prentice-Hall, Inc., 1978.
  Grade level: Professional
  Among the many strategies for teaching reading is the directed reading activity (DRA) modification, "instructional framework."

Holmes, Deborah. *Good Apple and Daily Breaks.* Carthage, IL: Good Apple, Inc., 1981.
  Grade level: 3-6
  Nine chapters follow the calendar of significant dates.

Hurwitz, Abraham B., Arthur Goddard, and David T. Epstein. *Number Games to Improve Your Child's Arithmetic.* New York: Funk and Wagnalls, Inc., 1975.
  Grade level: Pre-K-6
  The book provides oral, card, paper and pencil, dice, dominoes, counting, party, and language games for the young child.

Johnson, Marjorie Seddon, Thomas W. Lockman, and Richard J. Reisboard. *Critical Reading: A Teaching Guide.* Dansville: The Instructor Publications, Inc., 1977.
  Grade level: Professional
  This idea book will be useful in giving suggestions for determining the author's purpose, distinguishing fact from fiction, analyzing cause and effect, drawing inferences, recognizing propaganda techniques, and evaluation.

Kelner, Bernard G., and Joan B. Myers. *Key Competencies. Libraries: Elementary, Junior High, and Senior High.* Philadelphia: Philadelphia School District, 1980. ED 192780.
  Grade level: Professional
  Competency blueprints or profiles are shown for students in grades K through 12.

Kennedy, Leonard M., and Ruth L. Michon. *Games for Individualizing Mathematics Learning.* Columbus, OH: Charles E. Merrill Publishing Co., 1973.
  Grade level: K-6
  This book gives useful suggestions for making games, organizing the classroom to use them, and methods of storing and retrieving them. The areas covered are: meaning of numbers, operations on numbers, measurement, geometry, probability and statistics, and logic.

Kibler, Robert J., Donald J. Cegala, Larry L. Barker, and David T. Miles. *Objectives for Instruction and Evaluation.* Boston: Allyn and Bacon, Inc., 1974.
  Grade level: Professional
  Criterion reference and standardized tests and their component parts are compared and contrasted in terms of their usefulness to educators.

Krathwohl, D. R., B. S. Bloom, and B. B. Masia. *Taxonomy of Educational Objectives: The Classifi-cation of Educational Goals, Handbook II: Affective Domain.* New York: David McKay Company, Inc., 1964.
Grade level: Professional
This document has become a classic for those developing educational objectives in the affec-tive areas.

Kuhlthau, Carol Collier. *School Librarian's Grade-by-Grade Activities Program: A Complete Sequential Skills Plan for Grades K-8.* New York: Center for Applied Research in Education, 1981.
Grade level: K-8.
Many suggested ideas in this monthly activities book would be applicable for interest centers.

Lamberg, Walter J., and Charles E. Lamb. *Reading Instruction in the Content Areas.* Skokie, IL: Rand McNally and Co., 1980.
Grade level: Professional
This text provides useful guidance for establishing good study habits in the content areas.

Lee, Barbara Kaplan, and Masha Kabakow Rudman. *Mind Over Media: New Ways to Improve Your Child's Reading and Writing Skills.* New York: Seaview Books, 1982.
Grade level: Professional
This guidebook for parents presents suggestions for helping children interpret media. The authors advise the use of media as a starting point for discovering, developing, and extending children's interests. Some of the media covered are: television, books, comics, magazines, news-papers, and paperbacks. It also includes a section on the improvement of study and test-taking skills.

Lewis, Zella. *Developing Learning through Library Services.* Chicago: American Library Association Round Table, 1981. ED 211095.
Grade level: Professional
Suggested instructional activities in this curriculum guide include a wide range of library media topics. Many interpretation and organizational skills are represented. The skills arrangement would be helpful to library media specialists and classroom teachers for integrating content and library media research and study skills and processes.

Liesener, James W. *A Systematic Process for Planning and Communicating Media Programs.* Chicago: American Library Association, 1975.
Grade level: Professional
A plan for the integration of media skills instruction into the classroom teaching process is discussed.

Love, Marla. *20 Reading Comprehension Games.* Belmont, CA: Fearon Publishers, Inc., 1977.
Grade level: 4-6
A series of reproducible reading games reinforce reading/language arts skills. Some of the skills represented are: following directions, finding details, finding the main idea, drawing conclusions, locating information, and distinguishing fact from opinion.

Lowrie, Jean Elizabeth. *Elementary School Libraries.* 2d ed. Metuchen, NJ: Scarecrow Press Inc., 1970.
Grade level: Professional
Suggestions are given for experiences that support curriculum and for pupil information retrieval in the middle grades. The role of the classroom teacher in the school library is discussed.

Mallett, Jerry J. *Library Activities Kit.* New York: Center for Applied Research in Education, 1981.
Grade level: 1-8
Many ideas for games and learning centers are provided in this book of suggested activities for library skills instruction.

Margrabe, Mary. *The "Now" Library: A Stations Approach Media Center Teaching Kit.* Washington, DC: Acropolis Books, Ltd., 1973.
Grade level: Professional (1-8)
This book presents an individualized approach to teaching library skills through the use of learning stations. Behavioral objectives for 96 essential media skills that span the elementary grades are identified. Teaching stations (learning centers), student exercise sheets, and evaluative tests are included.

Middleton, Karen P. *Library Skills Instruction in the Fifth and Sixth Grades.* Bloomington, IN: Agency for Instructional Television, 1977. ED 157513.
Grade level: Professional
This author believes that the teaching of library location and usage skills is the joint responsibility of librarians and teachers. Location skills include: the use of the card catalog, the library's classification system, and published indexes. Usage skills include: identifying types of resources and the kinds of information found in each, selecting information for a purpose, evaluating materials, and synthesizing ideas from various sources.

Miller, Wilma H. *The Reading Activities Handbook.* New York: Holt, Rinehart and Winston, 1980.
Grade level: 1-8
This source includes diagnostic-prescriptive teaching suggestions and reproducible activity sheets for various reading comprehension skills. The section on study skills provides activities in: outlining, note taking, summarizing, locating information, and interpreting information from graphs and maps.

Moldenhauer, Janice. *Developing Dictionary Skills.* Carthage, IL: Good Apple, Inc., 1979.
Grade level: 3-6
Reproducible skills worksheets provide practice in alphabetical order, guide words, word meaning, syllabication, pronunciation, word structure, and etymology.

Mott, Carolyn, and Leo B. Baisden. *Children's Book on How to Use Books and Libraries.* New York: Charles Scribner's Sons, 1968.
Grade level: 3-8
Lessons on alphabetizing, book parts, the Dewey decimal system, dictionaries, encyclopedias, atlases, and writing book reviews are included in this book for children. Its cartoon illustrations help children learn the effective use of books and libraries.

Nichol, William T. *How Reference Resources Help Us.* Westchester, IL: Benefic Press, 1966.
Grade level: 4-8
Students are given examples of the use of print, nonprint, and reference sources in this book.

Nickel, Mildred L. *Steps to Service: A Handbook of Procedures for the School Library Media Center.* Chicago: American Library Association, 1975.
Grade level: Professional
Practical suggestions to facilitate library media services to students and teachers are given. Bibliographies for teaching library media skills are provided.

Oklahoma State Department of Education. *Curriculum Guide for the Teaching of Media Skills, K-12.* Oklahoma City: Oklahoma State Department of Education, 1975. ED 125655.
Grade level: Professional
This curriculum outline provides behavioral objectives, instructional activities, and resource materials to enable students to become independent users of library media centers. The elementary curriculum listings emphasize library orientation, parts of a book, and different resource materials.

Pavlovic, Lora, and Elizabeth Goodman. *The Elementary School Library in Action.* West Nyack, NY: Parker Publishing Company, Inc., 1968.
Grade level: Professional
Library-oriented activities are presented that could be adapted for teaching media skills within the subject areas.

Pelow, Randall, and Sally A. Chant. *The How-To Book of Survival Reading.* Dansville, NY: Instructor Publications, Inc., 1980.
Grade level: Elementary
Functional reading activities in which students locate and interpret information are given in this idea book. It is suggested that these activities be integrated into the most meaningful subject area.

Polette, Nancy, and Cathi Haddon Dame. *Using the Library Instructional Materials Center Effectively: Teacher's Manual.* Big Spring, TX: Creative Visuals (Division of Gameco Industries), 1969.
Grade level: 1-8
A set of 61 transparencies with an accompanying teacher's manual cover a wide range of library media skills.

Prostano, Emanuel T., and Joyce S. Prostano. *The School Library Media Center.* 3d ed. Littleton, CO: Libraries Unlimited, 1982.
Grade level: Professional
This book discusses the general organization and management of library media centers.

Rieke, Angela S., and James L. Laffey. *Pathways to Imagination: Language Arts Learning Centers and Activities for Grades K-7.* Santa Monica, CA: Goodyear Publishing Company, Inc., 1979.
Grade level: K-7
Ideas for learning centers and other activities are provided in a well-organized format. Sections are included on dictionary skills, etymology, and library skills.

Robinson, H. Alan. *Teaching Reading and Study Strategies.* 2d ed. Boston: Allyn and Bacon, Inc., 1978.
Grade level: Professional
Reading skills in the content areas and the application of study strategies are discussed in this textbook for teachers.

Roets, Lois F. *The Outline Wizard.* Santa Barbara, CA: The Learning Works, Inc., 1980.
Grade level: 3-6
Reproducible activity worksheets include practice exercises in the following: the parts of an outline, the writing of outlines, the gaining of information from outlines, the classifying of outline entries, and the writing of paragraphs from outlines.

Rossoff, Martin. *The School Library and Educational Change.* Littleton, CO: Libraries Unlimited, 1971.
Grade level: Professional
As library media skills are integrated into the curriculum, instructional practices change to meet student needs.

Sandt, Barbara. *Skill Builders: Vocabulary, Sentences, Paragraphs.* Los Angeles: Rhythms Productions, 1982.
Grade level: 3-6
Reproducible activity sheets provide student practice in dictionary, word meaning, and word parts skills.

Schnare, Sharon. "The Center Spot: The Dictionarea: A Place for Every Word." *Teacher* 96 (April 1979): 34-36.
Grade level: Professional
The article focuses on learning centers to provide student activities in the use of dictionaries.

Schwartz, Linda. *The Center Solution.* Santa Barbara, CA: The Learning Works, Inc., 1977.
Grade level: 3-6
Ideas, projects, and activities are listed for learning centers, including research and dictionary skill centers.

Schwartz, Linda. *Study Skills Shortcake.* Santa Barbara, CA: The Learning Works, 1979.
Grade level: 3-6
Reproducible skills worksheets provide student practice in using the dictionary, the encyclopedia, the thesaurus, textbooks, maps, charts, and graphs. Note-taking skills and outlining skills are also covered.

Schwartz, Linda. *Dictionary Dig.* Santa Barbara, CA: The Learning Works, Inc., 1980.
Grade level: 3-6
Reproducible activity skillsheets provide practice in the following: alphabetizing, guide words, pronunciation, syllabication, word structure, etymology, illustrations, and word meaning.

Singer, Harry, and Dan Donlan. *Reading and Learning from Text.* Boston: Little, Brown and Co., 1980.
Grade level: Professional
Reading in the content areas and the application of study strategies such as the directed reading activity (DRA) are discussed. A section on the varied instructional uses of discussions is very informative.

Smith, Jane Bandy. *Library Skills for Elementary Teachers.* Birmingham, AL: University of Alabama, 1976. ED 187329.
Grade level: Professional
This teaching guide includes a manual for self-instruction in basic library skills for elementary school teachers. Illustrated examples include organizational systems, library classification, library treatment of biographies and fiction, the use of indexes, book structure, and reference works.

Smith, Jane Bandy. *Library Skills for Middle Grades.* Birmingham, AL: University of Alabama, 1975. ED 186014.
Grade level: Professional

This teaching guide includes classroom activities for the following: use of alphabetical order, location of materials, Dewey decimal classifications, use of catalog cards, organizational systems, library vocabulary, call numbers, library resources, locating books, parts of books, use of indexes, use of bibliographies, use of multiple references, use of almanacs, use of current information sources, awareness of authors, and use of multiple resources.

Snoddy, James E., and J. Harlan Shores. "Teaching the Research Study Skills." In *International Reading Association Conference Proceedings. Part 1:* 13 (1968): 681-688. EJ 019181.
Grade level: Professional
This abstract reports on a study of twenty-eight sixth-grade students who significantly improved library research study skills by following a strategy involving short but frequent practice sessions.

Spellman, Linda. *Book Report Backpack.* Santa Barbara, CA: The Learning Works, Inc., 1980.
Grade level: 3-6
Reproducible worksheets provide follow-up activities to book reporting. Fiction worksheets concern setting, characterization, and plot. Nonfiction worksheets include: Science, travel, biographies, tall tales, mythology, fables, and etc.

Spellman, Linda. *Creative Investigations.* Santa Barbara, CA: The Learning Works, Inc., 1982.
Grade level: 3-6
Reproducible worksheets contain topics for thirty-six independent research investigations that appeal to students. Suggested art, research, and creative writing activities are provided for each topic worksheet. Procedural steps for writing a research report include instruction in the organizational skills of classifying, note taking, outlining, and constructing a bibliography.

Stauffer, Russell G. *Teaching Reading as a Thinking Process.* New York: Harper and Row Publishers, Inc., 1969.
Grade level: Professional
The author's reading-thinking plan is discussed. Many derivative study strategies have been based on this plan.

Strickland, Dorothy S., ed. *The Role of Literature in Reading Instruction.* Newark, DE: International Reading Association, 1981.
Grade level: Professional
A series of articles suggests that the use of literature is a most effective means of teaching reading skills.

Sullivan, Peggy. *Impact: The School Library and the Instructional Program.* Chicago: American Library Association, 1967.
Grade level: Professional
Problem-centered approaches to school library media management are presented.

Sulphur Springs Independent School District. *Guide for the Development of Library Skills and Services in the Sulphur Springs Independent School District, Grades K-12.* Sulphur Springs, TX: Sulphur Springs Independent School District, 1972. ED 066176.
Grade level: Professional

Behavioral objectives for library skills instruction are provided for grades K-12 in this curriculum guide. Suggested materials and activities are included for librarians, teachers, and students. The school district believes that library instruction should be part of the total curriculum and that the implementation of library instruction should arise from classroom assignments.

Taylor, M., and K. Liebold. *Libraries Are for Children: A Teaching Guide and Manual for Library Skills.* Bronx, NY: Fordham Equipment and Publishing Co., 1968.
Grade level: 3-7
A manual and accompanying ditto masters present a general approach to teaching the function of the library, the arrangement and types of materials, the Dewey decimal system, the card catalog, and a comparison of encyclopedias.

Thelen, Judith. *Improving Reading in Science.* Newark, DE: International Reading Association, 1976.
Grade level: Professional
Strategies to help students comprehend scientific materials are presented.

Thomas, Ellen Lamar, and H. Alan Robinson. *Improving Reading in Every Class.* 2d ed. Boston: Allyn and Bacon, Inc., 1977.
Grade level: Professional
Presentations on directed reading activities (DRA) and other study strategies are presented in this textbook.

Vacca, Richard T. *Content Area Reading.* Boston: Little, Brown, and Co., 1981.
Grade level: Professional
This college text provides methods for establishing good study habits for students.

Walker, H. Thomas, and Paula Kay Montgomery. *Teaching Library Media Skills: An Instructional Program for Elementary and Middle School Students.* 2d ed. Littleton, CO: Libraries Unlimited, 1983.
Grade level: Professional
Theoretical strategies for integrating media skills instruction and curriculum subject integration are presented. Practical activities for integrated library media skills instruction are included.

Wehymeyer, Lillian Biermann. *The School Librarian as Educator.* 2d ed. Littleton, CO: Libraries Unlimited, 1984.
Grade level: Professional
Suggestions are made for the establishment of a "learner-centered media center" in which the school media specialist is a teacher of students and teachers. Cooperative planning strategies for teachers and librarians are presented.

Weisburg, Hilda K., and Ruth Toor. *Elementary School Librarian's Almanac.* West Nyack, NY: Center for Applied Research in Education, Inc., 1979.
Grade level: Professional
A series of monthly activities accenting holidays and special events is presented. The varied activities include ideas, materials, and methods to enrich instructional programs for library media specialists and classroom teachers.

Welken, Marion L. *A Guidebook for Teaching Library Skills—Book Four.* Minneapolis: T. S. Denison, Co., 1967.
    Grade level: 4-7
An overview of the school library is given with activities related to parts of books, library arrangement, the card catalog, encyclopedias, and reference books.

Whitney, David C. *First Book of Facts and How to Find Them.* New York: Franklin Watts, Inc., 1966.
    Grade level: 3-6
This student book contains a good explanation of kinds of facts and the reference tools that will answer questions about facts. An introduction to the use of facts in critical thinking is also included.

Wilsher, Gary S. "For a Higher Interest Rate—Sign the Bottom Line." Kansas City, MO: Association for Educational Communications and Technology, 1978. ED 174204.
    Grade level: Professional
This teaching guide provides specific procedures for the development of teacher/library media specialist and student/teacher contracts. Several sample contracts for students in grades K-5 are included.

Wisconsin State Department of Public Instruction. *Skill Development in the K-6 Social Studies Program.* Madison, WI: Wisconsin State Department of Public Instruction, 1975. ED 125973.
    Grade level: Professional
This curriculum guide provides objectives and activities for the following: map and globe skills, research and critical thinking skills, the use of the library in research, note-taking skills, oral and written reporting strategies, interpretation and construction of tables and graphs, and questioning skills.

Zakalik, Leslie. *Study Skills Sorcery.* Santa Barbara, CA: The Learning Works, Inc., 1978.
    Grade level: 3-6
Reproducible activity worksheets provide student practice in using reference sources such as almanacs, atlases, dictionaries, encyclopedias, indexes, newspapers, and thesauri. Worksheets include practice activities in interpreting charts, graphs, maps, tables, and time lines. Organizational skills such as note taking, outlining, skimming, and summarizing are also covered.

Index